D0710591

Concept Learning
Designs for Instruction

PETER H. MARTORELLA
Temple University

with

ROSALIE S. JENSEN
Georgia State University

JOHN M. KEAN
ALAN M. VOELKER
University of Wisconsin

 INTEXT EDUCATIONAL PUBLISHERS
College Division of Intext
Scranton   San Francisco   Toronto   London

ISBN 0–7002–2389–4

Library of Congress Catalog Card Number: 70–188188

927754

To Mary

a unique concept

Preface

Essentially this book is about categorization. It deals with *why* sorting phenomena into categories is an important intellectual activity, *how* human beings carry out the process, and *what* may be done to assist others in efficiently discriminating and interpreting categories that our culture already has identified.

Trying to sort out the "blooming, buzzing confusion" of life into meaningful "heaps" is an ongoing task for children, adolescents, and adults. As one becomes more proficient in the sorting process, learning to combine and refine categories and to create new ones, his intellectual world enlarges.

A basic premise of this book is that the instructional procedures employed for the learning of *concepts* should be different from those for *other* learning outcomes such as facts, skills, and generalizations. To state the point another way, an instructional model for teaching a generalization should *not* be used to teach a concept.

The way for this book was paved by an earlier one, *Concept Learning in the Social Studies: Models for Structuring Curriculum*, and many elements have been borrowed from it. Its intent was to apply the literature concerning concept learning to one specific subject in the curriculum.

In this book the findings are extended, as appropriate, to *all* instructional areas. At the same time, separate chapters by subject-matter specialists—Rosalie Jensen, John Kean, Alan Voelker and the undersigned—discuss related developments and considerations in four specific curricular areas.

The opening chapter explores the nature of concepts, presents and illustrates an operational definition of a concept for instructional purposes, and discriminates between concepts and other basic related intellectual phenomena. In the second chapter, pertinent studies are reviewed and selected considerations for organizing instruction are inferred from them.

Chapter 3 explores in detail and illustrates models for concept learning abstracted from the works of Taba, Gagné, and DeCecco. These are generic designs in that they may be applied to a variety of different developmental levels and subject-matter areas.

The next four chapters deal respectively with mathematics, communication arts, science, and social studies. Each analyzes projects, studies, and issues related to concept learning in grades K–12 in a specific subject-matter area.

A schema for measuring concept learning is presented in Chapter 8, and sets of sample items for each of the four curricular areas are provided.

In Chapter 9, there are a series of exercises to assist the reader in internalizing some of the basic points in preceding chapters. These exercises are vehicles for translating some of the abstractions into demonstrable propositions, so the reader is urged to *perform* them himself. Since the Appendix has answers to the exercises, it should be read only *after* completing Chapter 9.

A concluding chapter outlines considerations that are basic to the efficient design of any instructional materials to be used for concept learning. A range of media is discussed, including texts, films, and computers, and an approach to individualization is suggested. Finally, a model of a theory of instruction is presented in order to illustrate how concept learning may be related to the total instructional process.

This book is intended for all who are concerned with the design of instruction—be they classroom teachers, supervisors, curriculum specialists, media developers, or educational psychologists. Its materials already have been used with success in a variety of contexts: preservice and inservice methods courses and workshops, clinics for designing instructional strategies and related media, seminars on principles of learning and instruction, and experimental research projects.

Let the reader determine this book's appropriate category.

PETER H. MARTORELLA

Philadelphia, Pennsylvania
March, 1972

Contents

Learning: Instructional Considerations for Students and
Teachers. A Theory of Instruction. Conclusion.

The Learner's Perspective. Exercises Related to Mathematics Instruction.

CHAPTER 1

The World of Concepts

David Ausubel tells us, "Anyone who pauses long enough to give the problem some serious thought cannot escape the conclusion that man lives in a world of concepts rather than a world of objects, events, and situations. . . . Reality, figuratively speaking, is experienced through a conceptual or categorical filter.[1] His message serves as a sharp reminder of the enormous compression of data that occurs when we communicate with concepts. As he notes, sighting a "house" is a good case in point.[2]

> When someone, for example, tells us that he sees a "house," he is not really communicating his *actual* experience, but a highly simplified and generalized version of it—an interpretation that reflects the cultural consensus regarding the essential (criterial, identifying) attributes of "house." His *actual* conscious experience of the event is infinitely more particularistic with respect to size, shape, style, hue, brightness, and presumed cost than the message communicated by his generic use of the term "house." If he actually tried to communicate his detailed cognitive experience, it would not only take him half a day, but he would still also be unable completely to express in words many of its more subtle nuances.

It would seem that it is the *critical attributes* of concepts that people share in common when they are able to meaningfully discuss their daily affairs. The professor, for example, probably has a different concept of automobile than the service station mechanic who repairs it, but enough agreement on the critical attributes of their concepts exists normally, so that the professor realizes that he can avail himself of the mechanic's services under certain conditions, and both can communicate concerning the problem. At a different level, since the au-

[1]David P. Ausubel, *Educational Psychology: A Cognitive View* (New York: Holt, Reinhart & Winston, Inc., 1968), p. 505.
[2]*Ibid.*, pp. 505–506.

tomobile has become such an engrained element in the American ethos, it is likely that all Americans, drivers and nondrivers, at an early age, share at least some critical or essential attributes in their concepts of automobile, such as "it is a motorized object that can move one from place to place."

Granting the personal nature of individual's concepts, concepts that students have which are identified by a common symbol should be essentially similar insofar as their critical attributes are shared in common. As Carroll has observed, it is probably a fact that universally people share certain properties in their concepts of such things as sun and man, for example, even though terminology and extended descriptive features and interrelationships will vary.[3]

In classrooms, the basic goal of setting all of the students to acquire the critical or criterial attributes of a particular concept should be the *initial* one for the teacher. Beyond this point, of course, provisions may be made for individual enlargement of the concept. The past experiences of the individual student, the way in which these experiences relate to new ones in the classroom, and the general reaction of students to the teaching situation, among other things, will influence the unique kind of conceptual network that each student acquires.

WHAT IS A CONCEPT?

What is not certain as one surveys the field of concept literature is whether the discussion is centered upon the learning of a common item. Those who do attempt to reduce confusion and improve communications by defining their terms are not infrequently unclear on the operational meaning of what they are discussing. Consider the following sampling of definitions from the literature.

> A *concept* is a kind of unit in terms of which one thinks; a unit smaller than a judgment, proposition, or theory, but one which necessarily enters into these.[4]

> In brief, concepts are properties of organismic experience—more particularly they are the abstracted and often cognitively structured, classes of "mental" experience learned by organisms in the course of their life histories.[5]

[3]John B. Carroll, "Words, Meanings and Concepts," *Harvard Educational Review*, Vol. 34 (Spring 1964), p. 184.
[4]Julius Gould and William L. Kolb (eds.), *A Dictionary of the Social Sciences* (New York: The Free Press, 1964), p. 20.
[5]Carroll, *op. cit.*, p. 180.

A concept may be thought of as "the common element shared by an array of objects" or "the relationship between the constituents or parts of a process."[6]

Concepts are artifacts extracted by verification from the contexts or sentences in which they occur.[7]

A concept is a generalized and abstract symbol; it is the sum total of all our knowledge of a particular class of objects. . . . In short, a concept is a condensation of experience.[8]

The basic concepts are essentially high-level abstractions expressed in verbal cues and labels.[9]

A concept is a general idea, usually expressed by a word, which represents a class or group of things or actions having certain characteristics in common.[10]

A concept . . . is something about an idea expressed in the words of our language.[11]

Frayer has suggested that a concept may be described as having at least six characteristics:[12] properties common to all cases of the concept, the concept rule, the properties that are irrelevant to the concept or which vary from case to care, a concept word, supraordinate concepts, and subordinate concepts. Figure 1–1 illustrates subordinate-supraordinate relationships between selected mathematical concepts, and specifies their relevant attribute values or common properties.[13]

Abraham Kaplan has distinguished between concepts and *conceptions,* the latter referring to one's particular application or interpretation of a concept.[14]

[6]F. H. George, *Cognition* (London: Methuen and Company, Ltd., 1962), p. 260.

[7]J. Bronowski and Ursula Bellugi, "Language, Name, and Concept," *Science*, Vol. 148 (May 8, 1970), p. 673.

[8]Gaston Viaud, *Intelligence: Its Evolution and Form*, trans. A. J. Pomerans (New York: Harper & Row, Publishers, 1960), pp. 75–76.

[9]Hilda Taba, "Techniques of In-Service Training," *Social Education*, Vol. 29 (November 1965), p. 465.

[10]Isaac J. Quillen and Lavone A. Hanna, *Education for Social Competence*, rev. ed. (Chicago: Scott, Foresman & Company, 1961), p. 187.

[11]Myles M. Platt, "Concepts and the Curriculum," *Social Education*, Vol. 27 (January 1963), p. 21.

[12]Dorothy A. Frayer, *Effects of Number of Instances and Emphasis of Relevant Attribute Values on Mastery of Geometric Concepts by Fourth- and Sixth-Grade Children*, Technical Report No. 116 (Madison, Wis.: Wisconsin Research and Development Center for Cognitive Learning, March 1970), pp. 10–11.

[13]*Ibid.*, p. 27.

[14]Abraham Kaplan, *The Conduct of Inquiry* (Scranton, Pa.: Chandler Publishing Company, 1964), pp. 48–49.

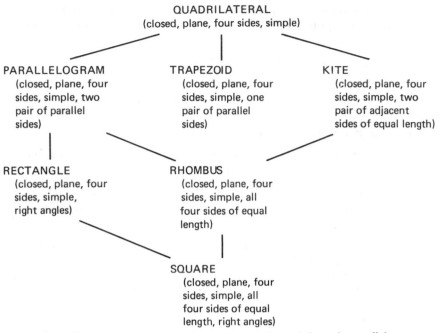

Fig. 1–1. Relationships among the concepts of quadrilateral, parallelogram, trapezoid, kite, rectangle, rhombus, and square. Relevant attribute values of each concept are indicated in parentheses.

A conception "belongs to" a particular person (although, of course, others may have very similar conceptions), and it will differ, in general, from time to time. My conception of an atom is different from a nuclear physicist's, largely because of ignorance, and different again from what it was before I was aware of nuclear reactions. Associated with the *usage* of a term is a *concept*, which may be said correspondingly to be a family of conceptions.

In appraising the plethora of definitions available in the literature, the psychologist Vinacke has noted of them that "one of their greatest weaknesses is the unfortunate tendency to regard words as concepts rather than to recognize that a verbal response is merely a label for the internal cognitive system, which from the psychological standpoint, is actually the concept.[15] A similar warning also has been raised by Hullfish and Smith:[16]

[15]W. E. Vinacke, *The Psychology of Thinking* (New York: McGraw-Hill Book Company, 1952), p. 100.
[16]H. Gordon Hullfish and Philip G. Smith, *Reflective Thinking: The Method of Education* (New York: Dodd, Mead & Company, 1961), p. 160.

It appears that the search for *a concept* is fruitless. No such entity is to be discovered, despite the inspired efforts over the ages of students of "mental life" or those of the analyses of behavior. And research is ill-conceived that investigates the formation and function of a "something" thought to be so well known that it need not be defined, with its existence taken for granted simply because there is a noun in the language that names it.

An Operational Definition of Concept

What is required by the teacher, in effect, is a concept of a concept that permits him to make inferences about appropriate instructional procedures. In this spirit, a definition is suggested which draws heavily upon the work of Bruner et al.,[17] and Viaud:[18]

> A concept is a continuum of inferences by which a set of observed characteristics of an object or event suggests a class identity, and then additional inferences about other unobserved churacteristics of the object or event.

By "suggests" it is meant that the organism involved is prompted to go beyond the immediate objects or events perceived, in the sense that inferences are made from what is directly observed. In turn these inferences then suggest additional ones to the organism. To illustrate, one reads in a text, for example, that Country A has been externally controlled by country B; from this statement the reader correctly or incorrectly infers "imperialism," which in turn suggests economic, political, and social domination of country A by B, and specifically, the loss of country A's sovereignty. Similarly, in a different situation, if smoke is observed and crackling heard, one quickly may infer "fire," which suggests, in turn, something to be avoided, the decomposition of matter, and flames; the latter then further suggests water, the need to escape and to seek assistance.

In these two cases, the report of the external control of the country and the sensing of smoke and crackling provided a set of observed characteristics, which suggested a class identity, denoted by a symbol, and then a chain of inferences from observed and unobserved properties.

An essential implication of the definition is that one can only accurately speak of concept Y that person X may have, or of the symbol— let it be called $f(Y)$—which stands in place of or suggests Y for X or

[17]Jerome S. Bruner, Jacqueline J. Goodnow, and George Austin, *A Study of Thinking* (New York: Science Editions, 1962), p. 244.
[18]Viaud, *op. cit.*, pp. 75–76.

other persons. To illustrate, if $f(Y)$ = democracy, then for X, $f(Y)$ may
stand in place of a series of interrelated ideas dealing with voting,
values, power, and the like which make up Y. Those who are unable to
infer Y from $f(Y)$ or a similar cue may be said to be potential acquirers
of Y, but, at that point, the concept is *non*existent for them.

A further implication is that concepts do not lie fallow in some
mental cavity of an organism, nor are they, strictly speaking, "carried
around," "strung together," or "held" by organisms. Concepts, rather,
assume an emergent character and come into being for the organism
as immediate perceptions lead to a classification process and eventually
to a network of inferences, based on past and present experiences. Prior
to the initiation of the network of inferences, the concept in question
is momentarily nonexistent for the organism.

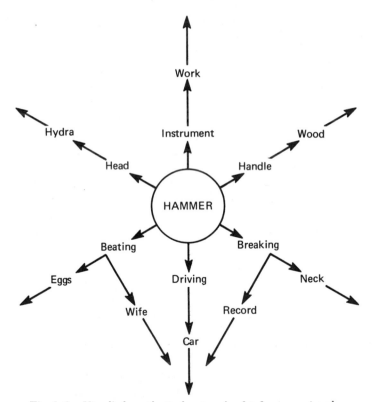

Fig. 1–2. Viaud's hypothetical network of inferences. An object or event is categorized as "hammer." This process generates
an inference network with "hammer" having the rule "an instrument for beating, breaking, driving nails, etc., with a solid
head at right angles to its handle." (Source: Gatson Viaud, *Intelligence: Its Evolution and Form*, E. J. Pomerans, trans., New York:
Harper, 1960, p. 76.)

This notion of concept as a sequence of inferential chains is illustrated by Viaud's schematic in Fig. 1–2, relating to the observed properties "solid-head-at-right-angles-to-handle."[19]

In Viaud's network of inferences, six attributes of "hammer" that typically might be considered by an observer are represented as *initial* inferences. These in turn suggest *additional* inferences—in some cases remote from the originally observed object, and in others interrelated. Adolescents reflect similarly divergent networks in their delight, for example, of *doubles entendres.*

Instructional Characteristics of Concepts

Concepts, for instructional purposes, may be thought of as a category of experience having a *rule* which defines the relevant category, a set of *positive instances* or *exemplars* with *attributes* and a *name* (though this latter element is sometimes missing). Thus "a natural elevation of the earth's surface rising to a summit" is a *rule* stating essential or criterial *attributes* with the *name* "mountain," of which "Fuji" is a positive *exemplar* or illustration. Rules then are the definitions or formulas specifying the attributes of the concept. Hunt and Metcalf refer to a rule as the "intension" of a concept, as opposed to its "extension," which is the set of items to which it is applied.[20] They cite the Beardsley's example of "city": "The extension of 'city' is London, Paris, New York, Berlin, Tokyo, Moscow, Nairobi, etc. The intension of 'city' is (roughly) the characteristic of being a politically independent area of high population density and large population total."[21]

Attributes in turn are those characteristics which are the identifying features of a concept, and which enable one to distinguish between exemplars and nonexemplars. Generalization of the criterial or critical attributes to all members of the class requires the learner to generalize among exemplars presented in a particular learning task, as well as to other exemplars he will encounter in the future. Stereotypes, for example, present an extreme example of *over*generalization, where the learner has formed rigid concepts which do not assimilate and accommodate experience. A teacher's role in these situations is to initiate the

---

[19] *Ibid.,* p. 76.

[20] Maurice P. Hunt and Lawrence E. Metcalf, *Teaching High School Social Studies: Problems in Reflective Thinking and Social Understanding,* 2nd ed. (New York: Harper & Row, Publishers, 1968), p. 89. See also David Elkind, "Conservation and Concept Formation," in David Elkind and John H. Flavell (eds.), *Studies in Cognitive Development: Essays in Honor of Jean Piaget* (New York: Oxford University Press, 1969), pp. 180–181.

[21] *Ibid.,* p. 89, as quoted from Monroe C. and Elizabeth L. Beardsley, *Philosophical Thinking: An Introduction* (New York: Harcourt Brace Jovanovich, 1965), p. 24.

process of qualifying such overgeneralizations by presenting new and objective information for concept modification. As DeCecco suggests,[22]

> If the child excludes members of some races, religions, and nationalities from the general concept *human being,* some instruction is strongly indicated. Or, if the child lists the attributes of one race as intelligent, socially responsible, sanitary, and achieving and the attributes of another race as stupid, irresponsible, dirty, and lazy, the teacher can provide a wider array of positive and negative examples for both races than the child may have experienced before.

Exemplars may be regarded as positive instances of the concept, nonexemplars as negative examples, and names as symbols commonly used by a culture to identify or label a concept. The absence of *one* or more criterial attributes from a rule will qualify an item as a *nonexemplar.* Thus "iceberg" (a body of ice, surrounded by water) is a *nonexemplar* of "island" (body of land surrounded by water), though it lacks only *one* common attribute, and similarly, "tree" is a nonexemplar, sharing no common attributes.

Exemplars, of course, may take many varied forms and include considerable extraneous or noncriterial material. A freehand drawing or high altitude photo of an island, for example, will provide an exemplar with only the three criterial attributes illustrated, while a film exemplar of Hawaii may include considerable detail irrelevant or noncritical to the concept such as palm trees, buildings, dancers, and leis.

Rules and Language

The importance of phrasing rules in a language appropriate for the student's age level should be underscored, since many of the problems connected with concept learning derive from linguistic barriers. Henry Johnson provides us with an apt anecdote on this point.[23]

> Was the seventh-grade girl who came home from a history lesson reporting that "General Arnold cut off both of General Burgoyne's legs" exercising her fool spot or was the fool spot in the textbook which informed her that "General Arnold cut off General Burgoyne's supporting column?

Language of course has long been considered to have a key causal relationship with concept learning. As Sapir has eloquently phrased it,

[22]John P. De Cecco, *The Psychology of Learning and Instruction* (Englewood Cliffs, N.J.: Prentice-Hall, Inc., 1968), p. 400.
[23]Henry Johnson, *The Teaching of History,* rev. ed. (New York: The Macmillan Company, 1940), p. 249.

"Language is a dynamo that we use principally for lighting little name plates, for labeling and categorizing things." Whorf's pioneer linguistic analyses similarly underscored how man is language-bound in all his intellectual activities. But, while vocabulary and concept development have a close relationship, it is one of contingency rather than equivalency, as has been indicated.

Neither correctly verbalizing a concept nor stating its corresponding rule guarantees, however, that one can identify exemplars of the concept. This qualification distinguishes symbol transmission from conceptualizing. Gagné has observed, for example, that "concepts may be aroused by verbal means. . . . But to be accurate tools for thinking about and dealing with the real world, concepts must be referable to actual stimulus situations."[24]

Symbol transmission, of course, can and does proceed in many classes without common conceptual referrents. Students may use terms such as, for example, "universe," "black power," "democracy," or "justice," either verbally or in writing, and still be conceptually ignorant of their basic meanings. The transmission of symbols, a student quickly learns, will often pass for "learning" in the conceptual sense in the classroom or in society at large. Both examinations and casual conversation with elders, he finds, frequently place emphasis upon symbol transmission and recognition rather than conceptualizing. Granted, there are hierarchical *levels* of symbol interaction that are expected, and these grow increasingly complex and sophisticated as one proceeds to graduate-level training.

The basic emphasis, however, frequently remains upon the manipulation of symbols as an end in itself, rather than as a vehicle or tool to conceptualize. Sigel has commented upon the educational implications of this phenomenon.[25]

> The use of language and interpretation of language in the socio-educational context deserves special attention. The teacher must be sensitive to the child's capacity for assimilating verbal language as well as be aware of the relationship between the child's language and his thought. . . . [T]he child's correct contextual use of a term is not necessarily indicative of his comprehension of that term or an accurate reflection of the child's ability to understand the logical basis of the concept.

Thus symbols often take on a *situational* meaning apart from their

[24]Robert M. Gagné, *The Conditions of Learning*, 2nd ed. (New York: Holt, Rinehart & Winston, Inc., 1970), p. 179.

[25]Irving E. Sigel, "The Piagetian System and the World of Education," in David Elkind and John H. Flavell (eds.), *Studies in Cognitive Development: Essays in Honor of Jean Piaget* (New York: Oxford University Press, 1969), p. 475.

conceptual meaning. A shrewd student confronted with a question from his teacher such as, "What do you like best about our country?" may discover that he can ease his conceptual burden by replying, "Our democratic process." By doing so, he reflects his grasp of the situational meaning of the terms "democratic process," indicating he recognizes these symbols can be positively related to characteristics of the United States. That the student may attach no conceptual meaning to the term is unimportant here, since chances are he will be rewarded with "That's a good answer, Johnny" from the teacher. He even may have learned from sad experience that an honest attempt to grapple conceptually with the question in the form of an answer, "Hot dogs, scary movies, and baseball," is frowned upon by the teacher, who categorized this latter response as "silly." Situationally silly, perhaps, but conceptually pregnant with meaning. Ausubel speaks to this point.[26]

> One reason why pupils commonly develop a rote learning set in relation to potentially meaningful subject matter is because they learn from sad experience that substantively correct answers lacking in verbatim correspondence to what they have been taught receive no credit whatsoever from certain teachers. Another reason is that because of a generally high level of anxiety, or because of chronic failure experience in a given subject (reflective, in turn, of low aptitude or poor teaching), they lack confidence in their ability to learn meaningfully, and hence perceive no alternative to panic apart from rote learning. (This phenomenon is very familiar to mathematics teachers because of the widespread prevalence of "number shock" or "number anxiety.") Lastly, pupils may develop a rote learning set if they are under excessive pressure to exhibit glibness, or to conceal, rather than admit and gradually remedy, original lack of genuine understanding. Under these circumstances it seems easier and more important to create a spurious impression of facile comprehension by rotely memorizing a few key terms or sentences than to try to understand what they mean. Teachers frequently forget that pupils become very adept at using abstract terms with apparent appropriateness—when they have to—even though their understanding of the underlying concepts is virtually nonexistent.

Ausubel's point is well illustrated by young children who are able to distinguish their right hand from the left, but have no notion of "right" or "left." Very small youngsters learn "the symbol game" quickly, as they discover that certain terms, spoken in certain contexts, evoke approval or disapproval from parents in the form of smiles, laughter, frowns, or other reinforcements. From the world around them

---

[26]Ausubel, *op. cit.*, p. 38.

youngsters are aware at a very early age that symbols have meaning apart from their conceptual relationship, and so, not surprisingly, when this phenomenon confronts them later in classroom situations it appears quite natural. For, as John Dewey long ago observed, "adults and children alike are capable of using even precise verbal formulae with only the vaguest and most confused sense of what they mean."

A recent cartoon showed an Eskimo parent and child sitting in an igloo reading the nursery rhyme about "Little Jack Horner" and the caption "What's a corner, Daddy?" The humor of the cartoon derives, in part at least, from the fact that nursery rhymes frequently are regarded as having *situational,* rather than *conceptual* import, much like a beer jingle. One need not know what curds and whey are to enjoy Miss Muffett's tale, so that argument goes.

The Eskimo youngster illustrates clearly what occurs when *conceptual* versus *situational* meaning is at issue. Conceptually, he requires an experiential basis, which he now lacks, in order to assimilate his new datum. In effect, he refused to treat the symbolic content as "just part of a nursery rhyme."

The relationship to classrooms and the import of conceptual versus linguistic manipulation for learning now may be clear. In the "nursery rhyme" sense, instruction *can* proceed with little concern for common conceptual referents; "freedom," "justice," et al., merely become the equivalents of "curds and whey." To the extent that teachers are sensitive to the need to have a common experiential basis with students in order to proceed with instruction, they, like the Eskimo parent, must answer before they move.

THE LEARNING OF CONCEPTS

Concepts and Inquiry

Even casual perusal of the educational literature produced over the last decade will reveal that the topic of "inquiry" has dominated much of our methodological discussions. Inquiry in curricular settings has taken a variety of forms, but generally has come to refer to instructional settings in which students are encouraged to volunteer or arrive at inferences and implications from observed subject matter. Deductive, inductive, or what has been called "seductive" procedures are used to generate such processes in students. Virtually all instructional materials that identify themselves with "inquiry" reflect either an explicit or implicit methodological model that bears at least a faint resemblance to John Dewey's notion of "reflective thinking."

While an adequate discussion of his pertinent views are beyond the scope of this work,[27] the nexus between Dewey's notion of reflective thinking and concept learning may be seen in the conceptualization process inherent in reflective thinking. One engaged in reflective thought necessarily is categorizing, organizing, and relating observations into an overall pattern, as well as inferring, and eventually verifying. Consistent too with Dewey's notions concerning the initiation of reflective thought, an act of concept learning may be seen as being triggered by the confrontation and delineation of puzzling, disturbing, curious, or problematical situations. Similarly, conceptualizing may be viewed as the conferring of significant meaning upon previously meaningless stimuli. As Dewey suggests,[28]

> Thought confers upon physical events and objects a very different status and value from those which they possess to a being that does not reflect. These words are mere scratches, curious variations of light and shade, to one to whom they are not linguistic signs. To him for whom they are signs of other things, the collection of marks stands for some idea or object. We are so used to the fact that things have meaning for us, that they are not mere excitations of sense organs, that we fail to recognize that they are charged with the significance they have only because in the past absent things have been suggested to us by what is present and these suggestions have been confirmed in subsequent experience. If we stumble against something in the dark, we may react to it and get out of the way to save ourselves a bruise or a tumble without recognizing what particular *object* it is. We react almost automatically to many stimuli; they have no meaning for us or are not definite individual objects. For an *object* is more than a mere *thing;* it is a thing having a definite significance.

Learning Situations

While man may live in a world of concepts, he appears to acquire them in different ways, some systematic and some informal. Figure 1–3

Learning a Concept of Relativity	Learning a Concept of Cowboy	Learning a Concept of Lightning
More Systematic Situations	Partly Informal, Partly Systematic Situations	More Informal Situations

Fig. 1–3. Continuum of learning situations.

[27]For a discussion of the Dewey model of reflective thinking applied to one dimension of classroom instruction in an analytic way, see James B. Kracht and Peter H. Martorella, "Simulation and Inquiry Models Applied to Environmental Problems," *Journal of Geography,* Vol. 49 (May 1970).

[28]John Dewey, *How We Think* (Boston: D. C. Heath & Company, 1933), pp. 19–20.

illustrates a simple continuum of learning situations that might occur for an individual.

Vygotsky, in a similar vein has characterized learning situations as "spontaneous" and "scientific."[29] Spontaneous concepts, he suggests, develop naturally from contacts with everyday life, as one interacts naturally with his environment. On the other hand, scientific concepts are those acquired in formal instructional sessions, either self-generated or externally generated. While these learning situations may be differentiated, they are frequently complementary or interactive. One may spontaneously or informally learn, for example, a concept of lightning, from which an interest is generated to seek out systematically or scientifically information concerning clouds and electricity. Although a concept of lightning may be acquired by many individuals in its basic form in informal or spontaneous contexts such as storms, it is possible also to have learned the concept first in a systematic or scientific fashion.

Having examined the work of Gagné, Guilford, Piaget, and Klausmeier, Dorothy Frayer has suggested that an act of concept learning involves the following seven processes.[30]

1. Cognition of the attribute values of concept instances.
2. Association of attribute values with their labels.
3. Cognition of an instance as an example or nonexample of the concept.
4. Association of a concept instance with its label.
5. Cognition of the characteristics common to all concept examples.
6. Cognition of the conceptual rule relating the common characteristics.
7. Cognition of the relationship between the concept and concepts subordinate and supraordinate to it.

Discussion of these and similar postulations concerning concept learning and their relationship to instruction will follow specifically in Chapters 2 and 3 and generally in the remaining chapters.

CONCEPTS AND OTHER INTELLECTUAL PHENOMENA

An assumption that permeates this book is that to be optimally efficient instructional procedures for the learning of *concepts* should be different from those used for other learning outcomes. In short, a teacher who wishes to teach a *concept* should follow a much different set of procedures than if he were attempting to teach a *skill, generaliza-*

---

[29]L. S. Vygotsky, *Thought and Language*, trans. and edited by Eugenia Hanfmann and Gertrude Vakar (Cambridge, Mass.: M.I.T. Press, 1962), p. 8.
[30]Frayer, *op. cit.*, pp. 14–15.

tion, theory, or other specified objective. *Until such distinctions have been made, there can be little progress toward developing curricular materials and learning contexts optimally appropriate for the specific instructional task delineated.*

As a way of distinguishing between intellectual phenomena, Edith West has suggested the following relationships.[31]

> Generalizations and theories are built up of specified relationships among concepts. Moreover, a new term or concept is developed to represent a newly discovered relationship among older concepts. For example, someone notes that a number of different categories have certain characteristics in common. He invents a new name to represent categories with these attributes (e.g., groups such as families and friendship groups are characterized by intimate face-to-face relations. The term "primary group" was invented to refer to all groups with this characteristic.) Or a scientist discovers a casual explanation. . . . In this sense, the concept becomes a shorthand notation for an explanatory law.

Her analysis of the relationship is essentially the same as that of Brownell and Hendrickson. The latter contend that any generalization states some abstract relationship among several concepts, and that, as such, it is more complex than any single component concept.[32] They argue that teachers should not attempt to teach generalizations among concepts that are not themselves "meaningful" (i.e., concepts that are clearly formulated, understood, and acquired). As a negative example, they offer the generalization, "In a democracy, every citizen is entitled to freedom of worship." A child who cannot answer questions such as "What is 'freedom of worship?' What is a 'citizen?' " they state, cannot really acquire the generalization intended.[33]

Vygotsky has called attention also to the systematic hierarchical network between concepts that is reflected in generalizations.[34] He provides the illustration of a child who has learned about "flower" and about "rose," but not the supraordinate-subordinate relationship between the two concepts. As the child becomes aware of the nexus between "flower" and "rose", he generates a concept system. "Concepts do not lie in the child's mind like peas in a bag, without any bonds between them" Vygotsky observed.[35]

[31]Edith West, "Concepts, Generalizations, and Theories: Background Paper No. 3," Unpublished paper, Project Social Studies, University of Minnesota, n.d., p. 4.
[32]W. A. Brownell and G. Hendrickson, "How Children Learn Information, Concepts, and Generalizations," *Learning and Instruction: Part I, Forty-ninth Yearbook, National Society for the Study of Education* (Chicago: University of Chicago Press, 1950), pp. 121–122.
[33]*Ibid.*
[34]Vygotsky, *op. cit.*, p. 111.
[35]*Ibid.*, p. 110.

An Operational Schema

For purposes of distinguishing in instructional procedures the relationship of concept to its complementary intellectual components, let us consider the following schema. *Data* comprise the fabric from which cognitive phenomena evolve; they are normative and transcend academic disciplinary boundaries, constituting the universe of discourse from which knowledge concerning a given topic may be drawn; data represent the unorganized sum total of information. *Facts*, in turn, are a component of data, representing the perceptual flow that a given organism generates from data. In this schema they are organized, selective elements of data, as shown in Fig. 1–4.

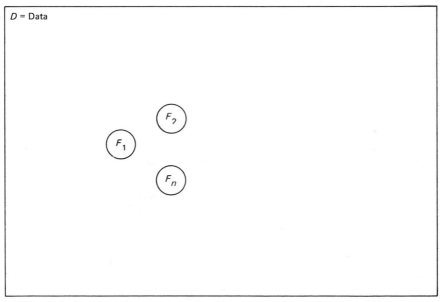

Fig. 1–4. Data and facts. The relationship of data to facts, where D = all the data pertaining to a particular topic and $F_1, F_2, \ldots (F_n)$ = specific facts pertaining to the topic.

Fact clusters in a special interrelationship then form as a *concept*, as shown in Fig. 1–5 with the category "dog." Figure 1–2 implies both a structural relationship among F_1, F_2, F_3, as well as the possibility that F_n may exist. The selection of *three* critical attributes in this illustration is, of course, purely arbitrary. C_1, in fact, may have n number of attributes, and so with any other concept.

Similarly, a hierarchical fact cluster or concept—animal, for exam-

Fig. 1-5. A concept of dog. The relationship of facts to a concept of "dog" within the context of relevant data, where D_1 = all data relating to dogs, C_1 = a concept of dog, and F_1, F_2, F_3, = facts about dogs that represent C_1's criterial attributes.

ple—may be considered, as in Fig. 1-6. Therein a stated relationship between concepts, cat, dog and animal (for example, "cats and dogs are animals") forms then a very basic *generalization*. At some point in its history a generalization, once tested and regarded as truth, may serve the status of a *fact*. "Cats and dogs are animals" may function as a component of the fact-cluster for the concept "pet."

Finally, a *theory* may be regarded as the set under which related concepts and interrelated fact clusters are subsumed in a special structure. This relationship is illustrated in Fig. 1-7, dealing with the theory "the origin of species."

A similar schema might be devised for a theory concerning the "origin of cities," where some of the following sample items might be subsumed.

(a) *Generalizations:* "All nations have cities;" "cities function as economic units."
(b) *Concepts:* city, nation, economy, defense, specialization.
(c) *Facts:* New York is densely populated; Los Angeles, Philadelphia, and Chicago have populations of over two million people. Tokyo is a geographic subdivision of Japan.

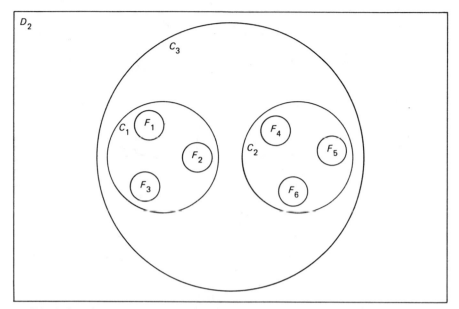

Fig. 1–6. The generalization: cats and dogs are animals. The relationship of sets of facts to concepts within the context of relevant data, resulting in a generalization, where D_2 = all data relating to animals, C_1 = a concept of dog and F_1, F_2, F_3 = facts about dogs that represent C_1's criterial attributes, C_2 = a concept of cat, F_4, F_5, F_6 = facts that represent C_2's criterial attributes, and C_3 = a concept of animal.

(d) *Data:* All known phenomena relating to the development of cities.

While these diagrams represent a severe distortion of the actual dynamic relationships in a data-fact-concept-generalization-theory continuum, several points to be considered for organizing concept-learning experiences follow from Figs. 1–4 through 1–7.

1. *Each component on the continuum has some subordinate or hierarchical relationship to other components.* Concepts are generated from *fact*-clusters, and in turn may organize into *generalizations;* all three comprise the stuff of *theories.* Formation of generalizations presupposes that subsumed concepts already have been learned, and theory acquisition requires the added dimension that a variety of concepts and generalizations be systematically interrelated. This nexus does *not* suggest, however, that the learning of facts must be a discrete step in advance of concept formation. A student easily may be exposed to a plethora of facts concerning government, yet never develop a concept. Conversely, however, he must acquire some fact relationship concerning critical attributes of government, if he is to develop a concept.

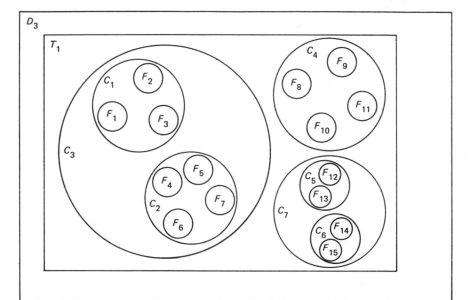

Fig. 1–7. A theory: the origin of species. The relationship of facts, concepts, and generalizations to a theory, a subset within the context of relevant data, where D_3 = a set of all data relating to the origin of species, T_1 = a subset, representing a theory on the origin of species, C_1 = a concept of apes and F_1, F_2, F_3 = a corresponding fact cluster, C_2 = a concept of man, F_4, F_5, F_6, F_7 = a corresponding fact cluster, C_3 = a concept of animals, C_4 = a concept of species, F_8, F_9, F_{10}, F_{11} = a corresponding fact cluster, C_5 = a concept of genes, F_{12}, F_{13}, a corresponding fact cluster, C_6 = a concept of sexual drives, F_{14}, F_{15} = a corresponding fact cluster, and C_7 = a concept of reproduction.

2. *In addition to organizing facts, learning a given concept may concurrently involve learning in advance a subordinate concept.*

Whatever the chronology of the learning sequence between concepts, clearly it must be a hierarchical one. In a geography-oriented lesson in an elementary class a teacher may be interested in introducing youngsters to maps and globes as models, which can predict phenomena in a real world. She isolates "equator" as the initial concept for students to learn and sets as the concept rule from her textbook: "an imaginary line around the earth which is everywhere equally distant from the two poles." Unfortunately for the teacher, "poles" and "earth" are two subordinate concepts that many of her students may not have learned, particularly if this is their first exposure to maps and globes. If she is cognizant of the problem, the teacher may "back up" and first develop the subordinate concepts. Otherwise, what many students are likely to learn is some variations of the themes: "It's the red line around the globe. It's the place where the halves of the globe are put together. It's the place where it's zero on the map. That's where it's real hot." These observations all might be facts noted also by one who *has learned* the concept, but in isolation they do *not* comprise the criterial attributes stated in the rule.

3. *A variety of data elements may provide the facts from which concepts are constructed.* Since the *same* facts need not be interrelated to generate a commonly shared concept, some attention is possible at least to the individual differences of students. A teacher who wishes to develop a concept of power need not require students to be restricted to a specific body of social science facts. Given a concept rule as a guide, the general data base might be (a) mayor's-office operations in Chicago, (b) Saul Alinsky's programs, (c) Theodore Roosevelt's foreign policies, (d) influence of advertisers on TV programming, (e) Stalin's regime. Self-generating historical parallels are provided at the level of concepts, without the artificial and vague linkage between events that teachers often laboriously strive to contrive.

4. *A student's conceptual development is a coefficient of his database dimensions.* While the selective organization of facts provides the main focus for a concept-learning task, it is important not to overlook the obvious role of the learner's data base. Typically it may have several dimensions: (a) teacher's background, (b) student's background, (c) classroom materials, (d) nonclassroom materials or data from home, mass media, etc. All the dimensions have limitations for a concept-learning task in that they already represent a *filtering* of data or a store of *facts.* Consequently, the teacher reflects rather her *fact base,* as does the student, as do curricular materials by reflecting the author's *fact base,* and as do the news media. The greater the screening out of relevant data, as represented, for example, by experience-deprived teachers, students, curricular materials, and nonclassroom materials, the more restricted is the student's opportunity to develop a given concept. This is the point that the historian Carl L. Becker makes in stating[36]

> If our memories of past events are short and barren, our anticipations of future events will be short and barren; if our memories are rich and diversified, our anticipations of what is to come are likely to be more or less so, too. But the main point is that the character of the pattern of the one, no less than its richness and extent, will depend on the character of the other.

[36]Carl L. Becker, *The Heavenly City of the Eighteenth-Century Philosophers* (New Haven: Yale University Press, 1932), p. 121.

The notion of data as discrete from facts suggests that students and teachers be more sensitive to broadening their data-seeking tools and to rejecting facile fact-compilation as an end. In the process of facilitating concept learning a teacher will assist students in acquiring the skills necessary for extending the dimensions of their data base as widely as possible. This approach might enable students to see their and others' daily life-experience flow as a pregnant source of data. In this sense they might perceive themselves in their cultural interactions as data generators as well as receivers, and become more sensitive to the data limitations of all curricular materials.

CONCLUSION

Man lives in a conceptual world which he builds through both informal and systematic interaction. Concepts enable us to simplify and organize our environment and to communicate efficiently with others. While each of us may be said to have truly unique concepts of objects or events, we share with others at least the critical or criterial attributes of the concepts. This minimal commonality should provide the basic instructional goal for teachers in classroom settings.

While concepts have been defined in varying ways, for instructional purposes an operational definition is the most useful. Drawing upon the writings of Viaud and Bruner and associates, it was suggested that "a concept is a continuum of inferences by which a set of observed characteristics of an object or event suggests a class identity, and then additional inferences about other unobserved characteristics of the object or event." A concept, for instructional purposes, may be thought of as having a rule which defines it, criterial or critical attributes which are stated in the rule, a name or concept word, and positive instances or exemplars. Though concepts are interrelated with other intellectual phenomena, such as skills, generalizations, theories, and the like, they have a discrete identity of their own which requires special instructional considerations.

SUGGESTED READINGS

Ausubel, David P., *Educational Psychology: A Cognitive View* (New York: Holt, Rinehart & Winston, Inc., 1968), Chap. 15.

Fine analysis of the dimensions of a concept learning from both an experimental and a general theoretical point of view.

Bruner, Jerome S., Jacqueline J. Goodnow, and George A. Austin, *A Study of Thinking* (New York: Science Editions, 1962).

A major work dealing with a variety of experimental and theoretical issues associated with the nature of cognitive processes. Considerable attention is paid to the role of symboling in concept learning.

Carroll, John B., "Words, Meanings, and Concepts," *Harvard Educational Review*, Vol. 24 (Spring, 1964), pp. 178–202.

Discusses the nature of concepts, the inadequacies in traditional concept-learning research, and various instructional problems in a lucid and well-organized fashion.

Dewey, John, *How We Think* (New York: D. C. Heath & Company, 1933).

A classical treatise on the nature of thinking processes.

Hullfish, H. Gordon, and Phillip G. Smith, *Reflective Thinking: The Method of Education* (New York: Dodd, Mead & Co. 1961), Chap. 10.

A well-written and succinct analysis of conceptualizing as a process and of its implications for classroom instruction.

Vygotsky, L. S., *Thought and Language*, edited and trans. by Eugenia Hanfmann and Gertrude Vakar (Cambridge, Mass.: M.I.T. Press, 1962).

A pioneer study dealing with the role of language in the formation of concepts. The clear analysis is particularly relevant for teachers.

CHAPTER 2

Studies of Concept Learning

The pattern that emerges from much of the psychological research on concept learning since the 1920's is generally consistent. The emphasis has been on studying both the clearly specifiable attributes that are critical to the concepts in question and the specific variables in the task required of the subject. Usually taken into account is the sequence in which the positive and negative examples are introduced to the subject and the amount of information about the concept that is provided. Frequently in experiments the procedure has emphasized the following type of task:[1]

> The subject is presented with a series of instances which are differentiated in some way: either the task of finding out in what way the several instances match up with one of a small number of names, or (in the simpler case) it is one of discovering why some instances are "positive" (i.e., instances of the concept the experimenter has in mind) or "negative" (not instances of the "concept"). Typically the stimulus material consists of simple visual material characterized by a number of clearly salient dimensions—e.g., the color of the figures, the geometrical shape of the figures, the number of figures, the number of borders, the color of the background, etc.

As the reader may suspect, what hampers the generalizability of these laboratory studies is their questionable relationship to concepts commonly learned in one's life experiences or to conditions under which everyday concepts are normally learned. Frayer has observed[2]

---

[1]John B. Carroll, "Words, Meanings and Concepts," *Harvard Educational Review*, Vol. 34 (Spring 1964), 198.

[2]Dorothy A. Frayer, *Effects of Number of Instances and Emphasis of Relevant Attribute Values on Mastery of Geometric Concepts by Fourth- and Sixth-Grade Children*, Technical Report No. 116 (Madison, Wis.: Wisconsin Research and Development Center for Cognitive Learning, March 1970), p. 2.

Laboratory experiments have generally utilized specially chosen concepts embodying only a few of the aspects which may influence learning of concepts encountered in daily life. Most concepts studied in the laboratory are comprised of characteristics already known to the learner. Thus, the effect of variables influencing the learning of those characteristics is minimized. Laboratory concepts usually do not have meaningful concept labels, even though associations between such labels may have a powerful effect on transfer and interference in learning. Also, a large amount of response learning may be required to acquire the labels.

Therefore, while a considerable quantity of research on concepts has been amassed, unfortunately, there is a serious question as to how much of the findings may be applied to classroom instruction with any degree of assurance. Remstad has captured the essence of this issue in his statement[3]

An examination of the scores of experimental studies devoted to various aspects of concept learning leads to the conclusion that psychologists have compiled a considerable amount of information which should be relevant to the learning of the types of concepts taught in schools. However, closer examination raises the question whether or not that which the psychologist in his experimentation has labeled a concept bears an adequate enough resemblance to the type of concept taught in the classroom to be of value to educators.

Similarly, Carroll has cautioned,[4] "It is not self-evident that there is any continuity at all between learning 'DAX' as the name of a certain geometrical shape of a certain color and learning the meaning of the term *'longitude'*."

Some of the more significant differences between concepts learned in the laboratory under controlled conditions and those concepts usually learned under normal classroom conditions have been summarized by Carroll;[5] the gist of the distinctions are

1. A new concept which is learned in school is usually a genuinely new concept rather than an artificial combination of known properties.
2. In the classroom, new concepts learned depend upon properties which themselves also represent difficult concepts.
3. Many difficult school concepts are of the *relational* variety

---

[3]Robert C. Remstad, *Optimizing the Response to a Concept Attainment Test Through Sequential Classroom Experimentation*, Technical Report No. 85 (Madison, Wis.: Wisconsin Research and Development Center for Cognitive Learning, 1969), p. 8.
[4]Carroll, *op. cit.*, pp. 179–80.
[5]*Ibid.*, pp. 190–91.

concerning which little has been revealed from experimental
data.

4. An important problem in school learning is remembering many
   words and concepts, many of which are often dissimilar.

5. The most significant difference between concept learning in the
   classroom and the learning of concepts in the laboratory is that
   the former is chiefly deductive and the latter, generally inductive.

Remstad has indicated two other important differences between
the two types of learning conditions:[6] (1) a student must learn a new
word or a new use for a known word along with the concept; and (2)
neither the exemplars of the concept nor the dimensions to be considered can be listed or can be observed completely, so that "an ambigu-
ous or complete attainment of a concept is impossible."

And a final limitation of concept-learning research *generally*,
Frayer notes, "has been the preponderance of studies employing young
adults as subjects. In order to discover possible developmental trends
in concept learning, experiments should be replicated at various age
levels."[7]

The remainder of this chapter will treat selected dimensions of the
concept-learning literature that appear to have some general applications to all subject-matter areas. Later specialty chapters will deal with
other specifically discipline-related literature.

SELECTED LABORATORY STUDIES

Bruner and Associates

One of the more important hallmark studies of concept learning
was that by Bruner and associates, *A Study of Thinking*, published in
1956.[8] This book reported on twenty laboratory experiments on concept attainment, the nature of which may be described as follows:
Subjects are presented with a board containing a number of objects.
Each object has a set of dimensions with corresponding values. Subjects
are informed that the items can be divided into two mutually exclusive
groups with membership defined by a rule consisting of certain attributes. An object is designated as a member of the group, and from this
the subjects are to discover the classification rule by selecting objects
and then having the experimenter designate their group membership.

---

[6]Remstad, *op. cit.*, p. 12.
[7]Frayer, *op. cit.*, p. 3.
[8]Jerome S. Bruner, Jacqueline J. Goodnow, and George Austin, *A Study of Thinking*
(New York: Science Editions, 1962).

The subject is to reveal the classification rule as soon as he recognizes it, at which time the concept is considered attained.

Since these studies have had considerable influence upon concept-learning research, an extended summary of them seems in order. The experiments generated extensive data concerning the distinction between concept formation and attainment, the different types of concepts that exist, a working definition of a concept, and the learning set that one has for a concept-learning task.

Concept Formation and Attainment. Concept or category formation in these studies refers to the act by which classes are constructed, whereas concept attainment is the process of learning what features of the environment are relevant for grouping events into externally defined classes. Concept attainment is the search for and testing of attributes that can be used to distinguish exemplars from nonexemplars of various categories.[9] The authors provide a list of the decisions involved in attaining a concept.

1. *The definition of the task.* What does the person take as the objective of his behavior? What does he think he is supposed to do?

2. *The nature of instances encountered.* How many attributes does each exhibit, and how many of these are defining and how many noisy? Does he encounter instances at random, in a systematic order, and does he have any control over the order in which instances will be tested? Do instances encountered contain sufficient information for learning the concept fully?

3. *The nature of validation.* Does the person learn each time an instance is encountered whether it is or is not an exemplar of the concept whose definition he is seeking? Or is such validation only available after a series of encounters? Can hypotheses be readily checked or not?

4. *The consequences of specific categorizations.* What is the price of categorizing a specific instance wrongly and the gain from a correct categorization? What is the price attached to a wrong hypothesis? And do the various contingencies—rightness or wrongness of a categorization of "X" and "non-X"—have a different price attached to them?

5. *The nature of imposed restrictions.* Is it possible to keep a record of instances and contingencies? Is there a price attached to the testing of instances as a means of finding out in which category they belong? Is there pressure of time to contend with, a need for speedy decisions?

[9] *Ibid.*, p. 33.

Types of Concepts. Bruner and associates distinguish between three classes of concepts: conjunctive, disjunctive, and relational, considering each class to relate a different mode of coupling attributes.[10]

A *conjunctive* concept is defined in terms of a common class of combined elements, an example being "island"—a body of land surrounded on all sides by water." *Disjunctive* concepts, on the other hand, take their identity from the fact that they have *alternate* attributes. An instance of this sort of concept, Bruner et al. tells us, is a strike in baseball. Since a strike may be a pitched ball resulting in any one of several different phenomena—a missed pitched or a foul ball or a ball thrown over a certain region of the plate—its category identity is preserved even though its attributes may vary any given moment. The third class, *relational* concepts, express a certain relationship among the attributes of a concept. An example thus might be waste, which may be seen as the relationship between the given state of an item or class and the value that one places on it.

It was found that subjects tended to prefer common-element or conjunctive concepts over the other types. Part of the process of attaining disjunctive and relational concepts appears to be confounded by the *set* that a subject has developed in attaining conjunctive concepts. Whether this phenomenon "is a universal characteristic of human thought and language of Western cultures," Bruner et al. are not prepared to say.[11]

Working Definition of a Concept. Based upon abstracting a description of the processes at work in concept attainment, they define "concept" in the following terms:[12]

> We have found it more meaningful to regard a concept as a network of significant inferences by which one goes beyond a set of *observed* critical properties exhibited by an object or event to the class identity of the object or event in question, and thence to additional inferences about other *unobserved* properties of the object or event. We see an object that is red, shiny, and roundish, and infer that it is an apple; we are then enabled to infer further that "if it is an apple, it is also edible, juicy, will rot if left unrefrigerated, etc." The working definition of a concept is the network of inferences that are or may be set into play by an act of categorization.

In general, it may be said that a "concept" minimally involves the process wherein an individual is confronted with the task of identifying

[10] *Ibid.*, p. 41.
[11] *Ibid.*, p. 238.
[12] *Ibid.*, p. 244.

and placing events into classes on the principle of using certain critical characteristics and ignoring others.[13]

Learning Frame of Reference. A final set of conclusions from the studies relates to the issue of the learner's psychological frame of reference in confronting a concept-attainment task.[14]

> One other matter of technique has to do with the use of indirect or "cover-story" methods of studying cognition, a mater that has bedeviled the field of concept attainment particularly. If one presents a concept-attainment task to subjects with the cover-story instruction that it is a task of rote memory (associating DAXes and CIVs with various curlicues), then the behavior of the subject will be geared to the objectives of the task as stated and his strategy will reflect the requirements set him. Let it be clear that the problem of setting the objectives in problem-solving and conceptualizing experiments is not a nuisance to be got rid of by "cute" instructions that conceal the purpose of the research. Objective-setting is a critical variable to be studied as a variable; it is neither a parameter one can hold constant with safety nor an embarrassment to be swept under the procedural rug.

Studies of Related Variables

The influence of *A Study of Thinking* upon concept research has been considerable, and a number of related studies have appeared in the past sixteen years.[15] A study by Bourne,[16] for example, supported the conclusions of Bruner et al. concerning the factors that affect strategies used in concept-learning tasks.

Examining a different dimension of concept learning, the effects of various types of different presentations, Kates and Yudin concluded that the presentation of all exemplars simultaneously was an optimal sequence strategy for concept learning.[17] In their study, students were given *successive presentations* in which examples were shown briefly and then removed, *focus conditions* sequences, in which two exemplars were always shown—a positive exemplar plus a new one (either positive or negative), and *simultaneous presentations,* wherein every

---

[13] *Ibid.,* p. 232.

[14] *Ibid.,* p. 243.

[15] Interestingly, however, this book appears to be less well known among educators than Bruner's more general books; for example, *The Process of Education* and *Toward a Theory of Instruction.*

[16] Lyle E. Bourne, Jr., "Factors Affecting Strategies Used in Problems of Concept-Formation." *American Journal of Psychology,* Vol. 76 (1963), pp. 229–238. See also the more recent collection of studies by Bruner and associates, *Studies in Cognitive Growth* (New York: John Wiley & Sons, Inc., 1966).

[17] Solis L. Kates and Lee Yudin, "Concept Attainment and Memory," *Journal of Educational Psychology,* Vol. 55 (1964), pp. 103–109.

new exemplar was shown *together with* all the previous exemplars. Their findings indicated a superiority hierarchy of *simultaneous presentations* to *focus condition* to *successive presentation.*

While the research findings concerning the ratios and orders of positive and negative exemplars in concept-learning tasks have been inconclusive,[18] Bourne and Guy, in a 1968 report, suggest some important variables for consideration.[19] From their study with laboratory-type concepts, they have concluded that both the concept rule and the nature of the learning problem must be taken into account as affecting the role of positive and negative exemplars.[20] This conclusion represents a qualification of Glaser's generalization, "as the information required to define the concept is increasingly carried by negative rather than positive instances, concept learning becomes increasingly difficult."[21]

One of the early studies to examine the effects of irrelevant information in nonconjunctive concept learning was conducted by Kepros and Bourne.[22] Haygood and Stevenson,[23] in extending this study, concluded that the effects of adding irrelevant stimulus information with nonconjunctive rules[24] paralleled those for conjunctive concepts—a linear decrease in performance results. The actual rate of decrease, they concluded, was highly dependent upon the specific characteristics of the conceptual problem.

Correspondingly, after a recent review of the related literature Frayer concluded: "In summary, emphasis of relevant attribute values by verbal cues has been shown to improve immediate concept learning performance, transfer, and retention."[25]

[18]For a review of the research, see Gilbert Sax, "Concept Formation," in Robert L. Ebel (ed.), *Encyclopedia of Educational Research* (New York: The Macmillan Company, 1969).

[19]Lyle E. Bourne, Jr., and Donald E. Guy, "Learning Conceptual Rules II: The Role of Positive and Negative Instances," *Journal of Experimental Psychology*, Vol. 77 (1968), pp. 488–494.

[20]*Ibid.*, p. 494.

[21]Robert Glaser, "Concept Learning and Concept Teaching," in Robert M. Gagné and William J. Gephart (eds.), *Learning Research and School Subjects* (Itasca, Ill.: F. E. Peacock, 1968), p. 15.

[22]P. G. Kepros and L. E. Bourne, Jr., "Identification of Biconditional Concepts. Effects of the Number of Relevant and Irrelevant Dimensions," *Canadian Journal of Psychology*, Vol. 20 (1966), pp. 198–207.

[23]R. C. Haygood and M. Stevenson, "Effects of Number of Irrelevant Dimensions in Conjunctive Concept Learning," *Journal of Experimental Psychology*, Vol. 74 (1967), pp. 302–304.

[24]Their nonconjunctive concepts were labeled "inclusive disjunctive" (either red *or* square *or* both) and "conditional" (if red, *then* square).

[25]Frayer, *op. cit.*, p. 24.

LABORATORY TO CLASSROOM: BRIDGING THE GAP

Wisconsin Research and Development Center

Researchers at the Wisconsin Research and Development Center for Cognitive Learning have worked extensively in recent years on concept-learning research in school settings with typical classroom concepts. Two recent studies by Remstad and by Frayer investigated the extent to which conclusions generated by laboratory studies concerning concept learning were generalizable to classroom conditions. Using upper-elementary-grade students and slide-tape presentations, Remstad specifically measured the effects of research-based mathematics instruction upon the learning of selected concepts, "quadrilateral," "isosceles triangle," "trapezoid," and "rectangle." Eight variables were examined.[26]

1. Amount of redundant information.
2. Mode of presentation of successive instances.
3. Ratio of positive and negative instances.
4. Order of positive and negative instances.
5. Amount of information in accompanying verbal cues.
6. Length of time the instances are available to students.
7. Length of time between instances.
8. Relative complexity of concept.

Among his conclusions were the findings that classroom instruction based upon principles of concept learning derived from laboratory studies *did* facilitate the learning of concepts and that verbal cues and time increments were significant variables.

Frayer similarly examined through the medium of *printed instructional materials* the effects of emphasizing relevant attribute values and varying the number of examples on the learning of the mathematical concepts, "quadrilateral," "kite," "trapezoid," "parallelogram," "rectangle," "rhombus," and "square."[27] As with the Remstad study, upper-elementary students in classroom settings were the experimental subjects. Each of the concepts were analyzed to determine their relevant and irrelevant attributes, their rules, appropriate exemplars and nonexemplars, and related subordinate and supraordinate concepts. A description of the lessons developed is given in Table 2–1.[28] Results of the study indicate "that variables that were effective in

[26]Remstad, *op. cit.*, pp. ix–x.
[27]Frayer, *op. cit.*, p. 38.
[28]*Ibid.*, p. 38.

laboratory concept learning may facilitate learning from printed instructional material."[29]

TABLE 2-1

DESCRIPTION OF GEOMETRY LESSONS

Lesson I.	Point, line segment, line, ray, angle
Lesson II.	Right angle, closed curve, simple curve, plane, polygon, parallel, adjacent, opposite, equal length
Lesson III.	Quadrilateral, kite, trapezoid, parallelogram, rectangle, rhombus, square
Lesson IV.	Relationships between the concepts included

The general program of the Center includes basic research to produce new information concerning learning variables and the processes of instruction, and the corresponding production of research-based instructional materials. Wherever applicable, school settings are used to test and revise materials. Two germane specific projects are the *Project on the Structure of Concept Attainment Abilities* and the *Situational Variables and Efficiency of Concept Learning Project.*

The former project cites as its goal, "a formulation of a model of structure of abilities in concept attainment in a number of subjects, including mathematics, science, and language arts, as well as social studies,"[30] while the latter project has established the following objectives:[31]

> To identify the conditions that facilitate concept learning in the school setting and to describe their management, to develop and validate a schema for evaluating the student's level of concept understanding, to develop and validate a model of cognitive processes in concept learning, to generate knowledge concerning the semantic components of concept learning, and to identify conditions associated with motivation for school learning and to describe their management.

Gagné and Ausubel

Two major researchers who have written and worked extensively in areas relating to classroom concept learning are David Ausubel and

[29] *Ibid.,*

[30] B. Robert Tabachnick, Evelyn B. Weible, and Dorothy A. Frayer, *Selection and Analysis of Social Studies Concepts for Inclusion in Tests of Concept Attainment,* Working Paper No. 53 (Madison, Wis.: Wisconsin Research and Development Center for Cognitive Learning, November 1970), p. iii.

[31] Frayer, *op. cit.,* p. iii.

Robert Gagné. Both have had considerable influence upon other researchers, the shaping of curriculum, and the analysis of learning conditions in naturalistic settings. Some of Ausubel's views have already been cited in the earlier chapter.

In his recent book, *Educational Psychology: A Cognitive View,* Ausubel has drawn upon his own research and others to state some general conclusions concerning concept learning.[32]

> Thus concepts and propositions are typically acquired during the post-infancy, preschool, and early elementary-school years as a result of inductive processing of verbal and nonverbal concrete-empirical experience—typically through autonomous problem solving or discovery. The young child, for example, acquires the concept of a chair by abstracting the common features of the concept from multiple incidental encounters with many different sizes, shapes, and colors of chairs and then generalizing these attributes. Reception learning, on the other hand, although occurring early, does not become a prominent feature of intellectual functioning until the child becomes sufficiently mature cognitively to comprehend verbally presented concepts and propositions in the absence of concrete, empirical experience (until he can comprehend, for example, the meaning of "democracy" or "acceleration" from their dictionary definitions). In other words, inductive concept *formation* based on nonverbal concrete, empirical problem-solving experience exemplifies early developmental phases of information processing, whereas simple concept *assimilation* through meaningful verbal reception learning exemplifies later stages.

The psychological processes involved in the highest form of concept formation, Ausubel has advanced in a thorough analysis, include the following exhaustive list of components:[33] (1) discriminating different stimulus patterns; (2) formulating hypotheses relating to abstracted common elements; (3) subsequent testing of such hypotheses in specific situations; (4) designating some of these into a general category or set of common attributes that covers all possible variations; (5) relating these attributes to similar ideas; (6) discriminating the new concept from similar concepts learned earlier; (7) generalizing the criterial attributes of the new concept to all members of the class; and (8) representing the new categorical content with a symbol commonly used in our culture.

Gagné's analysis of his own and other research on learning has led

---

[32]David P. Ausubel, *Educational Psychology: A Cognitive View* (New York: Holt, Rinehart & Winston, Inc., 1968), pp. 23–24.

[33]*Ibid.,* p. 517.

him to postulate the existence of at least *eight* clearly distinguishable types of learning conditions in a hierarchical arrangement, of which *concept* learning is Type 6, as indicated in Table 2–2.[34]

TABLE 2-2
GAGNÉ'S EIGHT CONDITIONS OF LEARNING

Problem solving (Type 8) requires as prerequisites
Rules (Type 7) which require as prerequisites
Concepts (Type 6) which require as prerequisites
Discriminations (Type 5) which require as prerequisites
Verbal associations (Type 4) or other *Chains* (Type 3) which require as prerequisites
Stimulus-response connections (Type 2)
Signal learning (Type 1) is *not* considered a prerequisite to the other types of learning

These eight different types refer to conditions under which distinguishable types of learning occur, and to the necessary prerequisite conditions for a new hierarchical learning to occur.

Concerning our focus, Gagné notes,[35]

> *Concept learning* refers to the acquisition of classification of object properties, objects, and events. Concepts may be concrete or defined. Beginning in the early grades and throughout his school career, the student will be asked to classify many things and events, from numbers to beetles to families to nations and forms of government.

In underscoring the distinctions between Type 5 and Type 6 learning, Gagné cites two cases of an individual's response to sets of keys.[36] In one situation he is given three look-alike keys for three different office doors. Eventually, however, through inspection of the key notches, he is able to distinguish between the keys. In a second situation, an individual categorizes two collections of keys as "padlock keys" and as "door keys," and when given an entirely new key, correctly identifies its category as one or the other. The former situation, according to Gagné, requires "different responses to the different members of a particular collection" or *discrimination;* while the latter case called for response "in a single way to a collection of objects as a class, which then

[34]Robert M. Gagné, *The Conditions of Learning,* 2nd ed. (New York: Holt, Rinehart & Winston, Inc., 1970), p. 66.
[35]*Ibid.,* p. 68.
[36]*Ibid.,* p. 156.

extends beyond the particular members that were originally present"
or *concept learning.*[37]

PIAGETIAN STUDIES

The work of Piaget[38] and his Geneva associates represents a vein
of findings which have had a profound effect upon American educators
in recent years. Among other conclusions, their studies suggest that the
attainment of such concepts as time, weight, color, and distance occur
developmentally as a youngster ages. More specifically, their findings
have generated a general schema providing, in Hooper's terms, "the
right kind of experience at the *right time* for the developing organism,"[39] suggesting what type of data is appropriate for learning at a
given stage and how it should be presented.

Basic to any discussion of Piaget's findings relevant to concept
learning are his concepts of "accommodation," "assimilation," "stages,"
and "equilibrium." A summary of their meaning follows.

Accommodation. When an individual encounters new circumstances where his sensorimotor organization does not fit, that modification process or reorganization that takes place within his psychological
structure may be considered as accommodation.

Assimilation. The process of internalizing or incorporating the ac-
commodative change may be considered as assimilation. These two
complimentary processes, then are simultaneously present in every
act, and together form the process of *adaptation.* Ginsburg and Opper
offer an illustration of how these processes may appear and interrelate.[40]

> Consider an example of adaptation in infancy. Suppose an infant of
> 4 months is presented with a rattle. He has never before had the
> opportunity to play with rattles or similar toys. The rattle, then is a

[37] *Ibid.*

[38] See for example J. Piaget, *The Child's Conception of Physical Causality* (London:
Routledge and Kegan Paul, 1930); *The Child's Conception of the World* (London: Rout-
ledge and Kegan Paul, 1951); *Judgment and Reason in the Child* (New York: Harcourt
Brace Jovanovich, 1929); *The Language and Thought of the Child* (New York: Harcourt
Brace Jovanovich, 1926); *The Moral Judgment of the Child* (New York: The Macmillan
Company, 1965); *The Origin of Intelligence in Children* (New York: International University Press, 1952); *The Psychology of Intelligence* (London: Routledge and Kegan Paul,
1950); and J. Piaget and B. Inhelder, *Ths Growth of Logical Thinking from Childhood
to Adolescence* (New York: Basic Books, Inc., 1958).

[39] Frank H. Hooper, "Piagetian Research and Education," in Irving E. Sigel and
Frank H. Hooper (eds), *Logical Thinking in Children,* (New York: Holt, Rinehart &
Winston, Inc., 1968), p. 423.

[40] Herbert Ginsburg and Sylvia Opper, *Piaget's Theory of Intellectual Development:
An Introduction* (Englewood Cliffs, N.J.: Prentice-Hall, Inc., 1969), p. 19.

feature of the environment to which he needs to adapt. His subsequent behavior reveals the tendencies of assimilation and accommodation. The infant tries to grasp the rattle. In order to do this successfully he must accommodate in more ways than are immediately apparent. First, he must accommodate his visual activities to perceive the rattle correctly; then he must reach out and accommodate his movements to the distance between himself and the rattle; in grasping the rattle he must adjust his fingers to its shape; and in lifting the rattle he must accommodate his muscular exertion to its weight. In sum, the grasping of the rattle involves a series of acts of accommodation, or modifications of the infant's behavioral structures to suit the demands of the environment.

Stage. Stage refers to a pattern of behavior that appears to characterize some definable period in an individual's life. Piaget's findings indicate four major periods in the intellectual development of an individual; sensorimotor (birth to eighteen months); preoperational (eighteen months to seven years); concrete operational (seven years to eleven years); and formal operational (eleven years and over). During the *sensorimotor* period the child passes through six successive stages and moves from being centered about the self to conceiving of objects independent of him and of his self-identity, and gradually coordinates his motor activities and perceptions. For Piaget, the ordering of the stages is invariant; a child must pass through stage one before stage two and may not skip steps.

Equilibrium. The notion of equilibrium refers to a state of harmony between elements that have been in disequilibrium. It involves compatibility with one's environment and an organism psychologically at rest. Of the concept and its relationship to the child, Ginsburg and Oper write:[41]

> Throughout development the child moves from states of a lesser to those of a greater degree of equilibrium. The tendency toward equilibrium results in an increase in coherence and stability; this stability is acquired by activity on the part of the child. The child is active in the sense that he compensates for changes in the world, either by means of overt actions, as in the sensorimotor period, or by internal mental operations, as in the older child. With age the equilibrium becomes more stable because the child can anticipate changes and compensate in advance.

Piaget and Structure

Much of the contemporary discussion concerning "structure" has been associated with Piaget, perhaps because of his frequent allusions

[41] *Ibid.*, p. 174.

to "mental structures." His position on the topic, however, bears a faint resemblance to the notion implicit in many so-called "structure-based" curricula where students are to be taught the unifying themes of a subject area. His statement makes his position on the matter clear.[42]

> The question comes up whether to teach the structure, or to present the child with situations where he is active and creates the structures himself. The goal in education is not to increase the amount of knowledge, but to create the possibilities for a child to invent and discover. When we teach too fast, we keep the child from inventing and discovering himself. . . . Teaching means creating situations where structures can be discovered; it does not mean transmitting structures which may be assimilated at nothing other than a verbal level.

Piaget's point is not that intellectual development proceeds at its own pace regardless of the teacher's efforts, but rather what usually is attempted in schools is ineffective—"You cannot further understanding in a child simply by talking to him."[43]

Piaget and His Contemporaries

Vygotsky, whose work represented a pioneer effort parallel to Piaget's, summarized the dimensions of concept learning from his own developmental perspective.[44]

> The principal findings of our study may be summarized as follows: The development of the processes which eventually result in concept formation begins in earliest childhood, but the intellectual functions that in a specific combination form the psychological basis of the process of concept formation ripen, take shape, and develop only at puberty. Before that age, we find certain intellectual formations that perform functions similar to those of the genuine concepts to come. . . .
> Concept formation is the result of a complex activity in which all the basic intellectual functions take part. The process cannot, however, be reduced to association, attention, imagery, inference, or determining tendencies. They are all indispensable, but they are insufficient without the use of the sign, or word, as the means by which we direct our mental operations, control their course, and channel them toward the solution of the problem confronting us. . . .

[42]Quoted in Eleanor Duckworth, "Piaget Rediscovered," in Richard E. Ripple and Verne N. Rockcastle (eds.), *Piaget Rediscovered*, Cooperative Research Project, No. F-040, (Washington, D.C.: U.S. Office of Education, 1964), p. 3.
[43]Duckworth, *Ibid.*, p. 2.
[44]L. S. Vygotsky, *Thought and Language*, trans. and edited by Eugenia Hanfmann and Gertrude Vakar (Cambridge, Mass.: M.I.T. Press, 1962), pp. 58–68.

The young child takes the first step toward concept formation when he puts together a number of objects in an *unorganized conger-ies*, or "heap," in order to solve a problem that we adults would normally solve by forming a new concept. The heap, consisting of disparate objects grouped together without any basis reveals a diffuse, undirected extension of the meaning of the sign (artificial word) to inherently unrelated objects linked by chance in the child's perception.

The extent to which Piaget's theories differ from those of contemporary American psychologists such as Gagné and Skinner has been sketched by Flavell and Wohlwill.[45]

For psychologists such as Gagné and more particularly those operating from within a Skinnerian framework, it seems that the problem of the child's "readiness to learn" can in fact be reduced to the question of whether he has mastered all of the steps in the sequence that precede and are prerequisites for the concept to be learned. This assumption appears to ignore the problem of horizontal transfer, i.e., the interrelationships among cognitive structures that are coordinate as to level.

INDUCTIVE CONCEPT LEARNING IN CLASSROOMS: CONCLUSIONS AND SPECULATIONS

Much of the recent discussion about instructional strategies has been filtered through the perspective of "inductive" or "discovery" and "deductive" approaches. By "inductive" it generally is meant that the learner is allowed (or forced) to infer conclusions from a basic fact base presented to him. In some forms of this approach the conclusions are predetermined and the fact basis provided is strung out sequentially in steps for a learner. Hilda Taba reflects this analysis in her statement.[46]

Inductive learning requires inductive teaching. Inductive teaching in turn requires the projection of a sequence of learning experiences by thinking backward: by determining what the students need to start with in order to end up with the expected concept, generalization, or intellectual skill. This projection of sequential learning experiences must also be cumulative in its impact, in the sense of starting

[45]John H. Flavell and Joachim F. Wohlwill, "Formal and Functional Aspects of Cognitive Development," in David Elkind and John H. Flavell (eds.), *Studies in Cognitive Development: Essays in Honor of Jean Piaget* (New York: Oxford University Press, 1969), p. 109.
[46]Hilda Taba, "Techniques of In-Service Training," *Social Education*, Vol. 29 (November 1965), p. 472.

with what students already know, understand, or can conceptualize and proceeding in an ascending hierarchy to the more complex and abstract ideas and the more demanding mental operations and inquiry techniques.

A deductive approach, on the other hand, parallels the process of deductive reasoning. Commonly it involves presenting a conclusion or rule and then attempting to verify it through the repeated illustration of appropriate facts. In a concept-learning task, according to the former approach, a learner would be required minimally to infer a rule for categorizing facts into a conceptual network from a series of positive and/or negative instances of a concept. The latter approach requires minimally an initial statement of the concept attributes, accompanied by appropriate exemplars and/or nonexemplars of the concept.

While considerable research energy has been expended on the general question of the relative merits of inductive versus deductive teaching procedures, no categorical claims for the superiority of either approach can be made for classroom instruction. As Wittrock notes in his review of the literature, it "precludes any important considerations about teaching or learning."[47]

This dilemma, in part, may be seen as the result of experimenters' failures to delineate operationally the nature of their "inductive" and "deductive" treatments. This failure, more than any other, is responsible for the lack of *cumulative* knowledge about the two approaches.

The serious problems that preclude broad generalizations also concern isolating and analyzing the varied dimensions of learning that may be affected by "inductive" or "deductive" approaches. One of the more carefully defined, multifaceted studies comparing the two approaches may illustrate some of these dimensions. Worthen, reporting on a study[48] comparing the effect of discovery and of expository presentations on the learning of mathematical concepts, defines his expository treatment in terms of five sequential steps: interjection of teacher knowledge, introduction of generalization, method of answering questions, control of pupil interaction, and methods of eliminating false concepts. Each step in turn has a series of specifications. Similarly with the discovery treatment which also has five steps: Interjection of teacher knowledge, introduction of generalization, method of answer-

[47]M.C. Wittrock, "The Learning-By-Discovery Hypothesis," in Lee S. Shulman and Evan R. Keislar (eds.), *Learning by Discovery: A Critical Appraisal* (Chicago: Rand McNally & Company, 1966), p. 45.

[48]Blaine R. Worthen, "A Study of Discovery and Expository Presentations: Implications for Teaching," *Journal of Teacher Education*, Vol. 19 (Summer 1968), pp. 223–242.

ing questions, control of pupil interaction, and method of eliminating false concepts.

To insure that teachers complied with and adhered to the two treatment models and thus insured discrete treatments, two measures, an observer rating scale and a pupil questionnaire, were used. Eight criterion measures then were made to determine the different dimensions of learning:

1. A concept-achievement test of initial learning.
2. A concept-retention test (at two later points in time).
3. Concept transfer test (to new situations).
4. Negative concept transfer test.
5. Written heuristic transfer (abstraction of a principle).
6. Oral heuristic principle.
7. Statement attitude scale (pupil reaction to the subject).
8. Semantic differential attitude scale.

Worthen's results indicated a variance in the superiority of the two approaches, *according to the dimension of learning isolated.* Apart from the instructional implications of his study, the important lesson for our focus herein is that overgeneralization about discovery or inductive versus deductive teaching is likely unless the microvariable manipulated is carefully specified, and the results interpreted in this limited sense. Had Worthen, for example, examined only *initial learning* and generalized to expository and discovery approach, the results would have shown a significant learning difference for the *expository* approach, and had he considered only *retention learning*, the *discovery* approach would have been shown to be superior.

By specifying an operational distinction between the two approaches, Worthen also avoids the logic controversy concerning whether induction and deduction may be regarded as discrete processes. Certainly in classroom instruction the products of inductive reasoning require verification through deduction at some point. Moreover, it is difficult to understand how induction can proceed without an information base grounded on deduction.

ORGANIZING INSTRUCTION: SELECTED CONSIDERATIONS

Some of the more crucial implications for the organization of curricular materials and strategies to facilitate concept learning concern the degree of extraneous or irrelevant material, the sequencing of exemplars, and variety in exemplars.

Degree of Extraneous or Irrelevant Material

In constructing or structuring materials for concept learning, teachers need to be exceedingly sensitive to the concept rule and its subsumed criterial attributes. These provide the focus for exemplars and nonexemplars and the parameters for relevant and irrelevant material. To the extent that subject matter is not directly relevant to selected attributes, it may be said to be extraneous. Apart from the direct insertion, deletion, manipulation, or even fabrication of subject matter, teachers may emphasize only relevant material by cueing techniques such as verbal cues (for example, statements or questions), written prompts (for example, instructions or arrows), learning sets (for example, immediate previous instruction in related concepts).

Sequencing of Exemplars

While a variety of variables appear to influence the selection of ratios and orders of positive and negative exemplars, both have a role in providing contrasts for a concept-learning task. Any illustration which is lacking in one or more critical attributes may be regarded as a nonexemplar; although for purposes of greatest contrast, it should lack all attributes.

With respect to the order of presentation, some evidence indicates that all exemplars and nonexemplars, clearly so-labeled, should be made available to the student after their initial presentation. In this fashion, he may refer back to them, noting similarities and contrasts, and generally reviewing salient features of the concept-learning task. This procedure contrasts with the frequent classroom pattern of introducing examples, removing them, and then introducing new illustrations.

Variety in Exemplars

The defining attributes of a concept appear to be learned more efficiently when a variety of different and varied illustrations are provided. In this situation a learner is permitted to develop inferences about commonalities, and hence about concept attributes, and then to test his generalizing in new situations. The minimum number of exemplars required, as well as the extent of the variety, will vary both with the complexity of the concept-learning task and the nature of the learner.

Instructional Strategies

The work of Festinger in experiments dealing with cognitive dissonance seems to suggest one clue for instructional strategies appropriate to revising concepts students hold, and provides a promising paradigm for further experimentation in subject areas.[49] On the basis of his research, Festinger has concluded that if an organism is placed in a situation where two cognitions are psychologically perceived as being in a dissonant relationship with one another, there is a tendency to attempt to modify one's cognitive structure to produce compatibility and thus reduce the dissonance. A general implication from his work, for example, is that teaching strategies which force students to grasp the dissonance between concepts established upon erroneous data, may serve to effect concept revision.

This notion is echoed in Sigel's summary of the implications for education of Piaget's research.[50]

> A major thrust of a teaching strategy is to confront the child with the illogical nature of his point of view. The reason for confrontation is that it is a necessary and sufficient requirement for cognitive growth. The shift from egocentric to sociocentric thought comes about through confrontation with the animate and inanimate environment. These forces impinge on the child, inducing disequilibrium. The child strives to reconcile the descrepancies and evolves new processes by which to adapt to the new situations. . . .

Similarly, Berlyne has concluded that in a wide range of cognitive activities, including concept formation, conflict must be playing a major role.[51] His work has reflected a variety of operational distinctions in levels of conflict or incongruity that suggest at least general applications to differentiated teaching strategies.

Finally, Bruner has stated that "it is usually when systems of representation come into conflict or contradiction that the child makes sharp revisions in his way of solving problems—as, for example, there may be a conflict between 'appearance' and 'reality,' the one being ikonic and the other symbolic."[52]

[49]Leon Festinger, "The Motivating Effect of Cognitive Dissonance," in Robert J. C. Harper et al. (eds.), *The Cognitive Processes* (Englewood Cliffs, N.J.: Prentice Hall, Inc., 1964), p. 513. See also his work, *A Theory of Cognitive Dissonance* (New York: Harper & Row, Publishers, 1957), for a more comprehensive treatment of the topic.

[50]Irving E. Sigel, "The Piagetian System and the World of Education," in David Elkind and John H. Flavell (eds.), *Studies in Cognitive Development: Essays in Honor of Jean Piaget* (New York: Oxford University Press, 1969), pp. 473, 486.

[51]David E. Berlyne, *Structure and Direction in Thinking* (New York: John Wiley & Sons, Inc., 1965), p. 247. See especially Chapter 9 on "Motivation of Directed Thinking: Conceptual Conflict," pp. 236–75.

[52]Jerome S. Bruner et al., *Studies in Cognitive Growth* (New York: John Wiley & Sons, Inc., 1966), pp. 11–12.

The traditional strategy of effecting concept learning through definitions, has received a surprising amount of support in recent years. This approach involves simply a precise delineation of the critical attributes of the concept the teacher has, and then a transmission of this definition to students through written or oral forms or both. Most of the systematic self-appropriated learning that has taken place, it would appear, has used this technique.

Such a technique, however, owes its success minimally to a number of factors which generally cannot be assumed in the classroom, except for the learning of trivial concepts: (a) students must have achieved a level of verbalization commensurate to that of the definer, (b) since the concept defined will involve other concepts prior to understanding it, such concepts must have already been learned by the students; (c) the definition is self-explanatory—that is, it raises no questions nor demands no clarification necessary for adequately understanding it.

Fancett et al. have suggested that the teacher entertain four basic questions before initiating a concept teaching session:[53] (1) What prior concepts must the students know in order to cope with the new content? (2) What additional or new concepts are implicit in the proposed content? (3) Will the students be able to relate the newly acquired concepts "to important ideas" and "reach for important generalizations?" (4) What methods, techniques, and materials will promote most efficiently the learning of the new content?

An example of how a psychologist might teach a child the concepts of "red" and "blue" has been provided by Mechner.[54]

> He might choose objects around the room, some red, some blue, and some other colors. First, he might show the child a set of three objects, two of them red and one not red. Each time he would ask, "Which one is not red?" thereby asking the child to discriminate the different, non-red one. He would repeat this with blue objects. Once these discriminations are established, he might start showing the child pairs of colored objects, asking each time, "Which one is red?" or "Which one is blue?" Then, he would increase the number of non-red and non-blue objects in each set until only one out of four or five objects is red or blue. In choosing the objects, he would be careful to include large ones and small ones, distant and near ones, coarse and smooth ones, dark and light ones, whole objects and parts of many colored objects. This would prevent attributes other than redness and blueness from becoming associated with the responses "red" and "blue" through inadvertent selection. With the properties of the ob-

---

[53]Verna S. Fancett et al., *Social Science Concepts and the Classroom* (Syracuse, N.Y.: Social Studies Curriculum Center, 1968), p. 44.

[54]Francis Mechner, "The Teaching of Concepts and Chains," in M. David Merrill (ed.), *Instructional Design: Readings* (Englewood Cliffs, N.J.: Prentice-Hall, Inc., 1971), pp. 256–66.

jects varied, the child would learn to generalize among objects having in common no characteristics other than their color. Once the child says "red" only to red objects, and never to non-red objects, and says "blue" only to blue objects, he may be said to have acquired the concepts of redness and blueness.

Teacher-versus-Learner Conceptual Levels

For instructional settings, perhaps one of the greatest general variables in a concept-learning task is the degree to which there is disharmony between a teacher's and a learner's conceptual levels. Subconcepts or related concepts germane to a new concept-learning task are often held in different proportions by teachers and students. This phenomenon is quite likely to occur, since both probably have constructed their related concepts from different experiences and networks of inferences.

Some of the more obvious instructional problems that may occur are

1. The teacher realizes that there is a discrepancy between his and students' conceptual levels and that some insight into his conceptual network is required.
2. The teacher discovers that he and students use a similar symbol to denote different conceptual networks.
3. The teacher discovers that he and some of the students use different symbols to denote similar conceptual networks.
4. The teacher finds that inter- and intraclass levels of related concepts vary considerably.
5. The teacher realizes that some combination of the first four problems exists.

In the first problem a teacher must either focus upon helping students learn related concepts *prior to* proceeding to learn a new concept or restructure his approach to correspond to the students' conceptual networks. Similarly, in Problem 2, the teacher must see beyond the trivial symbol similarity in communication patterns and work to restructure his approach. Problem 3, while it may result in much confusion, is the easiest one, since it involves only the learning of a new symbol—the conventionally accepted referent. Conversely, Problem 4 presents the greatest challenge to a teacher, and raises anew the fundamental question of individualized learning. Since each student's cumulative conceptual network is truly unique, it proceeds to assimilate and accommodate new information at both a rate and pattern equally unique. While it is quite likely that one's cultural context enforces in great measure a common configuration for encountering or perceiving data initially, the acquisition of conceptual networks appears to be highly individualistic, and hence highly complex.

Even if teacher's had total knowledge of each student's conceptual network—a fantastic achievement—he would be unable to use such material efficiently to structure a concept-learning profile for each student. The mass of information involved would be too great to cope with, both as it relates to students' backgrounds and as it concerns the teacher's own now expanding concept of the concept he wishes to teach.

Nature of the Concept Itself

While some evidence does indicate the desirability of prominently featuring only key or critical attributes in the development of concept illustrations, such a procedure is extremely difficult, if not impossible, for many abstract concepts. Normally what occurs in the development of textual materials is that extraneous or noncriterial attribute material is included in a concept illustration for the sake of developing and integrating a narrative. As an instructional sequence develops, related intellectual phenomena normally are discussed, along with the featured concept; hence they may function as distractors or extraneous material, and thus divert the learner from the intended concept.

Markle and Tiemann underscore this point,[55]

> Any typical teaching instance of a concept must include those properties which are critical to its class membership, by definition, but it will also include many properties which are irrelevant. What is critical and what is irrelevant may be quite apparent to the instructor but are rarely so apparent to the student.

In an instructional sequence, a narrative instance of the concept "democracy," for example, may mention the "White House," a concrete attention-catching referent for the child, but a *non*essential characteristic of democracy.

Similarly, whether a concept is conjunctive, disjunctive, or relational will influence the ease with which it is learned. Conjunctive concepts (a set of common attributes describes the concept) are easier to learn than disjunctive concepts (either one or the other of two or more sets of attributes describe the concept) or relational concepts (a relation between two or more attributes describes the concept). Examples of these three types of concepts in classes would be "rectangle" (conjunctive)—a four-sided plane figure with four right angles; "citi-

[55]Susan M. Markle and Philip W. Tiemann, "Conceptual Learning and Instructional Design," in M. David Merrill (ed.), *Instructional Design: Readings* (Englewood Cliffs, N.J.: Prentice-Hall, Inc., 1971), p. 289.

zen" (disjunctive)—a person who was born in the United States, *or* whose parents were born in the United States, *or* who has passed certain examinations;[56] and waste (relational)—the relationship between the given state of an item or class and the value that one places on it.

A learning task may become especially complex when a combination of abstract attributes, numerous attributes, and a nonconjunctive concept is involved. Using the legal concept of "tort," Carroll illustrates just such a combination.[57] "Tort" is outlined as having the attributes of (a) battery, (b) false imprisonment, (c) malicious prosecution (d) trespass to land, (e) interference to chattels, (f) interference with advantageous relations, (g) misrepresentation, (h) defamation, (i) malicious intent, (j) negligence, (k) causal nexus, (l) consent, (m) privilege, (n) reasonable risk by plaintiff, and (o) breach of contract.[58] The relationship of the numerous and abstract attributes, as described by Carroll, is both conjunctive and disjunctive.[59] Some of the difficulties inherent in an instructional sequences for such a concept are reflected in Carroll's comment, "Presumably, a person presented with a properly organized series of positive and nega tive instances of torts could induce the concept, provided he also understood such prerequisite concepts as *battery, misrepresentation,* etc."[60]

Operating within a different frame of reference, Vygotsky provides yet another illustration of how the psychological differences between concepts may be viewed. His concern is directed at the developmental aspects of youngster's conceptualizing, and he contrasts the growth of the concept of "brother" with that of social science concepts.[61]

> Let us take the concept "brother" . . . and compare it with the concept "exploitation," to which the child is introduced in his social science classes. Is their development the same, or is it different? Does "exploitation" merely repeat the developmental course of "brother"' or is it, psychologically, a concept of a different type? We submit that the two concepts must differ in their development as well as in their functioning and that these two variants of the process of concept formation must influence each other's evolution. . . .
>
> A child's everyday concept, such as "brother," is saturated with experience. Yet when he is asked to solve an abstract problem about a brother's brother, as in Piaget's experiments, he becomes confused. On the other hand, though he can correctly answer questions about "slavery," "exploitation," or "civil war," these concepts are schematic

[56]Maurice P. Hunt and Lawrence E. Metcalf, *Teaching High School Social Studies: Problems in Reflective Thinking and Social Understanding,* 2nd ed. (New York: Harper & Row, Publishers, 1968), p. 86.

[57]Carroll, *op. cit.,* pp. 198–199.

[58]*Ibid.*

[59]For an extended clarifying analysis of this point, see De Cecco, *op. cit.,* p. 404.

[60]Carroll, *op. cit.,* p. 199.

[61]Vygotsky, *op. cit.,* pp. 87, 108.

and lack the rich content derived from personal experience. They are filled in gradually, in the course of further schoolwork and reading. One might say that the development of the child's spontaneous concepts proceed upward, and the development of his scientific concepts downward, to a more elementary and concrete level. This is a consequence of the different ways in which the two kinds of concepts emerge. The inception of a spontaneous concept can usually be traced to a face-to-face meeting with a concrete situation, while a scientific concept involves from the first a "mediated" attitude toward its object.

Mechner has specified that the major problem in teaching difficult or complex concepts is less one of precedure than of definition.[62] His concern is more with getting agreement on specification of class definition than with developmental or other considerations, as he illustrates with the following example.[63]

> The reason why it would be difficult to teach the concept of "good rhythm in prose writing" is that it is difficult to develop a sufficient number of good rhythm examples and bad rhythm examples on which different experts would agree. Once the classes have been adequately defined, however, and a sufficient number of examples are available, the remainder of the teaching process poses few problems.

Edith West, in a different vein, has called attention to the importance of ascertaining the relative difficulty of concepts by considering certain conditions germane to the task.[64] She provides a chart (See Chart 2-1) to gauge the scale of difficulty of a concept in relation to selected criteria. While it does not provide definitive answers, it offers some broad guidelines. West cautions that "although all of these factors are related to the difficulty of concepts, no one factor can be used as a satisfactory criterion."[65]

She also has developed a general index, indicated in Chart 2-2, to weigh the relative importance or significance of concepts.

NEGLECTED AREAS OF RESEARCH ON CONCEPT LEARNING

In a paper cited earlier,[66] Frayer and Klausmeier have suggested that

[62]Mechner, op. cit., p. 278.
[63]Ibid.
[64]Edith West, "Concepts, Generalizations, and Theories: Background Paper No. 3," unpublished paper, Project Social Studies, University of Minnesota, no date, p. 8.
[65]Ibid., p. 7.
[66]Dorothy A. Frayer and Herbert J. Klausmeier, "Effects of Instructional Variations on Mastery of Geometric Concepts by Fourth- and Sixth-Grade Children," paper presented at the annual meeting of the American Educational Research Association, March 2–6, 1970, Minneapolis, Minn.

CHART 2-1
DIFFICULTY OF CONCEPTS
(These criteria must be considered together, not separately)

Criteria of Difficulty	Scale of Difficulty		
	Easy	More Difficult	Very Difficult
Distance from child's experience	Within direct experience	Within vicarious experience	Unrelated to past direct or vicarious experience
Distance from observed referents	Referrents are phenomena which can be perceived through senses — [Physical objects | Relationships / Processes — Speci-fied | Defined Operationally]	Referents are idealized types which do not exist in actuality	Referrents are phenomena which must be inferred from observations of other phenomena (constructs) — [Predis-positions | Configura-tions | Processes]
Scope of concepts	Narrow scope — Few concepts subsumed under it | Relates few concepts	Broader scope	Very broad scope — Many concepts subsumed under it | Relates many concepts
Certainty of presence of defining attributes	Always present		Tendency
Openendedness of concepts	Closed and so reliable	Not completely closed; somewhat unreliable	Open ended; vague boundaries; unreliable
Way in which attributes of concept are related	Conjunctive (joint presence of several attributes)	Disjunctive (presence of one or another attribute)	Relational — Specified relationship (ratio, product, verbal) — [Com-para-tive | One attri-bute affects another | All attri-butes inter-act]

SOURCE: Edith West, "Concepts, Generalizations, and Theories: Background Paper #3," unpublished paper, Project Social Studies, University of Minnesota, no date, p. 8.

CHART 2-2
IMPORTANCE OR SIGNIFICANCE OF CONCEPTS

Importance determined by following criteria:
1. What is the scope of the concept? (i. e., How many concepts are subsumed under it or related to it?)
2. How many generalizations relate the concept to other concepts?
3. How significant are the generalizations which use the concepts?
   (a) To what degree are they explanatory and predictive?
   (b) Are they empirical generalizations, theoretical generalizations, or part of a narrow or broad gauge theory?

Scale of Significance		
Unimportant	Of More Importance	Of Great Importance
Limited scope	Broader scope	Very broad scope
Few generalizations using concept	A number of generalizations using concept	Many generalizations using concept
Generalizations using concept of little significance: (a) Nonexplanatory or predictive (b) Empirical	Generalizations using concept of some significance: (a) Explanatory (and probabilistic) (b) Theoretical	Generalizations using concept of great significance: (a) Explanatory and predictive (b) Part of a narrow or broad gauge theory

SOURCE: Edith West, "Concepts, Generalizations, and Theories: Background Paper #3," unpublished paper, Project Social Studies, University of Minnesota, no date, p. 10.

Additional research should be carried out to establish the generality of the effect of emphasis of relevant attribute values and to determine other variables which may improve learning from texts. The value of this research strategy is that variables may be identified which could be incorporated into instructional material in many subject-matter areas.

A particularly fruitful area of exploration relates to the effects of printed instructional material upon the learning of specific concepts, about which little is known. "Validation of such effects," Frayer and Klausmeier note, "would have important implications for textbook writing."[67] They suggest a research paradigm:[68]

Research dealing with learning of subject matter concepts requires extension of the techniques used in laboratory studies. First,

[67] Ibid.
[68] Ibid.

concepts must be analyzed to determine their relevant and irrelevant characteristics. This analysis provides a rational basis for teaching the concept and testing for understanding. Second, variables manipulable in printed instructional material must be identified. These variables may include some not usually considered in laboratory studies, such as use of definitions, synonyms, and sentence contexts. Third, various aspects of concept learning should be tested. These tests should go beyond simple recognition of examples and nonexamples, to determine knowledge of relevant characteristics, definition, and relationships to other concepts. Finally, studies should be carried out with subjects of various ages to discover possible interactions between age and instructional variables.

Similarly, Glaser outlined seven key neglected research areas, based upon his recent survey of the relevant literature on concept learning. He urges research dealing with[69]

1. Concepts that are comprised of verbal, thematic, and meaningful dimensions and that involve a mediated response.
2. Concepts with definitional parameters that are altered with increased experience and knowledge.
3. Concepts in which the "salience or perceptibility of different dimensions differ as a function of societal norms, differing perceptual characteristics of the stimuli involved, or individual learner histories."
4. Concepts that are relational rather than conjunctive.
5. Concepts that more efficiently might be learned "deductively;" that is, by first stating a rule, then examining exemplars and nonexemplars.
6. Concepts that are based on a hierarchy of previously learned concepts.
7. Concepts "whose acquisition deemphasizes memory by providing the learner with a strategy which minimizes memory requirements, or by providing him with tools or job aids for memory storage."

CONCLUSION

A variety of basic conclusions concerning procedures for effecting classroom concept learning, some based on studies and some based on

[69]Glaser, op. cit., p. 27. For an extensive bibliography on concept learning, see the two works, Herbert J. Klausmeier et al., Concept Learning: A Bibliography, 1950–1967, Technical Report No. 82 (Madison, Wis.: Wisconsin Research and Development Center for Cognitive Learning, 1969) and Herbert J. Klausmeier et al., A Supplement to Technical Report No. 82, Concept Learning: A Bibliography, 1968, Technical Report No. 107 (Madison, Wis.: Wisconsin Research and Development Center for Cognitive Learning, 1969).

logical analyses, some general and some specific, have been generated in the literature. Woodruff, for example, has concluded that[70]

1. The basic process by which one acquires concepts of specific objects or events is the same for all concepts and for all students.
2. All of the things in a given class can be learned by one general kind of learning experience.
3. A student is prepared to acquire a new concept when he already has a store of concepts appropriate to understanding the new concepts.
4. Lessons contribute most to the progress of students when each one introduces one significant concept abstracted from a sequence of concepts, assuming that other learning factors are satisfactory.
5. The presentation of several concepts in a single lesson is confusing to students and learning proceeds more rapidly when concepts are presented singly.

Finally, Robert Glaser, in a succinct summary of the literature on concept learning and teaching, has concluded:[71]

> We know something about concepts consisting of nonverbal dimensions where the stimulus values are perceptually clear, and where the instance-non-instance boundaries are reasonable clear, and further, where such concepts involve rules that are taught by an inductive procedure. This kind of concept task seems to define the situation that prevails in two cases: (1) in non-verbal tasks and in concept learning with pre-verbal learners, that is, young children; this kind of situation is exemplified by the inductive learning of such concepts as triangle, quadrilateral, and circle; and (2) tasks for verbal learners where a concept to be learned is intricate to verbalize so that is needs to be learned by induction from exemplars. . . .

Interestingly, a 1968 article by the Kendlers on "Concept Formation," appearing in the recent edition of the *International Encyclopedia of the Social Sciences,* seems to suggest that we have not made as much progress as might be desired in resolving the substantive theoretical issues concerning concept learning.[72]

There is little doubt that the discrimination process is of primary

---

[70] Asahel D. Woodruff, *Basic Concepts of Teaching, Concise Edition* (Scranton, Pa.: Chandler Publishing Company, 1961), pp. 7–9, 115.

[71] Glaser, *op. cit.,* p. 27.

[72] Howard H. Kendler and Tracy S. Kendler, "Concept Formation," in L. Sills (ed.), *International Encyclopedia of the Social Sciences,* Vol. 3 (New York: The Free Press, 1968), p. 210.

importance in concept formation. The best method of teaching a concept would be to arrange the optimal conditions for discriminating between instances that belong to a concept and those that do not. Although such a principle would be generally accepted, there would be much disagreement about its specific interpretation. Whether optimal conditions for discrimination could be best arranged by reinforcing correct habits and not reinforcing incorrect ones, by encouraging suitable mediational responses, by training the organism to perceive crucial differences, by developing appropriate cognitive systems, or by some favorable combination of all of these factors—all these issues would be open to dispute. Basic to the disagreement are two related questions: Do these apparent differences always represent real differences? If so, does their resolution depend upon their being cast in precise mathematical language?

Moreover, the quotation captures aptly how apparent agreement by researchers on basic principles of concept learning may mask underlying sharp disagreements over appropriate corresponding instructional settings. This phenomenon is the challenge that confronts teachers as they look to "research" for guidance in designing instruction.

SUGGESTED READINGS

Ausubel, David P., *Educational Psychology: A Cognitive View* (New York: Holt, Rinehart & Winston, Inc., 1968), Chap. 15.

A rigorous, stimulating discussion of classroom-related experimental research on concept learning by the author and others, as well as some theoretical remarks concerning the nature of concepts.

Bruner, Jerome S., Jacqueline J. Goodnow, and George Austin, *A Study of Thinking* (New York: Science Editions, 1962).

A major work dealing with a variety of experimental and theoretical issues associated with the nature of cognitive processes.

Carroll, John B., "Words, Meanings and Concepts," *Harvard Educational Review*, Vol. 24 (Spring 1964), 178–202.

Discusses inadequacies in traditional concept-learning research, the different types of concepts, and the difficulties inherent in organizing classroom instruction in a lucid and well-organized fashion.

De Cecco, John P., *The Psychology of Learning and Instruction* (Englewood Cliffs, N.J.: Prentice-Hall, Inc., 1968), Chap. 10.

Lucid, well-written analysis of relevant research findings concerning concept learning, with suggested applications to classroom instruction.

Frayer, Dorothy A., *Effects of Number of Instances and Emphasis of Relevant Attribute Values on Mastery of Geometric Concepts by Fourth- and Sixth-Grade Children,* Technical Report No. 116 (Madison, Wis.: Wisconsin Research and Development Center for Cognitive Learning, March 1970).

Besides reporting on a major study of concept learning in a classroom setting, this two-part paper presents an excellent summary of relevant literature.

Gagné, Robert M., *The Conditions of Learning,* 2nd ed. (New York: Holt, Rinehart & Winston, Inc., 1970). A highly readable analysis of the author's views on learning, with a systematic discussion of each of the eight possible conditions for learning that he postulates.

Ginsburg, Herbert, and Sylvia Opper, *Piaget's Theory of Intellectual Development: An Introduction* (Englewood Cliffs, N.J.: Prentice-Hall, Inc., 1969).

A clear, highly readable introduction to some of Piaget's major ideas, including their research basis.

Glaser, Robert, "Concept Learning and Concept Teaching," in Robert M. Gagné and William J. Gephart (eds.), *Learning Research and School Subjects* (Itasca, Ill.: F. T. Peacock Publishers, Inc., 1969).

Succinct and lucid summary of possible instructional applications of selected concept-learning research and a delineation of major areas in which further research is required.

Klausmeier, Herbert J., et. al., *Concept Learning: A Bibliography, 1950–67,* Technical Report No. 82 (Madison, Wis.: Research and Development Center for Cognitive Learning, 1969); also by the same authors, *A Supplement to Technical Report No. 82. Concept Learning: A Bibliography, 1968,* Technical Report No. 107 (Madison, Wis.: Wisconsin Research and Development Center for Cognitive Learning, 1969).

An extensive bibliography of articles from fifty-one journals and Center publications, listed by topics and by authors without annotation.

Ripple, Richard E., and Verne N. Rockcastle (eds.), *Piaget Rediscovered,* Cooperative Research Project No. F-040 (Washington, D.C.: U.S. Office of Education, 1964).

Series of excellent papers from a symposium dealing with the work of Piaget and his Geneva associates.

Sax, Gilbert, "Concept Formation," in Robert L. Ebel (ed.), *Encyclopedia of Educational Research* (New York: The Macmillan Company, 1969).

Well-organized summary of research relating to concept learning.

CHAPTER 3

Instructional Models for Organizing Concept Learning

The use of models and modeling has become a widespread practice among professional educators. No professional conference of any significance would be complete without several papers revealing someone's new model of some phenomenon. Not surprisingly, as Parsons and Shaftel have perceptively noted, some educators have concluded that the building of models is equally if not more important than any use to which they might be put![1]

The development of models has become such a major part of current educational thinking that many large curriculum projects have defined this as their primary purpose. In one large school system of the Southeast, for example, the major curriculum effort of the past year has been the development of an "integrated model" for instruction. In this case the model itself has become disassociated from the phenomena which it was supposed to represent and the district staff has substituted working with the model for working with reality. Great amounts of physical and psychic energy and huge sums of money are being spent on developing the model while little serious attention is being given to its relevance to what is occurring in the schools.

In short, as philosopher May Brodbeck has observed, "the term has moreover a decided halo effect. Models are Good Things."[2]

Models and modeling, however, do serve very *practical* functions

---

[1] Theodore W. Parsons and Fannie R. Shaftel, "Thinking and Inquiry: Some Critical Issues," in Jean Fair and Fannie R. Shaftel (eds.), *Effective Thinking in the Social Studies, 37th Yearbook* (Washington, D.C.: National Council for the Social Studies, 1967), p. 141.

[2] May Brodbeck, "Models, Meanings and Theories," in May Brodbeck (ed.), *Readings in the Philosophy of the Social Sciences* (New York: The Macmillan Company, 1968), p. 579.

in our culture generally and in classrooms specifically. Much of the U.S. space program, for example, has been heavily dependent upon lunar-related models to train astronauts. In this case, particularly in the early phases of the moon-shot program, models proved to be the *only* vehicle for preparing trainees. Similarly, implicitly or explicitly, models in a variety of forms are widely used in classroom instruction. Coaches, for example, trade heavily in two-dimensional models to illustrate plays on a blackboard. Three-dimensional geometric figures help the mathematics teacher translate abstractions. In a similar fashion, a teacher's use of simulation games as models provide a measure of correspondence between a competitive gamelike situation and reality. More explicitly, teachers frequently put forth theory X or schema Y as "models" of how phenomenon Z operates in reality. A final, more expansive note on the importance of models is supplied by Marc Belth.[3]

> Not only are we dependent upon the specific models we have available for the detailed interpretations, explanations, descriptions, and definitions of the data we encounter, but the logic of our thinking, the range of expectations, the anticipation and acceptability of sequence and the determination of discontinuity are dependent upon the forms of the models we most frequently use.

Restrictions of Models

While models provide a variety of useful functions, certain precautions concerning their use should be underscored. Belth reminds us, for example, that "Although anything that we encounter can be used *as* a model, nothing in and of itself *is* a model. Models . . . are constructed for the purpose of enabling us to think about the world experienced."[4] And the further removed from the reality of its representation that a model becomes, the greater the danger that slavish reliance upon it will result in a distorted view of reality.

Kaplan has outlined six shortcomings of models of which users should be aware:[5] (1) overemphasis on symbols—the symbolic style may not *actually* specify the way in which terms actually are used; (2) overemphasis on form—concern with development of models may hinder direct progress in dealing with reality; (3) oversimplification—models are often simpler than the subject-matter they represent; (4) overem-

[3]Marc Belth, "The Study of Education as the Study of Models," in Martin Feldman and Eli Seifman (eds.), *The Social Studies: Structure, Models and Strategies* (Englewood Cliffs, N.J.: Prentice-Hall, Inc., 1969), p. 174.
[4]*Ibid.*
[5]Abraham Kaplan, *The Conduct of Inquiry* (Scranton, Pa.: Chandler Publishing Company, 1964), pp. 277–78.

phasis on rigor—models are often improperly exact and call for measures that cannot be obtained as specified; (5) map reading—the failure to realize that the model is just a "mode of representation, so that not all its features correspond to some characteristic of its subject-matter;" (6) pictorial realism—forgetting that a likeness between an object and a model exists only in a given perspective, that a model is not a literal statement. Kaplan concludes: "The dangers are not in working with models, but in working with too few, and those too much alike, and above all, in belittling any efforts to work with anything else."[6]

Brodbeck also cautions that "uncertainty, selection, idealization, and quantification are characteristic to a greater or lesser degree of most worthwhile theories."[7] She specifically warns against speculation theories for which little concrete evidence exists, the abstraction process involved in theorizing which tends to eliminate key variables extraneous to the theory, the tendency to idealize in abstraction by reference to conceivable but nonexistent constructs, and the propensity to quantify and misrepresent their significance. Illustrations of these four cases in the area of social studies, for example, might be: (a) man has a territorial instinct; (b) in capitalism, industries have as their goal the maximazation of profits; (c) a total or complete free-enterprise system; and (d) correlation analysis in geography. In the first case, some empirical evidence exists but its import is not overwhelming; case two presents a generalization that is partly accurate but incomplete and misleading. The third instance suggests a conceivable ideal construct but one that has never existed nor is ever likely to in a social system. While case four indicates a highly sophisticated mathematical-statistical procedure for determining correlations between variables, but it proves no causal relationship and may even correlate coincidental and insignificant factors.

Parsons and Shaftel suggest similar cautionary considerations related to the use of models. Their arguments relate to the possibilities that models may limit reflection by providing hasty closure and that they may become ritualistic procedures pursued as ends rather than means.[8] In their criticisms of a grade-one unit on Japan they provide an illustration of how models misused may seriously distort rather than facilitate instruction. Of the unit's mode of organizing information, they state:[9]

[6] *Ibid.*, p. 293.
[7] Brodbeck, *op. cit.*, p. 587.
[8] Parsons and Shaftel, *op. cit.*, pp. 141–147.
[9] *Ibid.*, p. 155.

The food, clothing, shelter, school, and holiday scheme for organizing the unit information and sequencing the activities of instruction will have the unfortunate result of structuring a categorical model which children can internalize and use as the basis for subsequent culture studies. The difficulty of breaking out of this model once it develops is evidenced by the facts that children in all grades habitually approach culture study this way now, and that their teachers continue to limit themselves to these same narrow categories. From a strictly anthropological point of view, the major problem with this model is that it is an inappropriate and insufficient model for cross-cultural study for both children and adults because it considers neither the cultural determinants of, nor the more significant aspects of, human behavior.

In addition to structuring too early cognitive closure, this unit raises the strong likelihood of ethnocentric reinforcement, itself a form of cognitive closure or rigidity. The major categories (food, clothing, shelter, family, holidays, and school) and the subcategories (occupation, cleanliness, and so on) are projections of the principal value foci in American culture. By using these particular categories to structure their information about Japanese culture, the unit calls the children's attention to the importance of these factors in life and provides them with opportunity for evaluating Japanese culture by comparing it with their own culture. Such comparisons invariably seem to be in favor of American culture, perhaps because of the nature of the categories of comparison.

Types of Models

When a model and its representation share a close one-to-one correspondence in many details, the model may be said to be *isomorphic*.[10] A miniature train, constructed to scale in every dimension provides an illustration of an isomorphism. In the same way, Brodbeck suggests, *theories* whose laws have the same form or are structurally similar can be seen as isomorphic, and may be considered a model for each other.[11] She offers the illustration of how the human brain frequently is compared to an electronic computer.

Kaplan has distinguished five different senses in which the term "model" is used:[12] (1) any theory stated in logically more rigorous or more mathematical sense than is found in normal parlance (e.g., "Rostow's theories of economic development); (2) a semantical model analogous to some data (e.g., "war on poverty"); (3) a physical model corresponding to reality (e.g., a globe); (4) a formal model which is a

[10]Brodbeck, *op. cit.*, p. 583.
[11]*Ibid.*, pp. 579–580.
[12]Kaplan, *op. cit.*, pp. 267–68.

model *of* a theory (e.g., computer simulation of human information processing).

Parsons and Shaftel have differentiated what they regard as "categorical" and "strategic" models in social studies curricula. The former term refers to those models usually developed at the end of an inquiry process to explain the transaction.[13] "Strategic" models, on the other hand, are those which provide a schematic illustration of a sequence of steps or processes.[14]

GENERIC MODELS FOR CONCEPT LEARNING

Given the benefits and limitations of models, instructional strategies for concept learning, to be optimally efficient, should be based upon some systematic paradigm. Also, such a model to have high credibility should have been shown to have applicability beyond the creator's notebook. In short, the model should have been tested in the real world in which it is to operate.

Every suggested instructional sequence for teaching a specific concept *does*, of course, reflect an explicit or implicit model that the designer has used—whether he is conscious of it or not. Not all such models, however, will incorporate important concept-learning considerations outlined in earlier chapters, nor in fact will all succeed even inefficiently in producing minimal concept learning. Two common general shortcomings of the instructional models for concept learning that are inherent, though not necessarily explicit, in many curricular materials K—12 are (a) there is no attention to key variables suggested by concept-learning studies, and (b) there is no differentiation between concept and other intellectual phenomena as learning goals. The former deficiency is revealed minimally in the failure to imply or specify critical attributes of the concept, include and contrast negative examples appropriately, and eliminate irrelevant detail or to cue the learner on relevant attributes. While the latter shortcoming is evidenced by the manner in which goals are specified and reflected in materials. Obviously these limitations are likely to apply equally strongly to nontextual instruction.

As noted in earlier chapters, a body of growing literature exists concerning systematic schema or models for concept learning. Some have been developed in reference to specific subject-matter areas and might more fruitfully be discussed in the specific treatment of each discipline's issues. These schema will be incorporated into the following

[13]Parsons and Shaftel, *op. cit.*, pp. 141–45.
[14]*Ibid.*

four chapters dealing with the mathematics, communication arts, science, and social studies. Some instructional models, however, have been offered as being generic in their application. The procedures outlined by Mechner and Frayer in earlier chapters would fall into this category.

Three generic models by De Cecco, Gagné, and Taba have been selected for a more thorough discussion, since they should have wide applicability to varied age levels and subject-matter areas. The three models also share several other characteristics: (1) they are based upon experimental research findings, (2) they provide explicit steps for instruction, (3) they share a similar concept of concept, and (4) they have been tried in a variety of classroom setting, either by the authors or others. On the other hand, the models differ sufficiently on such matters as sequential structure, evidence of minimal learning, and other nuances to provide contrasting considerations.

The primary value of generic instructional models is that they transcend specific isolated illustrations in a particular context and thus allow for varied applications. In this sense, instructional *models* allow for *teacher* individualization in a way that instructional examples do not. Adherence to a *model* commits a teacher only to follow a structural pattern *after* selecting whatever topics and materials *he* decides is within his and the class's competence and concern, whereas imitation of *examples* limits one to specific subjects.

Nevertheless, while teachers should concentrate upon internalizing *models* rather than specific applications, some examples may be helpful in suggesting translatability. Therefore, following each of the models, there will be a sample illustration of how it might be applied to classroom instruction.

De Cecco's Model

De Cecco's model was generated, in turn, by the basic model of teaching developed by Robert Glaser and presented in Fig. 3-1.[15]

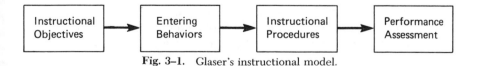

Fig. 3–1.   Glaser's instructional model.

[15]John P. De Cecco, *The Psychology of Learning and Instruction* (Englewood Cliffs, N.J.: Prentice-Hall, Inc., 1968), p. 11.

De Cecco's model of concept teaching appears in his text, *The Psychology of Learning and Instruction: Educational Psychology* and consists of nine steps.[16]

> Steps one and two pertain to instructional objectives. Step one requires a statement of the objective, and step two, a type of task analysis. Step two provides the student with the appropriate entering behavior. Steps three through six and step nine are specific instructional procedures for concept teaching. Steps seven and eight deal mainly with performance assessment.

These nine steps are listed in Table 3-1.[17]

TABLE 3-1
DE CECCO'S MODEL

Steps in Concept Teaching

Step 1.	Describe the performance expected of the student after he has learned the concept.
Step 2.	Reduce the number of attributes to be learned in complex concepts and make important attributes dominant.
Step 3.	Provide the student with clear verbal associations.
Step 4.	Provide positive and negative examples of the concept.
Step 5.	Present the examples in close succession or simultaneously.
Step 6.	Present a new positive example of the concept and ask the student to identify it.
Step 7.	Verify the student's learning of the concept.
Step 8.	Require the student to define the concept.
Step 9.	Provide occasions for student responses and the reinforcement of these responses.

In step 1 the teacher defines the parameters he wishes to place upon concept learning by indicating what type of performance will be considered as satisfactory. De Cecco's model itself does *not* specify the dimensions of concept learning to be achieved.

In the following step, a teacher determines the number of attributes in the concept rule and arrives at a plan for highlighting critical attributes. "Two general procedures," De Cecco indicates, "reduce the number of attributes of complex concepts: you can ignore some of the attributes and focus on those you think most important or you can code the attributes into fewer patterns."[18]

Step 3 is concerned with assuring that a student has the prerequisite verbal associations necessary for learning a new concept. To the extent

[16] *Ibid.*, p. 402.
[17] *Ibid.*, pp. 402–416.
[18] *Ibid.*, p. 403.

that verbal associations have not been established a teacher must develop them before proceeding to step 4.

During the next step students are introduced to positive and negative instances of the concept, sufficient in number to assure that all the critical attributes of the concept have been illustrated. Interestingly, De Cecco also notes of this step that "direct experience or realistic examples are usually not preferable to simplified presentations of the concepts, such as line drawings, cartoons, diagrams, and charts."[19]

In step 5 De Cecco recommends that examples be provided in close succession or simultaneously, with all exemplars available at all times for the student. In this way he does not have to rely on memory for preceding examples.

Steps 6, 7, and 8 deal respectively with providing contiguity and reinforcement, assessing students' performance, and stating concept rules.

In the final step, further occasions are to be provided for allowing students to respond to examples and to receive appropriate reinforcement.

De Cecco provides an illustration of a teaching session dealing with the concept "tourist."[20] Using his nine-step process as a guide we can illustrate each phrase of the lesson.

Step 1. Teacher initiates the lesson by telling class that she wishes to teach the concept of "tourist." She indicates further that students should be able to identify quickly examples of "tourist" at the close of the lesson.

Step 2. The teacher analyzes the concept and decides that it is a conjunctive concept with the critical attributes "activity," "purpose," and "residence." Related but noncritical attributes such as "mode of travel" were rejected on the grounds that their introduction would confuse students.

Step 3. Students indicate the necessary verbal association by responding correctly to the word "tourist" written on the blackboard.

Steps 4 and 5. The teacher presented her positive and negative exemplars as verbal narrations presented on large cards. Each card was left for examination after its presentation. Positive exemplars include vignettes such as "Mr. Phog lives in San Francisco but he is on vacation and he is visiting Rome to see friends and the city." Negative exemplars were of the variety, Americans who changed their residences to other countries. After presenting each exemplar the teacher waited for a response, and indicated whether it was correct.

Step 6. Students were provided with a new positive exemplar, Mr.

[19] *Ibid.,* p. 412.
[20] *Ibid.,* pp. 416–418.

Angelo returning to Italy to visit friends and vacation.

Step 7. The teacher presented new positive and negative exemplars, varying national origins, regions, and purposes for travel.

Step 8. Students were required to write a definition of "tourist," which was compared against her original set of critical attributes.

Step 9. The teacher reinforced correct responses and indicated errors. Students then were reminded of the original objectives, given a test dealing with new positive and negative examples, and were provided with their results immediately.

In this illustration, discrimination tasks and definitions were required of students as evidence of concept learning. The teacher makes an important decision in step two to distinguish certain attributes as critical and others as noncritical, and these divisions shape the character of her subject matter. It is useful to note that her subject matter, *while having a basis in reality, is, in fact, contrived.* Her concern for her objective in this case transcends any particular interest in pursuing for example, factual historical material.

One may also note that the procedures used in steps 4, 5, and 8 were possible largely because the students possessed certain verbal and maturational entry behaviors that *young* children would not be likely to have.

Gagné's Model

Gagné's work, as reported earlier, revealed the existence of eight distinguishable types of learning, each with correspondingly different conditions necessary to bring them about. As Gagné states,[21]

> To the person who is interested in knowing what principles of learning apply to education, my reply is: The question must be asked and answered with consideration of what kind of capability is being learned. The answer is different depending on the particular class of performance change that is the focus of interest. There are no "general" rules of learning known at present that can be used as guides in designing instruction.

Gagné has developed a similar set of specifications for instructional conditions necessary to bring about the learning of concepts. In his more recent writings, however, he has made a distinction between *concrete* and *defined* or *relational* concepts and the corresponding differential learning conditions that they require.[22] Concrete concepts,

---

[21]Robert M. Gagné, *The Conditions of Learning* (New York: Holt, Rinehart & Winston, Inc., 1968), p. v.

[22]*Ibid.*, 2nd ed., 1970.

according to Gagné, are those which have object referents or forms to which one can point—for example, "color", "tree," "cat," "shape."[23] Defined or relational concepts, on the other hand, have no observable referents but rather involve a relationship between two or more simple concepts.[24]

> The relational concept is, in a formal sense, one type of rule. The relation expressed by a defined concept may be used, as its name implies, to make it possible for the learner to identify the relation and distinguish it from others: the concept of *uncle* is distinguished from *aunt*, or the concept of *mass* from weight.

In these cases "uncle" is defined as "the brother of a parent", or "husband of a sister of a parent," and "mass" as "that property of an object which determines how much it will be accelerated by a given amount of force."[25] A defined concept must be learned entirely by means of verbal cues rather than reference to observable objects.

The implications of Gagné's more recent conclusions are that alternative instructional models must be considered, depending upon what *type* of concept is involved.[26] Consequently, both his models for Type 6—Concept Learning (concrete concepts), and Type 7—Rule or Principle Learning (including defined or relational concepts) will be considered.

Model for Concrete Concept Learning. The five-step model presented in Table 3-2 is taken from *The Conditions of Learning,* second edition.[27]

TABLE 3-2
GAGNÉ'S MODEL FOR CONCRETE CONCEPT LEARNING

Step 1.   Insure that the student repeats the concept name to acquire a stimulus-response connection.

Step 2.   Have the student identify several varied exemplars of the concept and specify its name.

Step 3.   Present several exemplars of the concept and several varied nonexemplars of the concept. (Having the students identify the discriminations by name is optional.)

Step 4.   Present additional exemplars of the concept all at once, and request students to specify the concept name.

Step 5.   Present the student with a situation containing a *new* instance of the concept, and ask him to identify the concept.

---

[23] *Ibid.,* p. 172.

[24] *Ibid.,* p. 190.

[25] Robert M. Gagné, "The Learning of Principles," in M. David Merrill (ed.), *Instructional Design: Readings* (Englewood Cliffs; N.J.: Prentice-Hall, Inc., 1971), p. 309.

[26] *Ibid.,* p. 311.

[27] Gagné, *The Conditions of Learning,* 2nd ed., pp. 175–177.

Steps 1–3 are included as part of the conditions for learning, but are identified as "prerequisites" to the learning of the concept, which, Gagné maintains, is actually learned in the last two steps.[28] Also, concerning step 5, Gagné explains:[29]

> It is not entirely clear whether the use of the final new example is necessary for the learning itself, or whether it is merely a test of what has already been learned. Quite probably the former is the case. At any rate, the instructor will probably wish to make a more reliable determination that concept learning has really happened, by asking the student to respond to one or two additional examples, each a novel one.

Model for Defined or Relational Concept Learning. In using this model, the assumption is made that simpler concepts related within the defined concept have already been learned. Table 3-3 outlines the steps in the model.[30]

TABLE 3-3
GAGNÉ'S MODEL FOR DEFINED OR
RELATIONAL CONCEPT LEARNING

Step 1. State the general nature of the performance to be expected of the student when learning is complete.

Step 2. Provide instructions to invoke recall of the component concepts that make up the rule.

Step 3. Provide verbal statements that will allow the student to organize the rule. (Such instructions may be verbatim statements of the rule, or a series of related statements.)

Step 4. Through questions, ask the student to illustrate or demonstrate the rule.

Step 5. (Optional) Through an appropriate question, require the learner to make a verbal statement of the rule.

Gagné again calls the reader's attention to the final step.[31]

> Note particularly that such a verbal statement is not essential to the learning of the rule, nor does it prove the student has learned the rule. Then why is it done? Probably for a very practical reason: the instructor wants the student to be able to talk about the rule later on, and so he teaches him the right words to say. This is important to note that this kind of verbal chaning ("learning the definition") is an unessential part of rule learning itself.

[28] *Ibid.*, p. 176.
[29] *Ibid.*, pp. 176–177.
[30] *Ibid.*, pp. 201–203.
[31] *Ibid.*, p. 202.

Both models will be related to classroom instruction, using the illustrations that Gagné himself has used.

Concrete Concept Illustration. Gagné illustrates the teaching steps necessary for the concept of "edge."[32]

Step 1. The instructor says the word, "edge," requests that it be repeated, and the student responds.

Step 2. The student identifies two or three edges, verbalizing the concept word each time an instance is encountered. The instructor may use questions such as, "What is this?" or "Where is the edge?"

Step 3. The student is provided with several new instances of edge and these are contrasted with nonexemplars. Gagné uses the examples of contrasting the edge of a three-dimensional object with its *side, top,* or *corner.* Having the student verbalize these distinctions is an optional step.

Step 4. Present several new examples of edge all at once, specifying that each is an edge. A "What is this?" type question may be used.

Step 5. The student is given a new context containing an instance of edge, (e.g., scissors), and responds correctly to a request to identify the concept. At this point, the concept has been learned.

Defined Concept Illustration. A concept from physics, "work," is used to illustrate the teaching of a defined or relational concept.[33] Work is defined by Gagné as "the product of the force acting on a body and the distance through which the body moves while the force is acting on it" or, more simply, "work = force × distance."[34] Subsumed under work, then, are the concepts "force," "distance," "equals," and "multiply."

Step 1. The student must be able to identify examples of the class "force," "distance," "equals," and "multiply" (or "product") and their appropriate sequential relationships.

Step 2. Insure that the students do know the concepts of "force," "distance," "equals," and "multiply," as assumed.

Step 3. Provide a verbal cue to the student by a statement of the concept rule, either verbatim or in some related fashion. For example, "work done is equal to the distance a body is pushed times the force acting on it" or the writing of the related equation on the board. [35] Such a statement is followed by one or more questions of the variety, "How much work is done on a block of wood pushed 2 feet by a force of 10 pounds?"[36]

[32]*Ibid.*, pp. 175–177; 181.
[33]Gagné, "The Learning of Principles," *op. cit.*, pp. 306–307.
[34]*Ibid.*, p. 307.
[35]*Ibid.*, p. 308.
[36]*Ibid.*, p. 309.

Step 4. In order for the student to demonstrate the concept rule by a series of different questions of the variety, "What is the work done in pushing a body of 1,000 grams a horizontal distance of 30 centimeters?" or "Show how to calculate the work done by a force of 50 pounds pushing a trunk along a floor for 10 feet."[37]

Step 5 (optional). Through an appropriate question, ask students to define "work" in their own words.

Taba's Model

Hilda Taba and her associates drew upon Piaget and others work in developing a sequential schema of cognitive processes or tasks.[38] The tasks were designed to move learners through a three-stage series of cognitive operations: concept formation, interpretation of data, and application of principles. Each task, in turn, is composed of a series of sequential steps, as illustrated in Chart 3-1.[39]

Task 1, that of *concept formation* and the one most directly germane to our concerns, is in reality designed more to *diagnose* the state of students' existing conceptual networks than to *teach* systematically a new concept. Through the sharing of each other's conceptual networks, however, students presumably do modify their conceptualizations. With free responses to open questions such as "What do you think of when you hear the word language?" students provide enumeration and listing information from which the teacher may diagnose the level of student backgrounds. Since verbal participation is normally very high for this activity, the teacher receives information from many (or all) students in the class. The remaining activities within this task require students to organize the information they have generated into groupings according to self-determined rationale, and then label the groups. The latter activity requires students to examine items within a group, determine the basis for relationships, and then check to be sure that the label fits. While, to be sure, students are likely to offer factually incorrect statements or offer apparently illogical groupings and labels, in this task, the teacher's role is *not* to challenge or correct, as Taba and her associates have noted.[40]

---

[37] *Ibid.*, p. 307.

[38] See the two project reports, Hilda Taba, Samuel Levine, and Freeman Elzey, *Thinking in Elementary School Children*, Cooperative Research Project No. 1574 (Washington, D.C.: U.S. Office of Education, 1964) and Hilda Taba, *Teaching Strategies and Cognitive Functioning in Elementary School Children*, Cooperative Research Project No. 2404 (Washington, D.C.: U.S. Office of Education, 1966).

[39] Taba, *Strategies, op. cit.*, pp. 39–40; 42.

[40] Hilda Taba et al., *A Teacher's Handbook to Elementary Social Studies*, 2nd ed. (Reading, Mass.: Addison-Wesley Publishing Company, Inc., 1971), p. 69.

CHART 3-1
TABA'S MODEL

Concept Formation		
Overt Activity	Covert Mental Operation	Eliciting Question
1. Enumeration and listing	Differentiation	What did you see? hear? note?
2. Grouping	Identifying common properties; abstracting	What belongs together? On what criterion?
3. Labeling, categorizing, subsuming	Determining the hierarchial order of items. Super- and sub-ordination	How would you call these groups? What belongs under what?
Interpretation of Data		
Overt Activity	Covert Mental Operation	Eliciting Question
1. Identifying points	Differentiation	What did you note? see? find?
2. Explaining items of identified information	Relating points to each other. Determining cause and effect relationships	Why did so-and-so happen?
3. Making inferences	Going beyond what is given. Finding implications, extrapolating	What does this mean? What picture does it create in your mind? What would you conclude?
Application of Principles		
Overt Activity	Covert Mental Operation	Eliciting Question
1. Predicting consequences. Explaining unfamiliar phenomena. Hypothesizing	Analysing the nature of the problem or situation. Retrieving relevant knowledge	What would happen if . . . ?
2. Explaining, supporting the predictions and hypotheses	Determining the causal links leading to prediction or hypothesis	Why do you think this would happen?
3. Verifying the prediction	Using logical principles of factual knowledge to determine necessary and sufficient conditions	What would it take for so-and-so to be true or probably true?

In all cases it is important that the students perform the operations for themselves, see the relationships between the items in their own ways, figure out a basis on which to group items, and devise the categories or labels for the groups. The teacher should not do any of these things for them. . . ."

On the other hand, each of the steps in concept formation is a prerequisite for the next one, and the order of steps indicated in Chart 3-1 must be adhered to.

Cognitive task 2, *interpretation of data,* aims at a *different* instructional outcome than concept learning and builds upon the highly personal conceptual verbalizations that have been generated by the students and have been left unchallenged by the teacher in task 1. Students now are required to translate and organize a given body of information, and then verbalize generalizations that are supportable on some logical bases.

The final task, *application of knowledge,* calls for the application of known or given information to a novel or unknown situation. One is required to analyze the dimensions of the problem, call up relevant information through devices such as retrieval charts, generate hypotheses, and test them.

While Taba's research on higher-level cognitive processes was done with social studies subject matter, the strategies developed have general application. Additionally, apart from its relationship to concept analysis, task one is an effective device for generating class discussion with any age group in any subject-matter area.

A recently published work by the Taba associates, several years after her death, has suggested a modification of the original three cognitive tasks into what are referred to as "seven major strategies" and "four minor strategies."[41] The former are for (1) developing concepts, (2) attaining concepts, (3) developing generalizations, (4) exploring feelings, (5) interpersonal problem solving, (6) analyzing values, and (7) applying generalizations.[42] Minor strategies are essentially related to types and sequences of *questions* that teachers will need to intersperse in classroom discussion to improve the efficiency and level of cognitive functioning.[43] These are (1) repeating students' responses, (2) rephrasing responses, (3) asking for explanations of predictions, and (4) asking for explanations of high-level responses.[44]

Apart from the addition of three affective strategies not in the original Taba studies and the making explicit of questioning procedures as minor strategies, the major modification germane to our concerns that the Taba associates have introduced is the inclusion of the *concept attainment* strategy. This strategy is essentially a modified version of the Gagné and De Cecco models; its basic steps are as follows.[45]

---

[41] *Ibid.,* pp. 64–65.
[42] *Ibid.*
[43] *Ibid.*
[44] *Ibid.*
[45] *Ibid.,* p. 71.

1. Teacher requests the student to repeat the concept word after her.
2. Concept instance is provided by having the student observe, listen to a description of, or read about it.
3. Additional instances are provided.
4. As in steps 2 and 3, nonexemplars are provided.
5. Student is required to correctly identify or discriminate an instance of the concept.
6. Student is required to define the concept.

To illustrate application of the Taba model to classroom situations, several varied contexts will be used, and two of the original cognitive tasks will be illustrated to provide contrast in instructional procedures. To highlight the most relevant of the two tasks, concept formation, each of the three steps within the task will be illustrated separately.

Concept Formation—Listing and Enumerating. In the following session, fourth grade children were shown a short filmstrip dealing with "Switzerland," and then were asked the question, "What did you see?"[46] Their responses are listed in Table 3-4 as they were generated verbally, and tabulated on the blackboard.

Concept Formation—Grouping. After all responses were exhausted, the questions was put to the class as to which items belonged

TABLE 3-4
TABA TASK 1: ENUMERATIONS AND LISTS

1. Skiers	17. Milking stool	33. Open-air	50. Table
2. Alps	18. Olaf	market	51. Clothes
3. Cabins	19. Milk cans	34. Stable	52. Gates
4. Goats	20. Exercise	35. Grocery	53. Spiked boots
5. Vegetables	21. Father	36. Cuckoo clock	54. Reins
6. Cows	22. Making	37. Windows	55. Christie
7. Fruits	cheese	38. Skis	56. Hats
8. Farms	23. Mountain	39. Roofs	57. Alpenstock
9. Mechanical	climbers	40. Bushes	58. Hockey Stick
toys	24. Snow	41. Mother	59. Rope for
10. Edelweiss	25. Grass	42. Trees	climbing
11. Jewelry box	26. Rocks	43. Houses	60. Ice
12. Watches	27. Other people	44. Wagons	61. Puck
13. Milk cart	28. Playyard	45. Apron	62. Tools for toys
14. Fields	29. School	46. Thermometer	63. Tools for clocks
15. Dog	30. Fences	47. Cheese pot	64. Mountain ledge
16. Nils and	31. Stone roads	48. Chair	
Gretel	32. Doorways	49. Workbench	

[46]Illustrations provided by Aldena Greene, Pennsbury School District, Fairless Hills, Pa.

together or might be grouped together. Responses were followed up with a question requesting a rationale for the grouping, or why the items belonged together. All groupings and rationale were accepted without challenge. Groupings are indicated by letters in Table 3-5. The reader will note that many items are in multiple groups. With this particular class, multiple classification occurred naturally. If this phenomenon had not, the teacher would have asked the class if some of the items could be put in more than one group to encourage the notion that the varied characteristics of all items allow many ways of categorization.

An alternative way of designating the grouping of items that may be more effective for young children is to use symbols rather than

TABLE 3-5
TABA TASK 1: GROUPING

CA	1.	Skiers	D	33.	Open-air market
A	2.	Alps	D	34.	Stable
A	3.	Cabins	D	35.	Grocery
D	4.	Goats	E	36.	Cuckoo clock
EDB	5.	Vegetables	EDBA	37.	Windows
D	6.	Cows	CA	38.	Skis
EDB	7.	Fruits	EDBA	39.	Roofs
D	8.	Farms	EDBA	40.	Bushes
E	9.	Mechanical toys	D	41.	Mother
A	10.	Edelweiss	EDBA	42.	Trees
E	11.	Jewelry box	ED	43.	Houses
E	12.	Watches	D	44.	Wagons
D	13.	Milk cart	FDC	45.	Apron
FDB	14.	Fields	FDCBA	46.	Thermometer
FDCA	15.	Dog	FD	47.	Cheese pot
ECBA	16.	Nils and Gretel	EDB	48.	Chair
DF	17.	Milking stool	E	49.	Workbench
DCBA	18.	Olaf	EDB	50.	Table
D	19.	Milk cans	ED	51.	Clothes
CB	20.	Exercise	EDB	52.	Gates
D	21.	Father	CA	53.	Spiked boots
DF	22.	Making cheese	FDC	54.	Reins
A	23.	Mountain climbers	A	55.	Christie
CBA	24.	Snow	DBA	56.	Hats
DB	25.	Grass	A	57.	Alpenstock
BA	26.	Rocks	CBA	58.	Hockey stick
EDCBA	27.	Other people	A	59.	Rope for climbing
CB	28.	Playyard	CBA	60.	Ice
B	29.	School	CBA	61.	Puck
EDB	30.	Fences	EB	62.	Tools for toys
EDBA	31.	Stone roads	EB	63.	Tools for clocks
EDBA	32.	Doorways	A	64.	Mountain ledge

letters to designate relationships. For example one might use these items.

□   ○   ☆   +   △   ∔   ⊙

Concept Formation—Labeling. Finally, the students were asked to suggest a name for each of the groups. The labels were: A = Winter Sports, B = School, C = Exercise, D = Farm, and E = Work:

Interpretation of Data. In this illustration, fifth graders were shown a film, "Japanese Boy—The Story of Taro,"[47] and then were asked the following sequence of questions. Commentary is added after each question.

1. "What did you see in the film?"

Students were encouraged to take some time to reflect, and responses were then accepted without challenge. This question provided students with an easy opportunity to verbalize anything that they were able to recall. After approximately ten minutes of free discussion the next question was raised.

2. "What were the feelings expressed by Taro in the film?"

This question focuses upon specific points that are to be compared and contrasted with other points. As students responded, they were asked to substantiate their claims by referring to specific elements in the film.

3. "What do you suppose were the reasons why Taro loved Noriocki so much?"

4. "What did the watch mean to Taro?"

5. "Why do you suppose the watch meant so much to him?"

This series of questions called for relating items to one another, and making interpretations. Again, students were requested to substantiate their opinions by reference to information in the film.

6. "How could we summarize what this film has presented?"

This concluding question asked the students to go beyond what was given to suggest a possible generalization. Insistence upon rationale was particularly important at this point to guard against extreme overgeneralization.

ANALYSIS OF THE GENERIC MODELS

Models and model building, carefully delineated and viewed in proper perspective, can provide a teacher with a useful instructional tool. They provide a focus and a rationale for subsequent classroom behavior and allow generalizability which transcends a specific instructional session or demonstration.

[47]The film is available from Encylopaedia Brittanica films.

Several selected generic models of how a concept-learning process might be structured were offered by way of suggesting some approaches for teachers to consider. Although the models all differ in varying degree, they share certain fundamental commonalities.

Use of Exemplars and Nonexemplars. All the models, in some respect, emphasize the selection of data and organization of facts around exemplars of the concept rule, and the use of nonexemplars as contrasts. The *most* structured delineation of procedures for the use of *exemplars* can be found in the Gagné and De Cecco models, although the *modified* version of the Taba strategies parallels them closely. The function of concentrating upon exemplars and nonexemplars, of course, is to highlight what a particular concept is through iteration.

Systematic Instruction. Not only is the element of organization of instruction critical to the models, but likewise the *sequence* of specific instructional moves and the emphasis of all attribute-related content. All three models suggest an invariant pattern of steps that should be followed in instruction. Additionally, there is a pronounced tendency to operationalize procedures as much as possible, even to the extent of specifying sample questions and questioning sequences, as with the Taba model. The vague admonitions that pervaded much of the early curricular materials dealing with concept learning is rejected by implication, if not specification.

Sensitivity to Prior Knowledge. Gagné's model most explicitly of the three indicates a sensitivity for the need to have prerequisite learning established. Structuring content for concept learning requires considerable attention to the knowledge base of students, since it presumes that the critical attributes of the concept rule are at least familiar to students. To the extent they are not, students cannot proceed to learn the concept in question. In this respect, a logical hierarchy of learning tasks or an abstracted projected cognitive structure is necessary for instructional design. While it is true that a learner's cognitive structure will not necessarily parallel any projected course that a teacher may surmise, a logical continuum of *prerequisite* concepts can be anticipated.

Practice Phenomenon. The models require a practice or exercise phenomenon in which the student tries his hand at manipulating, verbalizing, and discriminating material in the process of learning a given concept. This practice or exercise phenomenon differs from rote verbal drills, homework-associated tasks, or review sessions in that they ask students to explore fact-cluster relationships, to differentiate exemplars from nonexemplars, and to attempt creation of exemplars. Metaphorically, the student is requested to spin the web of a new cognitive structure and to assume some responsibility for selecting and organizing appropriate materials for the process.

Curriculum Organization. The models imply a radical shift in curriculum organization, and more specifically, the design of instructional materials, including all media forms. Traditionally, little attention has been paid to the design of curricular materials *with respect to differential learning outcomes.* The use of nonexemplars and sequential learning steps as systematically urged by the model authors is not a frequent pattern in the design of instructional materials. This point will be taken up in more detail in Chapter 10.

Evaluation. In both the De Cecco and Gagné models, evaluation is explicit though varied. De Cecco, in not distinguishing between concept types, includes *both* discrimination and rule elicitation as requisite tests for learning, whereas Gagné requires simple discrimination as a test for *concrete* concept learning and correct responses to related questions or *demonstration* as a test for *defined* concept learning. Gagné *does* include rule elicitation as an *optional* step for *defined* concept learning.

While not specifying as explicit a form of evaluation for the tasks of concept formation and interpretation of data, Taba's model *does* require careful analysis of student's feedback on the part of the teacher, so that appropriate questions may be raised, and correspondingly, the thinking level of the student's raised. In her formal research works, several instruments *were* used to empirically evaluate the models.[48]

CONCLUSION

Three generic models were outlined and translated into sample classroom illustrations to suggest their utility. To some extent, the models as applied to classroom instruction all differ in several characteristics. All, however, provide a basic component of what has been referred to as "concept learning." To be sure, these models in their translation do not encompass the multiple complex dimensions of facilitating the learning of *all* types of concepts, nor do they reflect a common or complete response on the issue of how the *ingredients* of a concept may be diagnosed for instructional purposes. As Markle and Tieman have noted,[49]

> Some concepts, like *catalyst* in chemistry, are clearly defined and easily discriminated from neighboring concepts. . . . Others, like *liberal* in political science, are subject to shifts in referrents depending on who is using the term and the historical period in which it is used. Some concepts, like *sentence*, seem to generate fair consensus on what be-

[48]Taba, *Strategies, op. cit.*
[49]Susan M. Markle and Philip W. Tieman, "Conceptual Learning and Instructional Design," in M. David Merrill (ed.), *Instructional Design: Readings* (Englewood Cliffs, N.J.: Prentice-Hall, Inc., 1971), p. 286.

longs in the set but almost none—at least to date—on what the critical attributes or properties of the class might be.

What the models *do* seem to provide is a more systematic and justifiable pattern for organizing subject matter toward an objective that all teachers ascribe to, but frequently seem unable to accomplish. To assume, as curriculum developers and practitioners so frequently have done, that the learning of concepts emanates systematically from the exposure to topically related facts clearly is unwarranted. There is, on the other hand, at least some empirical and considerable logical evidence to indicate that the paths charted by the models examined more closely approximate the most efficient routes to systematic concept learning.

SUGGESTED READINGS

Brodbeck, May, "Models, Meanings and Theories," in May Brodbeck (ed.), *Readings in the Philosophy of the Social Sciences* (New York: The Macmillan Company 1968), Chap. 33.

A discussion of the nature, functions, and limitations of models.

De Cecco, John P., *The Psychology of Learning and Instruction* (Englewood Cliffs, N.J.: Prentice-Hall, Inc., 1968), Chap. 10.

Provides an illustration of how a nine-step model for concept learning may be applied to the teaching of the concept "tourist."

Gagné, Robert M., *The Conditions of Learning*, 2nd ed. (New York: Holt, Rinehart & Winston, Inc., 1970), Chap. 7.

Presents a model for concept learning based upon the author's analysis of *eight* conditions for learning.

Kaplan, Abraham, *The Conduct of Inquiry*, Part II (Scranton, Pa.: Chandler Publishing Company, 1964).

An analysis of the nature, types, and functions of concepts and models from a philosophical viewpoint.

Taba, Hilda, *Teaching Strategies and Cognitive Functioning in Elementary School Children*, Cooperative Research Project No. 2404 (Washington, D.C.: U.S. Office of Education, 1966).

This and the earlier project report present sample classroom materials, evaluation procedures, and transcripts of classroom dialog relative to the three cognitive tasks.

Taba, Hilda, et al., *A Teacher's Handbook to Elementary Social Studies*, 2nd ed. (Reading, Mass.: Addison-Wesley Publishing Company, Inc., 1971).

Provides an extended analysis of the recent additions to the original Taba strategies.

Rosalie S. Jensen

CHAPTER 4

Concept Learning in the Mathematics Curriculum, K–12: Issues and Approaches

In order to describe important developments in mathematics education in the recent past and to point out continuing efforts which hold promise for the future, the writer of the present chapter has selected a limited number of persons and groups of people who represent various views and approaches. The most difficult task has been to narrow down the extensive efforts being expended in mathematics education by numerous people and to focus on particular persons and projects. Many contributions selected will be familiar to the reader; others will be unfamiliar to those readers outside the fields of mathematics and mathematics education.

A single thread will weave together the persons and projects pinpointed and will determine the order in which they appear. One of the basic unifying concepts in modern mathematics is that of a *function*. As each person or group is discussed, an example will be cited which pertains to the function concept. The order of presentation is determined by the complexity of the example in each case; thus, the writer has appealed to the popular spiral-curriculum approach used in mathematics teaching. We begin with Piaget, who provides us with an example of a particular type of function, called a *one-to-one correspondence*, and close by defining an abstract concept of function by means of exposition. A few examples which do not seem to be directly related to the function concept will be offered because they are of interest in their own right.

For the benefit of the nonmathematician, a *function* is a pairing of the elements of two sets of objects. The sets may consist of any kinds of objects. The essential characteristic of a function is that it pairs to each element in the first set a unique (one and only one) element in the second set. For the time being, this is all that is needed in order to proceed. The reader is cautioned, however, that as we move toward more advanced aspects of the function concept it may be necessary to read some sections several times through, slowly and carefully. Many mathematicians keep pencil and paper within reach so that they can work examples, filling in the missing details as needed.

We begin at an intuitive level, observing examples of functions appropriate for young children, and move progressively to abstract notions, advanced terminology, and mathematical symbolism. The reader is invited to work related exercises contained in Chapter 9. These are sequenced in the same order as the corresponding examples in this chapter.

JEAN PIAGET'S CONTRIBUTIONS

The importance of the work of Jean Piaget, especially in the area of early childhood education, can hardly be overstated. It is assumed that the reader is familiar with the types of experimentation and with the stages of cognitive development emphasized by Piaget. The objectives here will be to furnish some examples from Piaget's work with the young child that pertain to mathematical concepts and to cite several recent studies that have implications in the teaching of mathematics.

Piaget begins his article "How Children Form Mathematical Concepts" in this manner.[1]

> It is a great mistake to suppose that a child acquires the notion of number and other mathematical concepts just from teaching. On the contrary, to a remarkable degree he develops them himself, independently and spontaneously. When adults try to impose mathematical concepts on a child prematurely, his learning is merely verbal; true understanding of them comes only with his mental growth.

Some of Piaget's most widely discussed experiments involve the concept of conservation of number. In essence, a child is said to possess conservation of number (or the ability to conserve number) if he understands that the number of elements in a set is not changed if the spatial arrangement of the objects is altered. In order to test a child's ability to conserve, Piaget has designed a number of experiments involving

---

[1]Jean Piaget, "How Children Form Mathematical Concepts," *Scientific American,* CLXXXIX (November, 1953), p. 74.

two sets of objects which can be related by a special type of function called a *one-to-one correspondence*. Two sets are said to in *one-to-one correspondence* if each element in the first set is paired with exactly one element in the second set and if each element in the second set is the correspondent of exactly one element in the first set. Figure 4–1 shows a one-to-one correspondence between two sets. The arrows ⟷ indicate the elements which are paired under the correspondence. Two sets which can be put in one-to-one correspondence are called *equivalent sets*.

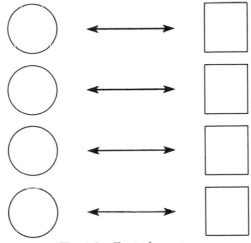

Fig. 4–1. Equivalent sets.

Piaget's experiments indicate that at the stage of intuitive thought, children realize that two sets of objects are equivalent if the two sets are arranged in a certain way but that they will say that there are more elements in one of the sets if its elements are rearranged spatially. Figure 4–2a illustrates the two sets in one arrangement, and Figure 4–2b shows the elements of one set spaced further apart. On the other hand, a child who has reached the stage of concrete operations[2]

> shows that he has spontaneously formed the concept of number even though he may not yet have been taught to count. Given eight red chips and eight blue chips, he will discover by one-to-one matching that the number of red is the same as the number of blue, and he will realize that the two groups remain equal in number regardless of the shape they take.

[2] *Ibid.*, 74.

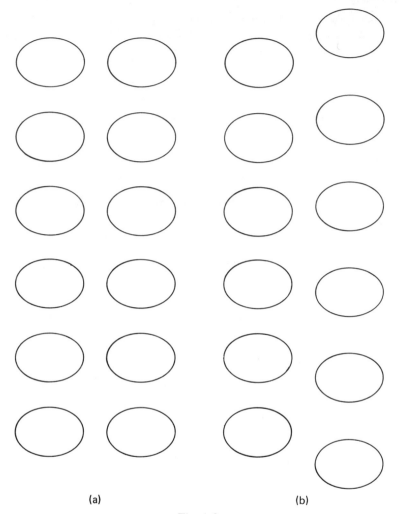

(a)   (b)

Fig. 4–2.

We will return to this concept of invariance, or conservation, of number in citing some experiments by other persons later in this section.

Let us consider some examples from areas other than number systems which are important to mathematics learning.

In studying the child's conception of spatial relationships, Piaget developed some ingenious experiments that can be easily performed by interested persons. He contends that the child's natural development of geometric concepts appears to be in some sense the reverse of the historical development of geometry. According to Piaget, the first formal geometry was the Euclidean system, dealing with figures, angles, and so forth; the next important development was projective geometry, concerned with perspective, and the most modern geometric development has been in the area of topology, which describes properties of figures that are not affected by continuous deformation (without tearing or joining). For instance, topology deals with properties of open and closed figures and with elements in the interior and the exterior of a closed figure. Piaget asserts that children begin with topological relationships. For example, at age 3 a child can copy a square or a triangle, draw a closed circle, and draw a cross with two separate lines. Considerably later they develop concepts of Euclidean and projective geometry simultaneously.[3]

The following experiment is one that Piaget designed to support his conjectures about the development of geometric concepts in the child. Piaget set up in modeling clay two little sticks about fifteen inches apart and asked children to place other sticks between the two in a straight line. Children under the age of four placed each new stick next to another, making a rather wavy line. "Their approach is topological: the elements are joined by the simple relationship of proximity rather than by projection of a line as such."[4] After age 4 the child may be able to produce a straight line of sticks if there is a straight line available to aid him. For example, the original sticks may be placed in such a way that the line of sticks between them should be parallel to the edge of the table on which the experiment is set up. Otherwise, the child may start building parallel to some line and change directions as he comes near to the second stick. If he is able to form the straight line, he does so by trial and error.

Now let us turn to the child at the stage of concrete operations.[5]

> At the age of seven years, on the average, a child can build a straight fence consistently in any direction across the table, and he will check the straightness of the line by shutting one eye and sighting along it, as a gardener lines up bean poles. Here we have the essence of the projective concept; the line is still a topological line, but the child has grasped that the projective relationship depends on the angle of vision, or point of view.

Piaget maintains that the child constructs concepts of Euclidean space as he forms notions of projective space. For instance, in lining up the sticks, the child may sight along a line and may place his hands parallel to each other to aid in giving direction. Piaget says that he is applying the principle of "conservation of direction," which is an Euclidean property[6]

[3] Ibid., p. 75.
[4] Ibid., p. 75.
[5] Ibid., p. 75.
[6] Ibid., p. 76.

Piaget and Inhelder have devised a clever experiment to test the child's development of measurement. A child is shown a tower of blocks on one table and asked to build a tower of the same height on another table. The rules of the "game" forbid moving the towers from one table to the other for comparison of height. The second table is of a different height than the first and the blocks from which the child is to construct his tower are of a different size than the blocks from which the first tower is built. Very young children, according to Piaget, build their tower to the same visual level as the other tower without regard to the heights of the tables. A slightly older child may lay a stick across the tops of the towers to assure that they are level. When he notices that the tables are not the same height, he begins to search for a standard of measurement.[7]

> Interestingly enough, the first thing that comes to mind is his own body. He puts one hand on top of his tower and the other at its base, and then, trying to keep his hands the same distance apart, he moves over to the other tower to compare it. Children of about the age of six often carry out this work in a most assured manner, as if their hands could not change position on the way!

When a child finds this method unreliable, he may attempt to use reference points on his body. The idea of an independent tool for measurement occurs eventually. A child's first effort along these lines will usually be to construct a third tower beside the first one and move his constructed tower to the other table. This is an indication to Piaget that the child has perceived certain properties of the relation "has the same height as." Call the first tower A, the tower on the other table C, and the movable tower B. (See Fig. 4–3.) The child apparently reasons that since B and A have the same height and B and C have the same height, it follows that A and C have the same height.[8]

A later development in the child's thinking leads him to choose a rod to replace the third tower. At first the rod is the same length as the tower, but later the child conceives of marking with his finger a certain place on a longer rod. Eventually he becomes aware that he can use a shorter rod which is applied a certain number of times. To Piaget, this last realization is the essence of understanding measurement, for he feels that measurement is a combination of separation into portions and of substitution. He believes, further, that measurement concepts develop later than the number concept, for it is more difficult to conceive

[7] *Ibid.*, p. 77.

[8] For the mathematically oriented, the child reasons that the relation "has the same height as" is symmetric and transitive.

(a) Given tower A, the child builds tower C.

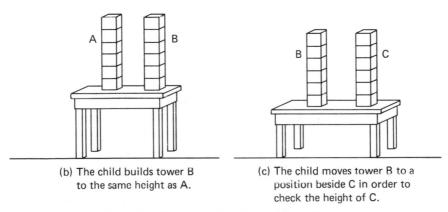

(b) The child builds tower B   (c) The child moves tower B to a
    to the same height as A.   position beside C in order to
                                          check the height of C.

Fig. 4–3. Piaget and Inhelder's tower of blocks.

of separating a continuous entity into units than to count discrete elements.[9]

Considering only the two examples cited, one can readily see that accepting Piaget's findings in the areas of geometry and measurement would lead the teacher in the primary grades to prepare very carefully her development of various concepts of geometry and to structure the measurement experiences of her pupils through a sequence of tasks leading from informal measurement to an appreciation of standard units.

For example, a sequence of activities for establishing the need for standard units of linear measurement might proceed along these lines. Pose a practical problem in the classroom such as the following: "Can

[9] *Ibid.*, p. 78. For a discussion, see: Leslie P. Steffe, "Thinking About Measurement," *Arithmetic Teacher*, Vol. 18 (May 1971), pp. 332–338.

we move this bookcase to that place against the wall between the window and the bulletin board? Since the bookcase is heavy, we do not wish to move it unless we know it will fit." Allow the children to suggest their own means of determining whether the arrangement will be suitable. They may attempt to solve the problem by extending their hands the width of the bookcase or by finding an informal measuring device such as a jump rope which can be stretched the width of the bookcase. They might try stepping off the width of the desk and comparing it with the space stepped off against the wall. In counting their steps, they may notice that shoe size determines the number of steps. When they realize that they cannot communicate their results in steps unless they choose a particular child's shoe as a standard, suggest other standards such as square tiles or blocks, chosen so that they are one inch on each side. When children understand that lining up and counting the tiles can be tedious, introduce the idea of a ruler which is marked off in inches. The numerals on the ruler coincide with the number of tiles it takes to measure a given length. Children can now measure up to twelve inches and read the nearest numeral indicated rather than counting a number of tiles. Need for a yardstick is motivated when the children find that lining up rulers can become as bothersome as lining up tiles. This progression, of course, will cover a rather extended period of time and will encompass many situations which necessitate linear measurement.

The writings of Piaget pose many questions with regard to the mathematics curriculum, particularly in the primary grades. Much research has been and is being conducted in an attempt to verify some of Piaget's findings and in an attempt to determine implications for the teaching of mathematics. Space does not permit a lengthy discussion of this research. Two questions will be pinpointed and discussed briefly.

The first of these questions is: Can children's progress through Piaget's stages of development be facilitated by outside intervention? There exists some disagreement among interpreters of Piaget as to his answer to this question. For example, Lydia Muller-Willis states:[10]

> I once translated a conference between Paul Rosenbloom and Piaget. Rosenbloom's stance was that it is possible, through creative teaching styles, to accelerate children's development. Piaget retorted, "Oh, you Americans, you are in a rush always!" His experiments have led to the conclusion that it is not possible to accelerate the pace very much. . . . Piaget does not say that education can do nothing, only that education is confined by the child's developmental sequence.

[10]Lydia Muller-Willis, "Learning Theories of Piaget and Mathematics Instruction," in W. Robert Houston (ed.), *Improving Mathematics Education for Elementary School Teachers: A Conference Report* (East Lansing, Mich.: Michigan State University, 1968),p. 41.

On the other hand, Adler prefers to interpret Piaget as follows:[11, 12]

> Piaget's critics have often complained that his emphasis on inward maturation and growth leaves no room for the effects of a stimulating environment. This view involves a partial misunderstanding of his theory, and the difficulty could be resolved easily by the realization that Piaget assumes continuous *interation* between the child and his environment. . . .
>
> The real cause of the failure of formal education must be sought primarily in the fact that it begins with language (accompanied by illustrations and fictitious or *narrated action*) instead of beginning with real practical action.

Because of space limitations only one experiment is cited here concerning attempts to accelerate progress.[13] The researchers, Harper and Steffe, studied the possibility of increasing the ability to conserve number in kindergarten and first-grade children through the presentation of a carefully constructed set of lessons. The thirty-minute lessons were taught one per week over a twelve-week period to some seven hundred kindergarten and first-grade children. The teaching progression in the lessons consisted of: (1) engaging children in physical activities; (2) manipulating concrete materials; (3) using semiconcrete examples on the flannelboard. The experimenters felt that they accomplished both aspects of their purpose, namely,[14]

> . . . first, to produce an instrument capable of testing children's strengths and weaknesses in the basic concept of conservation of numerousness; and second, to produce a set of lessons which would enhance children's acquisition of this basic number concept.

The study indicated a significant gain by the experimental group of kindergarten children in the area of conservation of number but indicated no apparent gain for the first-grade children. One implication is that further research is needed in finding a more effective technique for teaching fundamental number concepts.[15]

[11]Marilynne J. Adler, "Some Educational Implications of the Theories of Jean Piaget and J. S. Bruner," *Canadian Educational and Reserach Digest*, Vol. 4 (1964), p. 300.

[12]*Ibid.*, p. 301.

[13]For additional references and discussion, the reader is referred to: Vincent J. Glennon and Leroy G. Callahan, *Elementary School Mathematics: A Guide to Current Research*, 3rd ed. (Washington, D. C.: Association for Supervision and Curriculum Development, 1968), pp. 12–16.

[14]E. Harold Harper and Leslie P. Steffe, *The Effects of Selected Experiences on the Ability of Kindergarten and First-Grade Children to Conserve Numerousness*, Technical Report No. 38 (Madison, Wis.: Wisconsin Research and Development Center for Cognitive Learning), p. 31.

[15]*Ibid.*, pp. 31–32.

Even though the experiment cited indicates some success in increasing the ability of young children to conserve number, there are many other studies which show little or no gain.[16] An important variable in these studies may be the length of time over which the instruction was undertaken. Another significant variable may be the interaction of children permitted by some studies as opposed to the "clinical" atmosphere imposed by those studies undertaken in the isolation of the child from his peers.

The other question we cite is: What is the relationship between progression through Piaget's stages and mathematics achievement? Again we focus on a particular study, although other work has been done in this area. The study chosen is a study by Leslie P. Steffe conducted with a group of children who were near the end of their year of first grade. These children presumably had the benefit of instruction in counting and in addition. Steffe compared the ability of the children to conserve number with (1) the children's ability to solve addition problems and (2) their knowledge of addition facts. A child's ability on a number conservation test placed him in one of four groups, where each group had one-third of its members of IQ 114–140, one-third of its members of IQ 101–113, and one-third of its members of IQ 78–100. The group with the lowest scores on number conservation was labeled Level 4. The results indicated that the children in Level 4 "performed significantly less well on the test of eighteen addition problems and on the test of ten addition facts than did the children in the upper three levels."[17]

Concerning some earlier attempts to explore the relationship between conservation and arithmetic achievement, Glennon and Callahan conclude:[18]

> The evidence would suggest to the teacher that there is a relationship between Piaget's tasks and achievement in arithmetic as measured by standardized achievement tests. There is no indication that performance on conservation tasks is a better predictor of arithmetic ability than performance on IQ tests.

The studies cited tend to indicate that much more research is needed in the area of determining the implications of Piaget's work for teachers of mathematics in the early grades and in the preschool.

[16]For examples of studies indicating various results, see "Five: Training Results," in Irving E. Sigel and Frank H. Hooper (eds.), *Logical Thinking in Children, Research Based on Piaget's Theory* (New York: Holt, Rinehart & Winston, Inc., 1968), pp. 257–434.

[17]Leslie P. Steffe, "The Relationship of Conservation of Numerousness to Problem-Solving Abilities of First-Grade Children," *Arithmetic Teacher*, Vol. 15 (January 1968), p. 52.

[18]Glennon and Callahan, *Elementary School Mathematics*, p. 14.

JEROME BRUNER'S CONTRIBUTIONS

There can be no doubt that Jerome Bruner's writings have influenced the thinking of mathematics educators in the recent past. Concerning Bruner's *The Process of Education,* Shulman writes:[19]

> No single work embodied the letter and spirit of that psychology which undergirds the new curricula as did Bruner's short distillation of the deliberations of a conference of scientists and educators. . . . His writings did not initially stimulate those early renovative efforts in mathematics education. Yet at the end of the 1950's, he managed to capture their spirit, provide them with a framework of cognitive theory, and stimulate the development of their later forms and eventual successors.

It appears that Bruner, although not a mathematician himself, was able to provide at a crucial time an educational philosophy that appealed to mathematicians, mathematics educators, and curriculum planning groups.

The principal emphasis in *The Process of Education* is on the structure of the content to be taught. Bruner's stand on the importance of the basic concepts and unifying ideas of any discipline had appeal to those interested in the teaching of mathematics, for it implied that the modern reorganization of mathematics into structures or systems should be reflected in the mathematics curriculum from kindergarten to the university level. It should be emphasized that already attempts were being organized to formulate programs for the elementary school and the high school which did emphasize a restructuring of mathematics teaching to include new systems of knowledge and new ways of looking at older systems. (Some prominent programs will be discussed shortly.) Bruner's writings, however, appeared at a convenient time to provide a unifying psychological focus for the various groups impressed by the structure principle.

Bruner's emphasis on structure is not the only aspect of his general theory that has widespread appeal to members of the mathematics community. Discovery, as a means of learning mathematics, is a prominent doctrine in Bruner's addresses to mathematics educators. The twin themes of structure and discovery in Bruner's work make his writings compatible with the objectives of many of the mathematics programs that were designed in the late 1950's and throughout the 1960's.

[19]Lee S. Shulman, "Psychology and Mathematics Education," in Edward G. Begle (ed.), *Mathematics Education,* Sixty-ninth Yearbook of the National Society for the Study of Education (Chicago: University of Chicago Press, 1970), p. 25.

For a given concept, Bruner recognizes that there may be many successful approaches that could be classified under the heading "discovery learning." He recommends that each teacher develop his own approaches for eliciting discovery. One of the principal advantages of discovery is that discovery, "with the understanding and mastery it implies, becomes its own reward, a reward that is intrinsic to the activity of working."[20] Bruner does recognize practical problems in discovery learning situations such as the amount of time required, the problem of curriculum construction, and the problem of having some students left out in the process. He classifies these problems as technical ones which are outweighed by the excitement and self-confidence generated by the ability to discover. He concedes that much research is needed in order to find a balance between discovery learning and learning through exposition.

One of Bruner's most controversial and widely quoted statements is contained in *The Process of Education*. As the introduction to a chapter on readiness which focuses particular attention on Piaget's work, Bruner states: "We begin with the hypothesis that any subject can be taught effectively in some intellectually honest form to any child at any stage of development."[21] Considering mathematics learning specifically, it seems that many students find mathematics difficult and, when given a choice, reject it in favor of other subjects; thus this statement taken at face value appears to be at odds with reality. Bruner, however, does not imply that the formal, abstract end-products of mathematics can be understood by a child at any stage of development. He believes that subject matter can pass through certain stages of development:[22]

> Any domain of knowledge (or any problem within that domain of knowledge) can be represented in three ways: (a) by a set of actions appropriate for achieving a certain result (*enactive* representation), (b) by a set of summary images or graphics that stand for a concept without defining it fully (*ikonic* representation), and (c) by a set of symbolic or logical propositions drawn from a symbolic system that is governed by rules or laws for forming and transforming propositions (symbolic representation).

In attempting to reconcile the views of Piaget and Bruner, Shulman suggests that their main area of disagreement may lie in what they

[20]Jerome Bruner, "On Learning Mathematics," *Mathematics Teacher*, Vol. 53 (December 1960), p. 613.

[21]Bruner, *The Process of Education*, p. 33.

[22]Jerome Bruner, "Some Theorems on Instruction Illustrated with Reference to Mathematics," *Theories of Learning and Instruction*, Sixty-third Yearbook of the National Society for the Study of Education (Chicago: University of Chicago Press, 1964), p. 310.

accept as evidence that a child has learned a particular concept.[23] Thus at different stages of the child's development Bruner might accept certain actions as evidence that he had "learned" the concept or process. At a much later stage he would require a verbal or symbolic representation to insure that the child had mastered the concept.

Bruner suggests that "learning mathematics can be viewed as a microcosm of intellectual development." The student begins with physical activity—"a kind of definition of things by doing them;" he then represents and summarizes by images the operations he has performed; lastly, he grasps the abstract properties of the situation with the aid of notation, while at the same time continuing "to rely upon the stock of imagery he has built enroute to abstract mastery."[24]

A simple example from Bruner's writings is included here. The concept of *prime number* embodied in this example is developed in a set of exercises for the reader in Chapter 9.

Bruner describes a personal experience as follows:[25]

> I watched a ten-year-old playing with snail shells he had gathered, putting them into rectangular arrays. He discovered that there were certain quantities that could not be put into such a rectangular compass, that however arranged there was always "one left out." This of course intrigued him. He also found that two such odd-man-out arrays put together produced an array that was rectangular, that "the left out ones could make a new corner." I am not sure it is fair to say that this child was learning a lot about prime numbers. But he most certainly was gaining the intuitive sense that would make it possible for him later to grasp what a prime number is and, indeed, what is the structure of a multiplication table.

The child of whom Bruner speaks is engaging in the inactive stage of developing the particular concept of a prime number. Bruner believes that the activity described, or one like it, is extremely important in developing mathematical concepts. He says:[26]

> I am inclined to think of mental development as involving the construction of a model of the world in the child's head, an internalized set of structures for representing the world around us. These structures are organized in terms of perfectly definite grammars or rules of their own, and in the course of development the structures change and the grammar that governs them also changes in certain systematic ways.

[23]Shulman, "Psychology and Mathematics Education," p. 44.
[24]Bruner, "Some Theorems on Instruction Illustrated with Reference to Mathematics," p. 331.
[25]Bruner, "On Learning Mathematics," p. 614.
[26]*Ibid.*, p. 614.

Bruner particularly objects to imposing formal language and symbolism on the child before the child has proceeded through the sequence of building up the concept informally.

The type of discovery advocated by Bruner is only possible when the expectation of success outweighs the chance of failure.[27]

> It is founded on a kind of combinatorial playfulness that is only possible when the consequences of error are not overpowering or sinful. Above all, it is a form of activity that depends upon confidence in the worthwhileness of the process of mathematical activity rather than upon the importance of right answers at all times.

Bruner admits that once a learner has mastered a particular symbolic system it may be possible to by-pass the ikonic and enactive stages, but he warns that there is always a risk that the learner may not have "the imagery to fall back on when his symbolic transformations fail to achieve a goal in problem-solving."[28]

An important part of Bruner's theory is his notion of transfer. He states:[29]

> Virtually all of the evidence of the last two decades on the nature of learning and transfer has indicated that, while the original theory of formal discipline was poorly stated in terms of the training of the faculties, it is indeed a fact that massive general transfer can be achieved by appropriate learning, even to the degree that learning properly under optimum conditions leads one to "learn how learn."

If transfer is possible across broad domains of knowledge, then this fact has particular application in teaching mathematics, where we are concerned with a great variety of mathematical systems. An important question to be answered is whether it is possible for a student who is able to discover results inductively and to prove them deductively in one system can transfer this skill to other systems. This is a largely unsettled problem which will come up from time to time as we proceed in our discussion.

ZOLTAN P. DIENES' CONTRIBUTIONS

One of the foremost interpreters of a manipulative to semi-abstract to abstract sequence in the teaching of mathematics is Zoltan P. Dienes,

[27] *Ibid.*, pp. 613–614.
[28] Bruner, "Some Theorems on Instruction Illustrated with Reference to Mathematics," p. 314.
[29] Bruner, *The Process of Education*, p. 6.

who currently resides in Quebec, Canada. Not only has Dienes developed many activities, which he calls "games," for children, but also he has designed materials which are available commercially. Especially popular are his "Logical Blocks," to be described herein, his "Multibase Arithmetic Blocks," for teaching about numeration systems, and his "Algebraical Experience Materials."

Dienes' position on major issues in learning theory is compatible for the most part with those of Piaget and Bruner. His philosophy rests upon his notions of the nature of mathematics and the nature of mathematical thought. He says:[30]

> The problem of learning is essentially how to find a kind of "best fit" between the structure of the task and the structure of the person's thinking. For the process to be explained by any kind of intelligible theory, both these structures must be taken into account and at least some attempt made at quantitative description. This is, of course, a very difficult task and little is so far known. . . .

Since both mathematics and the "structure of the person's thinking" are important, we examine briefly Dienes' position on each before looking at his treatment of specific mathematical concepts.

Dienes does not conceive of mathematics primarily as a body of facts or as a collection of techniques, although he believes that techniques are quite essential for effective application of mathematical ideas. Instead, he regards mathematics as a "structure of relationships, the formal symbolism being merely a way of communicating parts of the structure from one person to another."[31] What is a mathematical concept in this scheme?[32]

> A mathematical concept usually contains a certain number of variables and it is the constancy between these, while the variables themselves vary, that constitutes the mathematical concept.

How does one achieve abstract concepts?[33]

> A mathematical abstraction is the result of considering some relevant properties of different mathematical situations and discarding at least for the moment all irrelevant ones. Mathematicians build up their abstractions during their research as a result of wandering about freely in the mathematical country they know so well and forming some idea that certain mathematical landscapes are somewhat familiar. When

[30] Z. P. Dienes, *Building Up Mathematics* (London: Hutchinson Educational Ltd., 1967), p. 27.
[31] *Ibid.*, p. 19.
[32] *Ibid.*, p. 30.
[33] Z. P. Dienes, *Mathematics in the Primary School* (London: Macmillan and Company, Ltd., 1966), p. 182.

they have explicitly become aware of what it is that makes these landscapes similar, a new abstraction is born, a new mathematical concept has been added to the already existing ones.

How is the activity of mathematical researchers related to the formation of concepts by children?[34]

Real concept formation of a lasting character and with positive transfer will, however, take place if children are given adequate experiences. These experiences must perforce be artificial ones, as there are very few, if any, "natural" mathematical situations in real life from which mathematical ideas could be abstracted in the same way as we abstract ideas such as colour, danger, beauty, etc. So the situations must be created. . . .

An important part of Dienes' development of mathematical concepts is the provision of a variety of situations and materials that embody the same idea. Dienes objects to the teaching of an abstract concept through only one set of materials. He feels that the abstract concept will be applicable to a wider variety of situations if the abstraction results from bringing together the common properties of a large number of different situations. For instance, in developing the concept of addition of whole numbers, Dienes would have us introduce a variety of embodiments of the abstract idea of addition. Figure 4–4 indicates some ways of presenting addition drawn from the writings of Dienes and from other sources.[35] Each section of the figure illustrates the addition "fact," 3 + 5 = 8.

Dienes describes three stages of concept formation through which children progress in achieving their basic notions of mathematics. Dienes calls the first step of his three-step progression in concept formation the "play" stage. At this level the child manipulates materials at will, experimenting with them in order to discover their relevant attributes. The role of the adult at this stage is to provide materials which embody the mathematical concept chosen. In the second stage the child engages in more directed activity even though he does not realize clearly what the end result of his learning will be. The stream of development during this stage will depend upon the concept and the child's way of thinking. The third level involves practice for fixing the concept or concepts developed and application of these concepts. During this stage the practice of one concept can act as play for a more advanced concept or principle. Dienes likes to think of the activities pursued as games. The child in his terms engages in "preliminary games," "struc-

---

[34] *Ibid.*, p. 183.
[35] Z. P. Dienes, "Fundamental Operations," *Mathematics in the Primary School* (London: Macmillan and Company Ltd., 1966), pp. 12–41.

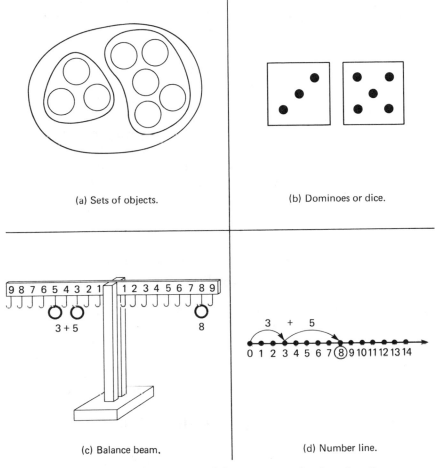

(a) Sets of objects.

(b) Dominoes or dice.

(c) Balance beam.

(d) Number line.

Fig. 4–4. Some means of demonstrating that $3 + 5 = 8$.

tured games," and "practice games" as he passes through the three stages.[36]

Dienes suggests that in a classroom setting children learn best by working in small groups of two or three with sets of assignment cards. The teacher in such a situation acts as a counselor and advisor. Dienes realizes that it is not a simple matter for a teacher to act as a friend and yet retain the last word on decision making in the case of conflicting opinions. He states, however:[37]

[36]Dienes, *Building Up Mathematics*, pp. 27–28.
[37] *Ibid.*, p. 35.

We have sufficient evidence now to say that any good teacher who has an easy relationship with his pupils is perfectly able to handle the disciplinary problems of this kind of situation if he is able to handle the other, more usual type of situation.

We make one further observation before considering Dienes' development of the concept of function. Dienes prefers that a child work out his own symbols for a concept prior to being given formal mathematical symbols. He concedes that research on the role of language is sketchy. On the other hand, reporting on some informal investigations at Harvard, he concludes that sometimes the creation of symbols by the child acts as an impetus to constructive thinking. Moreover, it appears that if formal symbols are introduced after multiple embodiments of a concept, the symbols are more likely to have meaning for a child, and the child is more likely to be able to use the symbols effectively in solving problems.[38]

The development to follow is based on the chapter "Relations and Functions" in *Building Up Mathematics*. We have attempted to construct the first example in such a way as to illustrate Dienes' three stages of development; however, because of the continuous interplay of language and manipulation, it is not possible to delineate precisely the move from one stage to another.

Dienes' development begins with the concept of relation, a more general concept than function, and then moves to a function, which is a particular type of relation. In order to have a relation, Dienes says, we must have two things: (1) a "universe of discourse," which consists of "all the things we are talking about"; (2) a symbol system, which allows us to refer to the elements in the universe. He continues:[39]

> Having established our universe, we can start relating members of this universe to other members of the same universe. Such relating would be what we are saying about the elements of our universe.

In other words, we begin with a set of objects, such as a set of persons, and we establish pairings between elements of the set on the basis of a given criterion or set of criteria, such as the pairings established by relations in everyday life such as "is the father of" and "is taller than." After children are familiar with examples drawn from familiar situations, they are given games and other activities which involve specially designed materials embodying the concept of relation. The following example describes an activity and notation for developing the idea of

[38]Z. P. Dienes, "Some Basic Processes Involved in Mathematics Learning," in Joseph M. Scandura (ed.), *Research in Mathematics Education* (Washington, D.C.: National Council of Teachers of Mathematics, 1967), p. 27.
[39]Dienes, *Building Up Mathematics*, p. 127.

a relation. For brevity, directions are given in the language of an adult audience.

Example 1. Suppose that we have a group of three children and a set of Dienes "Logical Blocks." A set of these blocks consists of 48 wooden or plastic "attribute blocks." The blocks vary in size (large and small), thickness (thick and thin), color (red, yellow, blue), and shape (circle, square, rectangle, and triangle).

At the play stage the children try various experiments, such as stacking blocks, making up stories about the blocks, or separating them into distinct sets according to specific criteria.

When they are ready to enter the next stage, the children look at assignment cards, which have been carefully sequenced. One card tells each child to select five blocks from the total of forty-eight blocks.

John selects as his set the following blocks: large thick red circle, small thin red circle, small thin blue square, large thin blue triangle, large thick yellow triangle. The set he has selected is called the *universe* with which John will now work. Each of the other members of John's group also chooses a universe.

The next task is for John to separate his set into subsets such that the blocks in each subset are alike in size. (Note that John's activity is somethwat directed, but that he still does not know what the final outcome will be.) John separates his set into subsets as shown in Fig. 4–5.

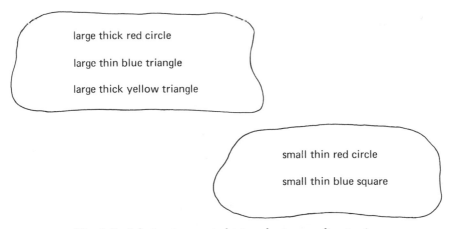

large thick red circle

large thin blue triangle

large thick yellow triangle

small thin red circle

small thin blue square

Fig. 4–5. John's set separated into subsets according to size.

At this point the teacher or the assignment cards may suggest the following type of notation: "(1) Choose any element of your original set of five blocks. Write a description of that block. Draw an arrow and place at the point of the arrow an element of your universe which is related to the first element by the relation 'is the same size as.' " For example, John writes:

small thin red circle $\longrightarrow$ small thin blue square

The directions continue: "(2) For each element of your universe indicate by arrows all other elements of your universe which are related to it by the relationship 'is the same size as.' (Remember that each block is related to itself.)" John writes:

small thin red circle $\nearrow$ small thin red circle

$\searrow$ small thin blue square

large thick red circle $\nearrow$ large thin blue triangle
$\rightarrow$ large thick red circle
$\searrow$ large thick yellow triangle

small thin blue square $\nearrow$ small thin red circle

$\searrow$ small thin blue square

John continues until he has also indicated all blocks related to the large thin blue triangle and the large thick yellow triangle under the relation "has the same size as."

This last task of listing all correspondents of each element in the universe would serve as part of the practice stage, fixing the idea that to each element the relation "has the same size as" assigns one or more elements of the universe. It might also serve as the preliminary stage for the development of certain important mathematical properties of the relation.

The example above does not provide an example of a function. In order to provide an example of a function, we must find a relation with a specific property characteristic of all functions. The property is this: Given any element of the universe, there must be one and only one correspondent under the relation. In our example above, the small thin red circle has two correspondents, namely, the small thin red circle itself and the small thin blue square. This single example, called a *counterexample*, is sufficient to prove that the relation is not a function. The reader is warned, however, that proving that a relation *is* a function involves either checking all correspondences in the relation or constructing a deductive proof.

Let us return to our group of three children and construct an example of a function.

Example 2. An assignment card directs the children to choose as their universe the set consisting of the following blocks: small thin red circle, small thick red circle, large thick blue triangle, large thick red triangle. The task is now to find the correspondents for each member of the universe determined by the relation "differs in exactly one attribute from." It is specified that the correspondents as well as the first elements must come from the universe. John records for his group as follows:

small thin red circle ⟶ small thick red circle

small thick red circle ⟶ small thin red circle

large thick blue triangle ⟶ large thick red triangle

large thick red triangle ⟶ large thick blue triangle

Notice that the relation indicated is a function only because the author chose the elements of the universe very carefully. There are many subsets within the set of Logic Blocks which would not yield functions under the specific relation "differs by exactly one attribute from." An example is given as an exercise in Chapter 9. As the play stage for this particular example, Dienes would probably have the children play a game. The game proceeds as follows: One child chooses any block and places it on the floor. The next child chooses any block which differs in exactly one attribute from the first and places it next to the first block. The third child selects any block remaining which differs in precisely one attribute from the second block. The game progresses with the children forming a "train" of blocks where each block differs from the previous one in exactly one attribute.[40]

SOME IMPORTANT PROJECTS

One modern curriculum project which has attempted to build upon the work of Piaget is the Nuffield Mathematics Project in Great Britain. The project also reflects thinking similar to that of Bruner and Dienes in its emphasis on problem solving, student discovery, and development of concepts through manipulative materials and everyday situations.

In the words of the project organizer Geoffrey Matthews,[41–42]

> The object of the Project is to "produce a contemporary course for children from 5 to 13." In England, children move from "primary" to "secondary" schools at the age of 11, and the change is often an abrupt one, from activity to more formal methods. The Project will try to bridge the gap and make the change-over more gradual. . . . The ultimate aim of this is simple: to produce happy children (and happy teachers) capable of thinking for themselves.

The Project, organized in 1964, began with the formation of a writing team consisting of teachers, who concentrated on writing Guides for

[40]Z. P. Dienes and E. W. Golding, *Learning Logic, Logical Games* (New York: Herder and Herder, 1966).
[41]Geoffrey Matthews, "The Nuffield Mathematics Project," *Arithmetic Teacher*, Vol. 15 (February 1968), pp. 101–102.
[42]*Ibid.*, p. 102.

classroom teachers rather than textbooks for children. Centers were set up around the country so that teachers could meet to discuss problems, to study mathematics, to exchange ideas, and to talk about how to use the Guides.

In describing the Project, Robert B. Davis, a well-known American mathematics educator, writes[43]

> ... the Nuffield Project seeks to identiy clearly-defined developmental stages in the child's growth and to hang curricular plans on these pegs —individualizing for each single child separately, so that the children do not move together as a group.

Because of the age range for which the Project is designed, two of Piaget's developmental stages are of great concern—the stage of intuitive thought and the stage of concrete operations.[44]

> Through a wealth of different materials the child is enabled to establish the 'invariance' of such things as number, substance or liquid. . . . Once invariance has been established the child is in a position to approoch, with confidence, any real problem that arises from the use of concrete materials.

During the concrete-operations stage, children are given questions to answer which initially require manipulation of concrete materials. For instance, children who are asked to find the volume of various rectangular "boxes" might fill each box with hollow cubes, then fill the cubes with sand, and pour the sand into containers of known capacity. After much labor one child in the group may realize that the volume can be obtained by multiplying the dimensions of the box.[45]

> Such a moment of enlightenment does not indicate that from then onwards the child will be able to cope with "formal operations" . . . but that he is entering the significant transitional stage. . . . They will discard real materials themselves at the appropriate moment, as the above example indicates, and eventually, when faced with a problem will ignore all available materials and approach it abstractly.

The writers of the Guides view mathematics as a practical subject which aids the child in giving order to his experiences, both inside and outside of the classroom. The primary rationale for the inclusion of mathematics in the curriculum is related to the notion of patterns and relationships. Mathematics is perceived as an experimental science;

---

[43]Robert B. Davis, *The Changing Curriculum: Mathematics* (Washington, D.C.: National Council of Teachers of Mathematics, 1967), p. 35.

[44]*Ibid.*, p. 35.

[45]Nuffield Mathematics Project, *I Do, and I Understand* (New York: John Wiley & Sons, Inc., 1967), p. 9.

therefore, in order to learn about a mathematical concept, a child should perform an experiment or series of experiments, form a hypothesis, and test his conjecture. If his hypothesis is false, he returns to the experimental stage; if his hypothesis is true, he attempts to generalize and/or apply his discovery to other situations. In general, he will wish to communicate his findings to his classmates and to the teacher. Young children will tell about their discoveries, and older children will write and draw diagrams to describe their findings. Children are encouraged to invent their own symbols to record information before they are taught formal mathematical symbolism for a particular concept.

Davis describes the actual classroom situation depicted in the film "I Do and I Understand" as follows:[46]

> . . . the English classroom resembles more closely a garage, or a machine shop, or a college laboratory class in physics. . . . The resemblance comes from the fact that most of the children are working at benches around the room, usually working in groups of two or three. Those who are not working at benches are usually laying out larger jobs on the floor, or working outside in the corridor, or even working outdoors in the school yard.

The teacher's role is one of providing materials, arranging the classroom for maximal efficiency, discussing the child's approach to a problem and his tentative findings, and responding to the child's questions in such a way as to aid him in evaluating his results and expressing his discoveries in acceptable language. Small group discussion as well as teacher-child discussion is very important. Topics for discussion and problems arise from both everyday activities and from activities contrived by the teacher.

We examine several activities from the book *Mathematics Begins* which are in part designed to lay the groundwork for a formal development of the concept of function later in the child's mathematical education. According to the philosophy of the Project, many such examples are needed before the abstract concept of function is introduced.

In one experiment children are given a set of objects and asked to classify them according to whether they float or sink when placed in a water tray.[47] Suppose that the set consists of the following objects: a cork, a leaf, a rock, a piece of metal chain, a wooden spool, a nail, a plastic car, a shell, a spoon. Perhaps the children make a game of their experiment and guess whether each object will sink or float before

[46]Robert B. Davis, "The Next Few Years," in William W. Joyce et al. (eds.), *Elementary Education in the Seventies: Implications for Theory and Practice* (New York: Holt, Rinehart & Winston, Inc., 1970), p. 55.

[47]Nuffield Mathematics Project, *Mathematics Begins* (New York: John Wiley & Sons, Inc., 1968), pp. 14–15.

placing it in the water. After the children test each item and separate the set into two subsets, the teacher helps them decide upon one or more ways of recording their findings. One method is illustrated in Fig. 4–6. The children draw the objects as members of one set and draw an

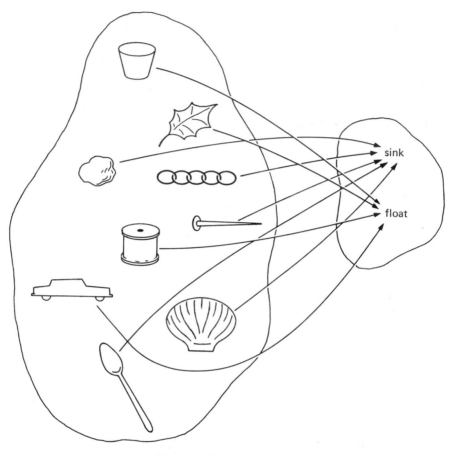

Fig. 4–6.   Recording subsets.

arrow from each of the objects to one of the words "sink" or "float," considered as members of a second set. If the children can write well, they may prefer to indicate their results as a set of "ordered pairs," where each object appears as the first member of a pair and is followed by "sink" or "float" as the second member:

> (cork, float)   (leaf, float)   (rock, sink)   (chain, sink)
> (spool, flloat)   (nail, sink)   (plastic car, float)
> (shell, sink)   (spoon, sink)

Notice that in both methods of notation each object of the original set is paired with a single element of the second set; therefore, we have represented a function. The writers of the Guides suggest many other kinds of representation for young children.

Let us consider a particularly important example of a function.[48] Suppose a situation arises in which children wish to record the results of adding the number 1 to each member of the set of numbers containing 0, 1, 2, 3, 4, and 5. A suggested way of recording is illustrated in Fig. 4–7. The diagram indicates that "Add 1" is a function which assigns to

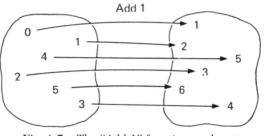

Fig. 4–7.   The "Add 1" function on the set $\{0, 1, 2, 3, 4, 5\}$.

each whole number in the first set one and only one element in the second set.

The operation of addition itself can be viewed as a function which assigns to each ordered pair of whole numbers a unique whole number. For instance, the function assigns to the ordered pair (2, 3) the number 5. Traditionally, we write the ordered pair as $2 + 3$ and the associated "addition fact" as $2 + 3 = 5$. In *Mathematics Begins*, the preferred notation for the ordered pair is (2, 3) and the addition fact is indicated by

$$(2, 3) \xrightarrow{\text{Add}} 5$$

A particular case of the "addition function" is illustrated in Fig. 4–8, where we have in the first set all ordered pairs of whole numbers to which the number 7 is assigned.

One of the important mathematics projects of the last decade was the Madison Project of Syracuse University. The Director of the Project, Robert Davis, contributed much from his own psychological orientation to the program.[49]

> His work with children emphasizes a low-keyed discovery approach, often in the format of competitive games which require the opposing teams to develop inductively the mathematical abstractions which contain the winning strategy.

[48] *Ibid.*, pp. 50–51.
[49] M. Vere DeVault and Thomas E. Kriewall, *Perspectives in Elementary School Mathematics* (Columbus: Charles E. Merrill Publishing Company, 1969), p. 65.

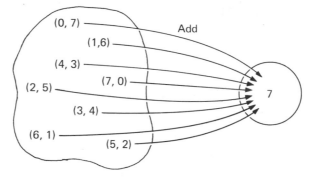

Fig. 4–8.   The "addition function" on the set of all ordered pairs of whole numbers with a sum of 7.

Davis describes the major objective of the program as building readiness over a period of years for concepts and techniques which are essential in high school and college mathematics.

In *Discovery in Mathematics* Davis explains that the project initially identified the fourth, fifth, and sixth grades as target areas for work because children at the intermediate grade levels are more curious and more interested in mathematical abstractions than are high school and college students. Further, he credits children in these grades with "retentive memory, shrewd analytical ability and incredibly honest logic."[50]

Based on their desire to bring children into an active role in the classroom, the originators of the Madison Project laid the foundation for their program on the following decisions: (1) to discard classroom lectures per se and long written exposition; (2) to replace traditional lectures by group discussions in which the teacher acts as moderator; (3) to leave tasks unstructured in the sense that the child is not told a specific method to use; (4) to lead the children into devising solutions to problems and generalizations through a carefully planned sequence of questions; (5) to replace systems of external rewards and punishments by the child's intrinsic reward of having accomplished something through constructive efforts.[51] In addition, the Project attempted to identify and emphasize basic notions rather than specific results, such as formulas, and to encourage student "discovery" of patterns and similarities in situations through trial and error. At an advanced stage children might wish to at-

[50]Robert B. Davis, *Discovery in Mathematics* (Reading, Mass.: Addison-Wesley Publishing Company, 1964), p. 2.
[51]*Ibid.*, pp. 8–9.

tempt verification of some of their conclusions through a study of "mathematical truth."[52]

The following game is an example of an activity designed to develop ideas pertaining to a certain type of function and its "rule."[53] There would be no attempt by the teacher using the Madison Project materials to define the concept of function formally at this point.

Example 3. A small group of children is selected to make up a particular type of rule. For instance, the group might decide on the rule, "whatever number you give me, I'll double it and add four." The group members keep the rule a secret from the other members of the class. The other children suggest numbers. As each number is given, the group tells the number which results from applying the rule. Someone keeps a table of the results, such as the one in Fig. 4–9.

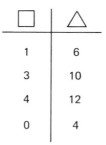

$\square$	$\triangle$
1	6
3	10
4	12
0	4

Fig. 4–9. Some pairs of numbers that
satisfy the rule ($\square \times 2$) + 4 = $\triangle$.

From the number pairs in the table, the children attempt to guess the rule. They learn that by choosing their numbers wisely, they will see a pattern which determines the rule. At some point they attempt to write an algebraic expression. For this rule, the expression would be:

$$(\square \times 2) + 4 = \triangle$$

In future lessons this idea would be extended in various ways.

A particular device for which Davis is well known is called "torpedoing." After a child has discovered a pattern and is confident that his conjecture is valid, Davis slips in a problem which does not fit the pattern. This is not an attempt to shake the child's faith in his ability to discover; it is instead a device to aid the child in seeing that his particular discovery is a specific case of a more general pattern. Davis cites this method as a stimulus for the two processes that Piaget calls "assimila-

[52]Robert B. Davis, "The 'Madison Project' of Syracuse University," *Mathematics Teacher*, Vol. 53 (November 1960), pp. 572–573.

[53]Robert B. Davis, *Mathematics Teaching—with Special Reference to Epistemological Problems*, Monograph Number 1, *Journal of Research and Development in Education* (Athens, Ga.: University of Georgia, 1967), p. 35.

tion" and "accommodation." When torpedoing is practiced in the atmosphere of a secure and friendly classroom with an understanding teacher, the imbalance produced by the introduction of the "counterexample" can be followed by the balance and gratification of being able to discover the more general pattern or rule.[54]

In recent years, Davis has changed somewhat in his views on the application of his type of discovery learning. Admittedly influenced by prominent English mathematics educators, he now prefers dividing a class into small groups in an attempt to take the teacher away from the front of the classroom. In this context he spots two weakensses in his book *Discovery in Mathematics*. He describes the first weakness as follows:[55]

> . . . Discovery uses rhetorical questions. With the teacher guiding discussion, and with thirty children to offer contributions, these rhetorical questions served very well to arouse interest and to focus attention. However, when three or four children are working together by themselves, they often take these rhetorical questions very literally, and find that, among them, they do not possess the resources to dispose of these questions. . . . Hence, whether carefully selected rhetorical questions are valuable or obstructive depends upon the social organization of the classroom.

The other weakness is a technical one which has to do with the order in which the components of equations are written.

A more recently developed program, which is reminiscent of the Madison Project, is entitled Special Elementary Education for the Disadvantaged (SEED). This project takes into elementary school classrooms, university professors, who develop abstract concepts for children through a combination of demonstrations and questions. The reader who is interested in learning more about this project is referred to the article in *Think*, an IBM publication, found in the list of suggested readings at the end of this chapter.

Few mathematics programs have drawn as much attention as the innovative projects of the University of Illinois Committee on School Mathematics, under the direction of Max Beberman. Other project directors readily admit the influence of Beberman and his group on recent mathematics programs. Robert Davis states[56]

> Like nearly all "new" mathematics programs, the Madison Project owes a great debt to Max Beberman of the UICSM Project, who

---

[54]Davis, "Discovery in the Teaching of Mathematics," pp. 118–119.
[55]Davis, *Mathematics Teaching—with Special Reference to Epistemological Problems*, p. 41.
[56]Davis, "The 'Madison Project' of Syracuse University," p. 575.

(among his other contributions) proved the existence theorem that an improved program of school mathematics can be brought into actual use.

In describing the effect of the UICSM program on the revolution in school mathematics of the early 1960's, Wooten says[57]

> Under the ebullient leadership of Max Beberman, the UICSM produced, tested, and publicized a sequence of experimental text-books and teacher manuals that presented the mathematical world with a startlingly new and bold conception of the way they felt math-ematics should be presented to high school students.

The Committee on School Mathematics was established in 1951. With financial support from the University of Illinois, the Carnegie Corporation, and the United States Office of Education, the group de-veloped a sequence of mathematics courses for grades 9 through 12. The National Science Foundation supplied money for summer insti-tutes for training teachers in the use of the materials, which were clearly different from conventional secondary school textbooks.

In his writings, Max Beberman explains some of the underlying principles behind the development of the program. For one thing, there is an attempt to integrate various areas of mathematics that have traditionally been taught as rather distinct and separate subjects. In an article published on graphing in 1956, Beberman and his co-author explain:[58]

> Our emphasis upon both algebraic and geometric concepts stems from our firm conviction that an understanding of mathematics rather than a narrow view of any one of its branches should be the goal throughout all mathematics courses.

Beberman describes another prominent feature of his philosophy as follows: "Somewhat related to the notion of discovery in teaching is our insistence that the student become aware of a concept before a name has been assigned to the concept."[59] This is an indication of Beberman's preference for considering a formal statement of a process or the for-malization of a concept only after the student has an opportunity to discover the procedure or concept and has gained practice in its ap-plication.

The UICSM in 1962 turned its attention to the development of

[57] William Wooten, *SMSG: The Making of a Curriculum* (New Haven: Yale Univer-sity Press, 1965), p. 266.

[58] Max Beberman and Bruce E. Meserve, "Graphing in Elementary Algebra," *The Mathematics Teacher*, Vol. 49 (April 1956), p. 266.

[59] Max Beberman, *An Emerging Program of Secondary School Mathematics* (Cam-bridge: Harvard University Press, 1958), p. 33.

materials for underachievers in grades 7 and 8. The textbooks for seventh-grade students deal with fractions, decimals, and percents, and the materials for eighth-graders are concerned with informal geometry. Each course consists of four workbooks designed to motivate underachievers through activities of a constructive nature. It is difficult to describe the ingenuity with which these materials have been designed. Particularly clever are certain developments in *Stretchers and Shrinkers* (the series on the arithmetic of rational numbers) which are embedded in situations inside factories that stretch and shrink sticks.

In some of their earlier books, the UICSM developed the idea of a "function machine." A function machine is pictured as a box into which one can drop a pair of numbers in a specific order, or a single number, depending on the nature of the machine. The machine acts on the "input," the number or pair of numbers, yielding a single "output." For example, suppose we wish to represent the function "Add 1" (introduced in Fig. 4–4) for the set of numbers 0 through 5 by means of a machine. Such a machine would take the actions illustrated in Fig. 4–10.

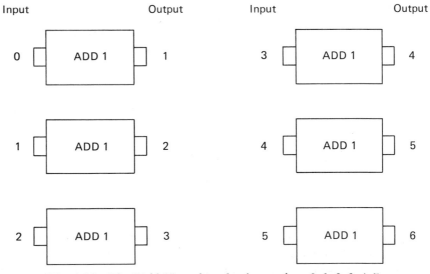

Fig. 4–10.   The "Add 1" machine for the numbers 0, 1, 2, 3, 4, 5.

The utilization of function machines, although they are not called this, is an integral part of the development in the series *Stretchers and Shrinkers*. In these textbooks for underachievers, ordinary expository passages are replaced by nonverbal devices such as pictures, cartoon sequences, diagrams, and graphs. The cartoon characters (see Fig. 4–11) lead the student into the solution of problems involving length, money,

Fig. 4–11. Reprinted from University of Illinois Committee on School Mathematics, *Stretchers and Shrinkers*, Teacher's Edition, Book 1 (New York: Harper & Row, Publishers, 1969), p. 8.

weight, and time. The student also learns skills such as factoring a number into prime factors, estimation, and operations on whole numbers, fractions, decimals, and percents. The development of computational procedures for multiplication of whole numbers is accomplished through "stretching" machines, procedures for division of whole numbers through "shrinking" machines, and procedures involving operations on fractions through "fraction" machines. (See Fig. 4–12 for an example of each type of machine.)

The series *Motion Geometry* for eighth-grade students utilizes geometric functions, called *transformations*. The technical names for the transformations are replaced by informal terms. A geometric transformation called a translation is named a *slide*, a reflection is titled a *flip*, and a rotation is called a *turn*. In a mathematical sense, these transformations can be thought of as functions on points in the Euclidean plane. Figure 4–13 indicates a figure and its image under a particular slide, which is indicated by a "slide line" and a "slide arrow." The student learns how to construct images under the transformations, to represent the transformations, and to follow one transformation by another. Eventually he learns about the more conventional topics in Euclidean geometry pertaining to lines, rays, familiar shapes, area, and perimeter.

It is hoped that these imaginative, carefully constructed materials for underachievers will succeed in bringing them up to a level appropriate for entering a ninth-grade course in algebra.

In 1959 a report was published which had a direct influence on the high school mathematics curriculum and a more indirect, but important, influence on the elementary school curriculum. Entitled *The Report of The Commission on Mathematics: Program for College Preparatory Mathematics*, it was the product of the work of a committee

Stretching machines do multiplication
by whole numbers.

Shrinking machines do division
by whole numbers.

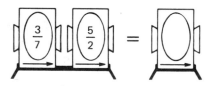

An abundance of problems with fractions
is provided for the student.

Fig. 4–12. Reprinted from "The Slow
Learner Catches on with . . . the UICSM
Mathematics Program," Advertising Bro-
chure, Harper & Row, Publishers, with per-
mission.

appointed by the Mathematics Examiners of the College Entrance Examination Board. The Examiners were concerned about the curriculum
they were testing. In particular, they wondered whether their advanced test devoted to trigonometry, advanced algebra, and solid
geometry reflected what the schools were teaching and what they
should be teaching. Moreover, the Examiners knew that curricular
changes being made in many colleges were certain to influence programs for college-bound students.

    The Report of the Commission was an acknowledged attempt to
influence the secondary school curriculum. The following quotation
will serve to indicate the spirit of mathematics as viewed by the mem-

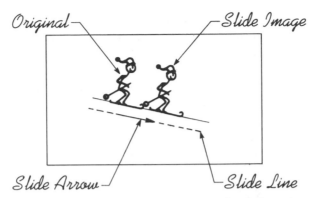

Fig. 4–13.   Reprinted from University of Illinois Committee on School Mathematics, *Motion Geometry*, Teacher's Edition, Book 1 (New York: Harper & Row, Publishers, 1969), p. 35.

bers of the committee and to state the case for revision of the exisitng curriculum:[60]

> Mathematics is a dynamic subject, characterized in recent years by such impressive growth and such extensive new applications that these have far outrun the curriculum. Moreover, the traditional curriculum fails to reflect adequately the spirit of contemporary mathematics, which seeks to study all possible patterns recognizable by the mind, and by so striving has tremendously increased the power of mathematics as a tool of modern life.

Not only did the Commission prescribe a curriculum outline for college bound students, but also they stated objectives of mathematics in general education. These objectives are:[61]

1. An understanding of processes of arithmetic, elementary graphical methods, and simple statistics, and the ability to use arithmetical processes and elementary algebraic formulas.
2. A knowledge of general properties of geometric figures and an understanding of relationships among figures.
3. An understanding of the notions of axiom, rules of inference, and methods of deductive proof.
4. "An understanding of mathematics as a continuing creative endeavor with aesthetic values similar to those found in art and music."

[60]Commission on Mathematics, *Report of the Commission on Mathematics: Program for College Preparatory Mathematics* (New York: College Entrance Examination Board, 1959), p. 9.
[61]*Ibid.*, p. 11.

To accompany their Report, the Commission devised Appendices, which are designed to provide mathematical background for teaching some of the topics included in their curricular outline. In order to develop the concept of function, the writers first develop the concept of ordered pairs and the concept of relation. Some of the development suggested in the Appendices has been incorporated by the author in the programmed unit contained as an exercise in Chapter 9. The notion of relation has been bypassed because of space limitations.

As a result of attempts to implement the Commission's Report and as a result of innovative programs such as those of the UICSM, more content began to prevade the textbook series in the so-called "new math" programs of the sixties.

Another significant effort has been expended by members of a committee which assembled first in 1963 and subsequently produced a document entitled *Goals for School Mathematics: The Report of the Cambridge Conference on School Mathematics*. They offered their recommendations simply as a "discussion document," and they recognized that it would not be appropriate to put it forward as a prescribed curriculum because of the lack of teachers qualified to teach the concepts and skills embodied. The content discussed for grades K–12 would encompass concepts now taught in about three years of college mathematics.[62] The first Cambridge Conference was followed in 1966 by a conference on teacher training for elementary teachers.

The Cambridge Conference on the Correlation of Science and Mathematics in the Schools was held in 1967. Their Report includes educational objectives of an integrated curriculum, specific topics in the mathematics-science curriculum, suggestions for teacher education, and recommendations for immediate implementation of their recommendations. With regard to instruction, the drafters of the Report state:[63]

> The failure to grasp a concept has both the direct effect of preventing a child from going on to dependent concepts and the indirect effect of discouraging him from making the effort to learn even in totally unrelated areas. A success, on the other hand, facilitates later learning both directly and psychologically. We shall argue therefore for a high degree of individualization of instruction coupled with as many and as varied illustrations of each new concept as possible.

[62] *Goals for School Mathematics: The Report of the Cambridge Conference on School Mathematics*, Educational Services Incorporated (Boston: Houghton Mifflin Company, 1963), p. 1.

[63] *Goals for the Correlation of Elementary Science and Mathematics: The Report of the Cambridge Conference on the Correlation of Science and Mathematics in the Schools* (Boston: Houghton Mifflin Company, 1969), p. 14.

One of the most extensive efforts ever undertaken in the writing, evaluation, and revision of materials for teaching mathematics originated in 1958. The organizers of this project shared in common with the members of the Commission on Mathematics the beliefs that (1) modern life demands more knowledge about mathematics on the part of all citizens than life in the past and that (2) the number of skilled mathematicians must be increased to meet the needs of a technological society. One problem that the originators faced was the fact that they could not know precisely what mathematics would be needed in the future. If they were to construct an effective program they felt that (1) the program must offer an improved curriculum that included skill in basic processes and understanding of underlying concepts and structure, (2) the program must attract capable students, and (3) the project must include training for teachers.[64]

The School Mathematics Study Group (SMSG) project that emerged did not in the beginning adopt any particular psychological theory of learning, although the director, E. B. Begle, has at various times expressed his own leanings. Concerning the objectives of the project, Begle says:[65]

> . . . the basic job of the SMSG is not to defend any orthodoxy, old or new, by passing judgment on questions of educational policy, but rather to make contributions to the data on which such judgments must be based.

When a formal structure was adopted for the SMSG in 1961, the bylaws for the group stated their prime purpose as fostering research and development in the teaching of mathematics. It was decided that the contributions of the SMSG should be principally in the areas of course development and provision of teaching methods.[66]

The direction of movement in outlining courses and preparing experimental textbooks proceeded from high school to kindergarten. The manual written for kindergarten teachers stresses the fact that concepts are more important than precise vocabulary. The writers suggest that the teacher encourage active manipulation of materials on the part of children. While a child should be allowed to describe his ideas in his own language, the teacher should use words such as "match," "join," "set," and so forth, that can be transfered to mathematical situations.[67]

---

[64]Edward G. Begle, "SMSG: The First Decade," *The Mathematics Teacher* (March 1968), p. 239.

[65]*Ibid.*, p. 240.

[66]*Ibid.*, p. 239.

[67]School Mathematics Study Group, *Developing Mathematical Readiness in Pre-School Programs* (Stanford: Stanford University, 1967).

To gain an idea of the interplay of informal and formal treatments of a particular topic, we consider the development of the concept of function from the Teacher's Commentary for the 1961 Revised Edition of the course entitled "Intermediate Mathematics." Because of limitations of space, only an outline can be offered here.

The concept of function is introduced as a "pairing" notion. It is suggested that the teacher draw examples of functions from the classroom. For instance, suppose we pair each student in the class with his first name. Notice that: (1) this pairing may not be a one-to-one correspondence, that is, two or more students may have the same first name; (2) each member of the class has only one first name; (3) every name represented is paired with at least one student. In terms of sets, we are really dealing with three sets. The first set is the set of students in the class. This set is called the *domain* of the pairing established. The second set is the set of names of students in the class and is called the *range* of the pairing. The third set is the set of all possible first names. This set contains the range as a subset.

After considering some examples in the classroom, the teacher and students discuss exercises in the student's textbook. These examples deal with numbers, geometric figures, and everyday situations. In some of the exercises it is difficult or impossible to specify the domain and range precisely. These exercises should lead to lively class discussion, where students discover that there is not always one correct, precise answer in mathematical situations.

The teacher is advised to lead the students into a formal definition of function by associating the notion of function with the idea of a box (function machine) that has an input, a mechanism for turning the input into an output, and an output. The "rule" for a function may be thought of as the mechanism inside the box. It may not be possible to formulate a rule; moreover, in advanced mathematics the emphasis is placed on the pairings themselves rather than on a rule for determining the pairings. Thus the abstract concept of function is the idea that we have a pairing between elements of two sets such that to each element of the first set (domain) there is paired a single element of the second set (range). In terms of the machine analogy, to each input there corresponds precisely one output.[68]

In more recent years, the textbooks for grades 7, 8, and 9 have been revised for low achievers, and the kindergarten and first grade programs have been revised for culturally different children. A wide range

[68]School Mathematics Study Group, *Developing Mathematics for High School, Intermediate Mathematics*, Part 1, Teacher's Commentary, rev. ed. (New Haven: Yale University Press, 1961), pp. 145–150.

of other types of materials have ben prepared including films for in-service work with teachers, supplementary units of various kinds, translations in foreign languages, and programmed materials. In all, several hundred persons have worked in developing materials of various types for the SMSG project.

ROBERT M. GAGNÉ

It is assumed that the reader is already familiar with Gagné's theory; therefore, several aspects of Gagné's work that have particular implications for the teaching of mathematical concepts will be considered here.

Discovery techniques of learning have played a prominent role in many "modern" mathematics programs. What is Gagné's position on discovery learning? Gagné asserts that there are different "varieties" of learning. Some of these types involve making "simple connections," the learning of "verbal associates," the learning of "concepts," the learning of "principles," "problem solving" (regarded as a form of learning), and learning the "heuristics of discovery." After analyzing the role of discovery in these various kinds of learning, Gagné concludes that discovery plays a significant role in several of the varieties. For example, concept learning[69]

> appears to require a process of discovery in the sense that an internally generated process of representation is involved. In adults, who have available suitable verbal mediators, concept formation in a novel situation appears to be a most rapid kind of learning. Laboratory studies of effective conditions for concept learning seem to be singularly lacking. But the employment of a high degree of guidance . . . seems to be a necessity for efficient learning.

In order to approach the teaching of a given concept, Gagné recommends that the instructor (1) state the end result of instruction as a behavioral objective, (2) analyze the prerequisite knowledge needed, and (3) structure a sequence of steps that will lead to an understanding of the concept. The understanding would be displayed in an observable way. For instance, the learner might be given examples and asked to choose the ones which exemplify the concept.

The concept chosen by the author for analysis and instruction is embodied in the following abstract definition of function. The reader

[69]Robert M. Gagné, "Varieties of Learning and the Concept of Discovery," in Lee S. Shulman and Evan R. Keislar (eds.), *Learning by Discovery: A Critical Appraisal* (Chicago: Rand McNally & Company, 1966), p. 149.

is expected to understand the definition only *after* completing the short programmed instructional unit contained in Chapter 9.

Definition. Given two sets A and B (where A may be the same as B), a *function from A to B* is a set of ordered pairs (a,b) such that
   (1) *a* is an element of A and *b* is an element of B, and
   (2) each element of A is the first element of one and only one ordered pair.

Stated in behavioral terms, the task required of the student to indicate an understanding of the concept is the following:

Task. Given a set of ordered pairs *(a,b)*, determine whether the set represents a function from the set A to the set B.

In order to lead the reader into performing this task, and thus into showing a grasp of the particular definition of the concept of a function, the author identified certain prior concepts that are needed, and constructed a program incorporating the necessary prerequisite knowledge and leading to a development of the desired concept. Because of limitations of space, the examples within the program and the exercises that follow are simple and should not be construed as comprehensive in scope. The reader is invited to complete the unit of instruction in Chapter 9 before proceeding in this chapter.

DAVID P. AUSUBEL

One of the foremost advocates of sound expository teaching in the mathematics curriculum is David Ausubel. Ausubel is not opposed to discovery learning as such, but he does cite what he feels are some misconceptions about discovery learning and some limitations of its application.

In particular, Ausbel objects to the stance that all discovery learning is meaningful and that all reception learning (that is, learning where the content is taught to the learner in "more or less final form") is not meaningful. He states:[70]

> . . . reception and discovery learning can each be rote or meaningful, depending on the conditions under which learning occurs. In both instances meaningful learning takes place if the learning task is related in a nonarbitrary and nonverbatim fashion to the learner's existing structure of knowledge.

[70]David P. Ausubel, "Facilitating Meaningful Verbal Learning in the Classroom," *Arithmetic Teacher*, Vol. 15 (February 1968), p. 126.

One limitation of discovery learning is that a child sometimes spends a great amount of time solving a trivial problem, whereas the teacher could demonstrate the solution in a few minutes. Ausubel feels that the scientifically unsophisticated child learns more from models and diagrams than from following a laboratory manual in rote fashion. He asserts further that the emphasis on creative problem-solving has actually produced its own kind of rote learning. Instead of memorizing formulas, students are led to the memorization of problem types and forms of solution of each type.[71]

Besides objecting to the time consumed by discovery and to the rote behavior that it may ellicit, Ausubel objects to using discovery as the primary means of teaching persons who are beyond the concrete stage of development. Even with children at the concrete state, he maintains that "the act of discovery is not indispensable for intuitive understanding, and need not constitute a routine part of pedagogic technique." Ausubel contends that[72]

> for teaching simple and relatively new ideas either verbal exposition accompanied by concrete-empirical props, or a semiautonomous type of discovery, accelerated by the judicious use of prompts and hints, is adequate enough.

He seriously questions the utilization of discovery techniques as a vehicle for learning in adults.[73]

> For older learners are able to draw on transferable elements of their overall ability to learn concepts abstractly. Hence, they are able to move through the concrete, intuitive phase of intellectual functioning very rapidly.

If expository teaching is properly structured, adolecents and adults can proceed immediately to an abstract level which is general, clear, precise, and explicit. Even so, when confronted with new subject matter in an area in which they are unsophisticated, they may profit from concrete aids in the very early phases of instruction.[74]

In the following expository passages several concepts are introduced and illustrated with examples. The examples are chosen on the basis of their simplicity. In order to generalize the concepts to more

[71]David P. Ausubel, "Some Psychological and Educational Limitations of Learning by Discovery," *Arithmetic Teacher*, Vol. 11 (May 1964), p. 291.

[72]*Ibid.*, p. 292.

[73]David P. Ausubel, "Can Children Learn Anything that Adults Can—And More Efficiently?" *Elementary School Journal*, Vol. 42 (February 1962), p. 271.

[74]Ausubel, "Some Psychological and Educational Limitations of Learning by Discovery," p. 293.

complex situations, we would need much more time and space.

As a review, we summarize the concept of function. A *function* pairs with each element of a first set one and only one element of a second set. The defining property of a function is that it pairs each element of the first set with exactly one element of the second set.

Consider examples of functions presented earlier. In his example of the child arranging shells, Bruner described each of the child's arrangements either as a rectangular array or as a rectangular array with one shell left over. With respect to this example, we may conceive of a function which pairs with each set of shells one or the other type of arrangement.[75]

In Fig. 4–7, the "add 1" function on a specific set of numbers is represented. If we denote the function as a set of ordered pairs, which we will call P, we have

$$P = \{(0, 1), (1, 2), (2, 3), (3, 4), (4, 5), (5, 6)\}.$$

Looking at the ordered pairs, we note that each first element is the first element of one and only one ordered pair in the set. Let A be the set of all first elements of ordered pairs in P and let B be the set of all second elements. We obtain

$$A = \{0, 1, 2, 3, 4, 5\} \quad \text{and} \quad B = \{1, 2, 3, 4, 5, 6\}.$$

The set A is called the domain of P and B is called the *range* of P. The following definition applies to functions in general:

Definition. Let F be a function considered as a set of ordered pairs. The set of all first elements of ordered pairs in F is called the *domain* of F and the set of all second elements is called the *range* of F.

Consider the following examples of functions.
1. Let $R = \{(0, 0), (1, 2), (2, 4), (3, 6), (4, 8), (5, 10)\}$.
   The domain of R is $\{0, 1, 2, 3, 4, 5\}$, which we have named A, and the range is $\{0, 2, 4, 6, 8, 10\}$.
2. Let $T = \{(0, 0), (1, 1), (2, 4), (3, 9), (4, 16), (5, 25)\}$. The domain is again the set A, and the range is $\{0, 1, 4, 9, 16, 25\}$.

Each of the functions presented was selected carefully so that it could be represented by a "rule." The rule for a function tells how to pair each element of the domain with a correspondent. Given the domain and the rule, we determine the range by finding the set of correspondents for elements of the domain.[76] For example, given the

---

[75]We assume that if the child makes an arrangement with one left over, he has done so only after exhausting all possibilities for making a rectangular array. For example, 15 shells can be arranged as a 3 by 5 rectangular array. Fifteen shells can also be arranged as a 2 by 7 array with one left over. We assume that the set of 15 shells will be paired with the term "rectangular array."

[76]The preceding statement is an oversimplification, but our examples are not complex and will allow us in each case to determine a range.

domain $A = \{0, 1, 2, 3, 4, 5\}$ and the rule "add 1," we add 1 to each element in the domain and write the resulting numbers as a set, the range.

Consider these examples:

3. Let A be the domain of the function with rule "multiply by 2." The function can be represented as

$$R = \{(0, 0), (1, 2), (2, 4), (3, 6), (4, 8), (5, 10)\}.$$

The range is the set of second elements, $\{0, 2, 4, 6, 8, 10\}$.

4. Let A be the domain of the function with rule "square," that is, "multiply by itself." We obtain the representation

$$T = \{(0, 0), (1, 1), (2, 4), (3, 9), (4, 16), (5, 25)\}.$$

The range is $\{0, 1, 4, 9, 16, 25\}$.

The reader is invited to work exercises in Chapter 9 which furnish additional examples of functions on specific sets and their rules. Again, it should be noted that the examples and exercises have been chosen for their simplicity. The general study of functions provides many complex examples which challenge some mathematicians for a lifetime.

SUMMARY

Contributions to the improvement of the mathematics curriculum come from many sources. Groups of mathematicians and educators attempt to pinpoint those concepts and skills which will be of most value to the student. The same group or other groups attempt to design programs and materials that will teach these concepts and skills most effectively. Efforts are made to access, revise, and improve the courses and the materials constructed. Some individuals and groups try to discover *how* students learn concepts and skills in order to create theories of learning mathematics. Examples of significant efforts along all of these lines have been provided: the Commission's Report and the Cambridge Conference Reports offer aid in selecting concepts and skills; the Nuffield Mathematics Project team, the Madison Project group, the UICSM, and the SMSG provide programs, materials, and suggested activities for presenting content effectively and seek to access the effectiveness of their programs and materials; theorists and researchers such as Piaget, Bruner, Dienes, Gagné, and Ausubel seek to describe how learning takes place and to prescribe means of accomplishing various educational objectives that they feel are crucial.

It is only through the cooperative efforts of many individuals and groups that a theory of learning mathematics will emerge that is rich enough to encompass the needs of the individual student, the needs of the subject matter, and the needs of society, and that this theory will be applied in designing a more effective mathematics curriculum.

SUGGESTED READINGS

Ausubel, David P., "Facilitating Meaningful Verbal Learning in the Class-room," *Arithmetic Teacher*, Vol. 15, No. 2 (February 1968), 126–132.

Ausubel explains the distinctions between "receptive" and "discovery" learning and between "meaningful" and "rote" learning; further, he discusses the nature of meaningful receptive learning and reasons why reception is the most efficient means of acquiring concepts and factual information.

Bruner, Jerome S., "On Learning Mathematics," *Mathematics Teacher*, Vol. 53, No. 8 (December 1960), 610–619.

In this article, which is the text of a speech delivered by Bruner, he describes the roles of discovery, intuition, translation, and readiness in mathematics education.

Bruner, Jerome S., "Some Theorems on Instruction Illustrated with Reference to Mathematics," in Ernest R. Hilgard (ed.), *Theories of Learning and Instruction*, Sixty-third Yearbook of the National Society for the Study of Education (Chicago: University of Chicago Press, 1964), pp. 306–335.

The objectives of the author are (1) to set forth some theorems about the nature of instruction; (2) to illustrate these theorems with reference to mathematics; (3) to remark on the role of research in supporting curriculum construction.

Davis, Robert B., "Discovery in the Teaching of Mathematics," in Lee S. Shulman and Evan R. Keislar (eds.), *Learning By Discovery: A Critical Appraisal* (Chicago: Rand McNally & Company, 1966).

Davis provides examples of discovery experiences of children, explains why discovery is important in mathematics instruction, and lists some goals of the Madison Project.

Davis, Robert B., "The Next Few Years," *Arithmetic Teacher*, Vol. 13, No. 5 (May 1966), 355–362.

Davis summarizes his ideas about the most urgent changes needed in elementary school mathematics.

Dienes, Zoltan P., *Building Up Mathematics* (London: Hutchinson Educational Ltd., 1967).

After surveying current practices in teaching mathematics and describing his own theory of mathematics learning, Dienes discusses the teaching of concepts in the areas of arithmetic, elementary algebra, linear algebra, functions and relations, and geometry.

Dienes, Zoltan P., *Mathematics in the Primary School* (London: Macmillan and Co., Ltd., 1966).

Dienes discusses the teaching of number concepts, arithmetical operations, and geometric concepts. He describes principles of abstraction, generalization, motivation, and classroom organization.

Gagné, Robert M., "The Acquisition of Knowledge," in Joseph M. Scandura (ed.), *Research in Mathematics Education* (Washington, D.C.: National Council of Teachers of Mathematics, 1967), pp. 6–20.

Gagné describes how a learner begins with an array of relevant learning sets and acquires new learning sets at progressively higher levels until he achieves the desired concepts and skills.

Gagné, Robert M., "Varieties of Learning and the Concept of Discovery," in Lee S. Shulman and Evan R. Keislar (eds.), *Learning By Discovery: A Critical Appraisal* (Chicago: Rand McNally & Company, 1966).

Gagné describes different types of learning and theorizes as to the necessity of discovery for each variety. He feels that concept learning requires discovery "in the sense that an internally generated process of representation is involved."

Henderson, Kenneth B., "A Model For Teaching Mathematical Concepts," *Mathematics Teacher*, Vol. 60, No. 6 (October 1967), 573–577.

Henderson offers a model for teaching concepts and points out how his model may be used in training mathematics teachers and in research.

Lavatelli, Celia Stendler, *Piaget's Theory Applied To An Early Childhood Curriculum*, A Center for Media Development, Inc. Book (Boston: American Science and Engineering, Inc., 1970).

Lavatelli applies Piaget's theory to the construction of a curriculum for four-, five-, and six-year-old children. She provides suggestions for teaching mathematical concepts in the areas of classification, seriation, measurement, and geometry.

Nuffield Mathematics Project, *I Do And I Understand* (New York: John Wiley & Sons, Inc., 1967).

The writers of the teachers' Guides for the Nuffield Mathematics Project state their philosophy of mathematics instruction and give suggestions for implementing their program in the classroom.

Nuffield Mathematics Project, *Mathematics Begins* (New York: John Wiley & Sons, Inc., 1968).

Mathematics Begins is a Guide for teachers of the early grades (the Infant School in Great Britain). It includes suggestions for work in classification and graphing, shape and size, and mathematical operations.

Piaget, Jean, "How Children Form Mathematical Concepts," *Scientific American*, Vol. 189 (November 1953), 74–79.

Piaget summarizes some experiments involving children's development of concepts involving number, geometry, and linear measurement as they progress through the stages of intuitive thought and concrete operations.

Rosenbloom, Paul C., "Implications of Piaget for Mathematics Curriculum," in W. Robert Houston (ed.), *Improving Mathematics Education for Elementary School Teachers; A Conference Report* (East Lansing, Mich.: Michigan State University, 1967), pp. 44–49.

Rosenbloom discusses reasons why Piaget's works have been neglected until recently in this country. He suggests implications of Piaget's theory for prospective elementary teachers and explores briefly the question of whether stages of development can be accelerated.

Sealey, Leonard G. W., "An Outline of Curricular Changes in Great Britain," in *Mathematics Reform in the Primary School* (Hamburg: UNESCO Institute for Education, 1967), pp. 106–114.

Sealey presents a summary of concepts and general topics chosen for the primary schools by the Schools Council for Curriculum and Examinations and describes the Nuffield Foundation Mathematics Project.

Shulman, Lee S., "Psychology and Mathematics Education," in Edward G. Begle (ed.), *Mathematics Education*, Sixty-ninth Yearbook of the National Society for the Study of Education, Part I (Chicago: The University of Chicago Press, 1970), pp. 23–71.

Shulman focuses on some important and varied learning theories and their applications to mathematics education.

Van Engen, "The Formation of Concepts," in Howard F. Fehr (ed.), *The Learning of Mathematics: Its Theory and Practice*, Twenty-first Yearbook of the National Council of Teachers of Mathematics (Washington, D.C.: National Council of Teachers of Mathematics, 1953), pp. 69–98.

Van Engen discusses "meaning" in mathematics, the nature of a concept, the attainment of concepts, and implications for the teaching of mathematics.

John M. Kean

CHAPTER 5

Concept Learning in the Communication Arts Curriculum, K–12: Issues and Approaches

> I doubt that an over-all structure in the discipline called English can be satisfactorily demonstrated. It remains, as someone has said of history, "a sack of snakes."
>
> Graham C. Wilson[1]

What makes people cringe when the speaker of another dialect talks? What makes some people love Walt Disney productions? What makes others look down their noses at them? What makes some people love TV? Why do others refuse to have it in their homes? Why do some parents believe *Catcher in the Rye* is obscene and subversive? Why do a lot of teachers push its use? The responses to these questions are not simple. Indeed such questions must become the core of a very thorough study of why we communicate in the ways we do. Questions like these defy factual or simple answers. There is in fact no true response to any of these questions. But before we can even begin to analyze them we must begin to deal with the developmental tasks in schooling that are necessary to concept development. We cannot agree on what concepts are appropriate in the language—communication arts until we have made some reasonable guesses such as: What concept load is involved in our opening question? What conceptions or misconceptions about

---

[1]Graham C. Wilson, "The Structure of English," in G. W. Ford and L. Pugno (eds.), *The Structure of Knowledge and the Curriculum* (Chicago: Rand McNally & Company, 1964), p. 85.

117

the nature of language, ethnic groups, geographical isolation, social isolation, self concepts, psychology, life styles, and so on, must be treated in order to understand why people cringe at the sound of another dialect. Even when the concepts related to the question are spelled out and agreed upon, there remains a question of values. Understanding the language and everything else may not stop people from cringing with distaste because they may still *prefer* to have everyone else speak as they do.

We have ordered our world through our symbols. How we respond to the above question or other questions on the uses of television and of books will depend in large on how we use these symbols to make generalizations about our environment and how we want to react to it. Our language provides us with a way of articulating to ourselves and to others our reasons for acting and reacting to the world around us.

In this chapter the writer will try to explicate the meaning of concept learning principles as applied to the English language arts (communication arts), how we might decide on concepts to be learned, to provide illustrations of concepts taught in the communication arts, to describe some of the curricular implications of concept teaching in the communication arts, and finally, to deal with some issues that are still to be fully debated in regard to concept teaching in the communication arts.

We may choose to cluster the concepts that we identify under broad structures. We could classify under "encoding" and "decoding" skills. We could classify concepts under the traditional tripod of language, literature, and composition. We could classify them under speaking, reading, writing, and listening. How we would choose to cluster them may be extremely important because of the limitations that naming something often implies. We are involved in many curriculum arguments now because of the many avenues of learning that our current curricular naming system prohibits us from explaining. For example, English courses in high school do not often reflect what we want to read and discuss—comparative literature, for example. Reading, writing, speaking, and listening have traditionally imposed limits that make it difficult for us to think about film and television in the elementary school. We tend to treat film as an add-on rather than as a presentation media that needs to be explicated carefully with children if they are to use both their expressive and receptive communication capabilities with any kind of skill. Moffett reminds us of the paradox that language curriculum building presents.[2]

> Language learning must go beyond and below language itself. The factors that determine how people produce and receive discourse are

___

[2]James Moffett, *A Student-Centered Language Arts Curriculum, Grades K–13* (Boston: Houghton Mifflin Company, 1968), p. 501.

not at bottom linguistic, but psychological and social. Forms of language and literature, choices made in composing and comprehending, reflect the inner facts of mental operation and the outer facts of human transaction.

What are concepts in the communication arts? We could taxonomically begin to brainstorm a whole series of possible concepts. For example, identifiable concepts might be phoneme, morpheme, grapheme; noun phrase, verb phrase, sentence, paragraph; hyphen, quotation mark, comma, period, capitalization, punctuation; tragedy, history, comedy, burlesque, farce, satire; mass media, newspaper editorial; poetry, prose, sonnet, verse; propaganda, censorship, obscenity; pantomine, choral speaking, story telling; word attach skills. Just spelling out such lists can in itself be confusing. If we look underneath a number of the racks in communication arts we can become even more confused. To describe oral language development and how children can use language, we develop lists like talking, conversing, sharing, planning, discussing, reporting, explaining, evaluating, problem solving, creative expressing, as well as many others. Behind these aspects of oral language uses there are others such as articulating, discriminating sounds, both in speaking and listening. Beyond these mentioned we can deal with the modes of literary invention that have long oral language use such as the lyric, the dramatic, and the epic. The list appears to be almost infinite, and perhaps it is. Finding reasonable ways to grasp and organize a "list of concepts" that children ought to deal with in school is exceedingly difficult. Perhaps it should not even be attempted.

What concepts do children need? How have we traditionally gone about determing what functional concepts children need if they are to become sophisticated communicators? Currently many concepts that we use in the communications arts are influenced by taboos, or legal precedent, or alchemy like observations, or common sense and even sometimes by rationally developed empirically validated deductions; but concepts seem to be lost in the dark ages of our early attempts to define the structure of language and communication. We have gone from parsing to descriptive grammar to generative grammar; from one cultivated form of speech to recognition of dialects, to bilingualism, to standard speech and back again all without any real attempt to grapple with the language values that will enable us to structure our learning. The failure to grapple with these values has left us without a clear sense of the concepts we want to teach.

We have only begun to refine our ideas about concept learning in school. We have finally begun to confirm our suspicions that the "wrong" concepts are really being learned in school (i.e., the definitions students must learn *about* language have hindered their development of fluency and control in using it). We have taken the concepts of English and refused to provide the exemplars that would enable children to make distinctions among grammar, usage, correctness, appropriateness. We have called differences in usage ungrammatical; we have said language items were correct or incorrect when they might better be called appropriate or inappropriate. We have told children our own version of the famous Pooley statement "Good usage is what is comfortable to the speaker and the hearer in a given situation." But "wrong usage" remains whatever differs from the teacher's usage, not what is different from the student's.

We have not moderated our practice by applying our rhetoric to ourselves. We have, through our own ignorance, criticized what is dynamic about the language while clinging to the shibboleths of our idiom. Take the case of the double negative. "Don't use a double negative because two negatives make a positive." This suggests a false analogy between the English language and mathematics. A double negative can be and often is used for emphasis. How many times have you misunderstood a double negative used this way?

There are many ways to deal with the double negative: it can be put into a historical context i.e., Shakespeare's emphatic use of it; examples of it can be shown in developmental cycles (No, No, John,/ John!), and in dialects. All these are more useful than merely to prohibit it.

The same kind of simplistic interpretation has led us to fail to treat much poetry or folk literature as oral. We have read when we should have been listening. We have written when we should have been speaking. We have made some progress since the *New England Primer* but we have not yet accepted the consequences of what we are learning about communications for the curriculum. It is almost as if we had accepted an "Ignorance is bliss" philosophy in a situation where Gray's longer statement makes more sense, "Where ignorance is bliss/ 'Tis folly to be wise." Perhaps it's finally time for folly.

This rambling introduction might be viewed as an attempt to suggest that concept learning in the language arts is not to be attacked directly. This is not the intent. Conceptualizing is basic to language learning. If we are to help children transform their experiences into transmittable messages, we have to help them learn to *conceptualize*. We have to help them learn the sustaining concepts that help us communicate with each other. There is a philosophical assumption underlying most of what will be discussed here that needs to be stated now. We can and do learn to communicate clearly without any formal intervention program called schooling. The personal communicating experiences that we have in our families and with our peers enable us to shape our language needs to fit most occasions. However we have increasingly developed more complex relationships with the world around us that suggest "normal communicating needs" expand in some kind of proportional relationship to our exposure to them. Schools have as one of their goals the helping of children to make use of the extraordinarily complex and sensitive symbols and presentation modes that man has been able to generate. Control over language, over media, can be developed only by some kind of a structured intervention program that gives children access to the wider ranges of human behavior and enables them both to transform their experiences into symbols and to use these symbols to improve their lives and to examine their values—to identify them, to evaluate them, or to change them. It has been suggested a number of times in this book that we cannot make generalizations without first forming concepts. Forming concepts in communications arts is the topic of this paper, but forming concepts is not *the* task of the communications arts. It needs to be kept in mind that we are not talking about a concepts curriculum but about the role of concepts in communications curricula. The communications curriculum can cover phoneme grapheme correspondences as well as the humanities.

CONCEPTS AND OTHER COMMUNICATION ARTS PHENOMENA

Concepts can be defined (a) structurally, in terms of readily perceptible or specific properties, (b) semantically, in terms of synonyms or antonyms, (c) operationally, in terms of the procedures employed to distinguish one concept from others, or (d) axiomatically, in terms of logical or numerical relationships.[3]

As noted in an earlier chapter, Gagné has outlined eight categories of learning which form a learning hierarchy, from simple to complex, with each succeeding category dependent upon learning of the preceding one which may be useful for relating concept learning to other learning types in the communication arts. His system included (in order from simplest to most complex) signal learning, stimulus-response connections, chaining, verbal associations, multiple discriminations, *concepts*, principles, or rules and problem solving.[4] In order to form

[3]H. J. Klausmeier, et al., and D. Frayer, *Strategies and Cognitive Processes in Concept Learning*, U.S.O.E. Cooperative Research Project No. 2850 (Madison, Wis.: U. of Wisconsin, 1968).
[4]Robert Gagné, *The Conditions of Learning*, 2nd ed. (New York: Holt, Rinehart & Winston, Inc., 1970).

language principles we need language concepts; to form concepts we need discrimination.

Gagné's heirarchy seems to lend itself to a consideration of the acquisition and use of communications skills because it begins with basic conditioning, but does not assume this to be a sufficient course to structure all higher learning within the communications arts. Yet for schooling purposes his distinctions may be too refined because of our inability to clearly distinguish what happens when children are engaged in school-learning activities. For example, in various early learning projects there is a deliberate attempt to set up situations in which children engage in a series of experiences which are highly drill-oriented. These are ordinarily structured so that children learn a given type of oral language pattern, not through any attempt to describe or discuss it but simply by the teacher's providing stimuli and asking children to respond appropriately. Negation, for example, is taught by a series of pictures or objects, with children responding again and again until all possibility of the proper response being extinguished is gone. Teacher: "This is a girl." (Shows child picture of a girl.) T: "Is this a girl?" (Shows a picture of a bull.) T: "No, this is not a girl." "Jimmy, is this a girl?" (Shows picture of a car.) Child is supposed to say "No, this is not a girl." This type of pattern is repeated until the response is automatic. Frequent repetitions of the drill insure that the child will have ample opportunity to learn. Signal learning and stimulus response learning appear to be the predominant modes used in such exercises.

A child is probably engaging in *chaining* learning at some stage as he learns to make manuscript letters. This learning follows learning of a more sophisticated type, as when a child begins to use verbal associations and multiple discrimination learning to link the appropriate grapheme with the appropriate sound, and, indeed, as he began to relate his visual image to the kinesthetic ones that his fingers provided. Thus a child will be using any number of learning modes at approximately the same time as he engages in learning some communication task.

Multiple discrimination learning becomes evident when one examines some psycholinguistic oral language programs. For example, the Chicago experimental *Psycholinguistic Oral Language Program: a Bi-Dialectal Approach*[5] has children engage in sessions in which the teacher provides some discussion stimulus and then asks the kids to respond first in *Everyday Talk* and then in *School Talk*—the emphasis in the program is on getting the children to differentiate their speech patterns on the basis of major grammatical differences between the

[5]Lloyd Leaverton, Director, *Psycholinguistics Oral Language Program: A Bi-Dialectal Approach, Part I* (Chicago: Board of Education, 1968).

speech of the child's home and the standard English of the school. For example, Everyday Talk would include, "He be working," while school talk would include, "He is working." But note the children are also learning concepts: *Everyday Talk* and *School Talk*. They have numerous examples of each. At some times they are learning by definition, at other times by separating the attributes of the concepts themselves. In this situation no conscious principles or generalizations are being learned. However, learning the concepts Everyday Talk and School Talk will eventually enable them to deal with generalizations about language, and culture, or language as a system, which will be discussed later in this chapter.

Problem solving, according to Gagné, means that the learner brings to bear upon the problem everything he has previously acquired in the form of stimulus response, verbal associations, multiple discriminations, concepts and principles in order to achieve some solution. In the language arts much of what is done in composition and creative writing at the upper levels could be defined as problem solving. The child learns how to evoke feelings through his writing; or as he decides what boundaries he will put on his stories; or as he uses the analytical tools in writing to describe an experience or report on some event. Writing poetry is problem solving in a play sense for many of us. Reading two different poets' interpretations of some feeling or event in society and making comparisons of their value systems is problem solving in its grandest sense. It allows us to make changes in our value system; it at least allows us to reaffirm in different ways the value system we already have.

Yet to talk about concept learning in the language arts through Gagné's learning hierarchy may, as suggested earlier, be too sophisticated in school situations. Concept learning as defined for schooling purposes can best be characterized by a definition offered in one of the most useful books providing direction for early learning. "The learning of concepts [is] the acquiring or using of a common response or label for two or more completely identical objects or stimuli."[6] It is perhaps more appropriate to examine concepts and relationships within concept hierarchies that have been used to model program materials for schools.

Klausmeier refined the notion of concepts by describing supraordinate,[7] coordinate, or subordinate concepts which basically define the relationships among concepts. A supraordinate has some but not all of

---

[6]Susan Gray et al., *Before First Grade* (New York: Teachers College Press, 1966), p. 25.

[7]This word is variously spelled and pronounced by various authors. Except when quoting directly this paper will use *supraordinate*.

TABLE 5-1
Analysis of the Concept "Noun Phrase"

The information from which the *noun phrase* items were written is as follows:

Attributes: One or more words, contains an optional noun marker plus a noun (or noun substitute such as pronoun, two-word noun, or gerund) diagramed NP——➤(NM) + N, takes several positions in a sentence—subject group, completer after *be*, object of verb, object of preposition, indirect object of verb.

Attribute value examples: (e.g., noun markers) *some of the, several, many, one, the, a, their, my.*

Attribute value nonexamples: (e.g., nonnoun markers) pretty, run, ordinarily, wasted, important.

Concept label: noun phrase.

Concept examples: *seven men, he, all the gold, only the lonely, our aunt.*

Concept nonexamples: *have been slowly declining, going to go, happy.*

Relevant attribute values: noun phrase position, noun, noun marker.

Irrelevant attributes: meaning, gender, adverb, verb.

Concept definition: A word or group of words appearing in any one of five positions in a kernel sentence and which consists of a noun in the last slot and any noun markers preceding it (or in shorthand NP——➤ (NM) + N).

Supraordinate concept: sentence, sentence constituent.

Coordinate concept: verb phrase, subject group.

Subordinate concept: noun phrase completer, noun, noun marker, subject group.

Principles: The subject group of a kernel sentence is a noun phrase. The noun phrase following such prepositions as *to, in, over,* etc., is the object of the preposition.

Problem situation: Find the noun phrases in a given sentence.

From Dorothy A. Frayer, Wayne C. Fredrick, and Herbert J. Klausmeier, *A Schema for Testing the Level of Concept Mastery* (Madison, Wis.: Wisconsin Research and Development Center for Cognitive Learning, April 1969).

the relevant attribute values of the given concept. A coordinate has the *same* number of relevant attributes as the given concept but differs in the particular attribute values which are relevant. A subordinate has all of the relevant attribute values of the given concept and others in addition.[8] In the communication arts *noun phrase* is a concept: *sentence* is a supraordinate concept, *verb phrase* a coordinate concept and *noun* a subordinate concept. (See Table 5-1.) *Exposition* is a concept, *discourse* is a supraordinate concept and *evocation* a coordinate concept.

The relationship between Gagné's hierarchy and that definition provided by Klausmeier might he displayed graphically for conven-

[8]Klausmeier et al., *op. cit.*

ience. Yet it does not appear advisable to do so. Gagné puts conceptual learning within a context that takes us from simple learning to extraordinarily complex learning. Klausmeier, on the other hand, provides us with a system that enables us to examine the multiple meanings and hierarchies within the category of concept. Klausmeier's definition enables us to cluster, group, and relate the concepts that we can name, and hence evaluate the nature of concepts that we might want to use to help children learn.

An endless game can be played that begins with the question: "When is a concept a supraordinate concept?" "When is a supraordinate concept a principle?" As we follow language definitions from phonemes to morphemes to syntactic patterns, from words to phrases to clauses to sentences to paragraphs to essays, it becomes impossible to set down a complete scheme of concepts. It seems best to remember that we are always working in subsystems of some larger system. Consequently whatever aspect we are focusing on, our target is *the* concept and whatever we can describe as part of it becomes a subordinate concept, etc. Such a definition would probably not satisfy Gagné. It is much too easy to get caught up in names of concepts and to forget that concepts are, to a large extent, alinguistic. In Carroll's description, "Concepts are essentially nonlinguistic (or perhaps better, *alinguistic*) because they are classes of experience which the individual comes to recognize as such, whether or not he is prompted or directed by symbolic language phenomena."[9] This is true even when we discuss the concepts that have obvious linguistic or communication power. Perhaps a reasonable illustration might relate to traditional male interpretations of the female as primarily cuddly, warm, supportive, sexy, dependent or otherwise restrictive adjectives. Use of such words as "chick" to describe a female suggests such a limited perspective, but the conceptualization of women in this fashion is not dependent upon the use of the word.[10]

When we are discussing opera or vampire movies or Hitchcock mysteries, we convey meaning only because our listeners or readers have had some experience with movies, mysteries, or opera. This is true whether our audience has been to many operas and seen many old movies on television or very few. If our exposure to Chinese and Afri-

---

[9]John B. Carroll, "Words, Meanings and Concepts," *Harvard Educational Review* Vol. 34, No. 2 (Spring 1964), p. 201.

[10]It may be the use of such words that eventually compels us to reexamine our ideas and to modify our concepts. Women today are forcing men to think about what "chick" means and what it implies about attitudes toward women. As with focusing attention on any habitual, derogatory expression, the intention is to reach and change the thinking behind the usage.

cans and Indians has been limited to Charlie Chan, Tarzan, and Lone Ranger movies, then our understanding of people will be limited by that lack of experience. We are given to characterizing the "inscrutable Chinese," the "shuffling nigger," the murdering savages, the shiftless, drunken, outlandish, uncivilized aborigines, because we make our generalizations on concepts that are bound in grossly ignorant data. Language in these cases may only be a single attribute of behavior which we then apply to many other nonrelated attributes.

The idea might be better illustrated by noting the fright of young children when parents talk about "bloodsuckers" (meaning ticks) and the children's prior experience has been with 8-mm horror movies and horror comics (before they could read) that showed vampires doing their evil deeds. We form concepts about the lark or about spooky noises in exactly the same way. Contemporary church music may elicit spectral rather than spiritual images in children's minds because they associate organ music with Boris Karloff in the attic instead of with the choir director's attempts to praise God. Although it makes sense to define concepts as alinguistic, linguistic and communications concepts do in fact exist as a part of this alinguistic class.

Throughout this chapter the reader will probably find much to quarrel with in terms of what is a concept and what is something else. I have tried to be consistent wherever possible. We have traditionally used a number of terms to describe certain phenomena in language and in communication generally. We are only beginning to realize that linguistic sciences, or verbal language, or dialects, or lexicography, semantics, psycholinguistics, metalinguistics, and so on do not define communication. Models of communications learning that assume these distinctions are the only necessary ones are probably doomed to failure. Earlier in this paper we emphasized that language does not operate in a vacuum; that there are social and psychological bases that provide a context for language. Carroll has said that concepts are *a*linguistic, not necessarily related to language. We can add that there is cognitive perceptive development, i.e., nonlinguistic experience that interacts with linguistic experience to determine a child's linguistic competence.[11] Operating in this context, it is reasonable that all curricular development of the language program should include the experience of treating language within the larger contexts that surround it.

Yet this chapter deals with communications teaching in schools. Much of what we know about communication in school is tied to lan-

[11]For an excellent discussion of the state of our understanding of this view, see Lois Bloom, *Language Development, Form and Function in Emerging Grammars* (Cambridge, Mass.: M.I.T. Press, Research Monograph No. 59., 1970).

guage. Any paucity in attention to nonverbal behavior and kinesics does not preclude their consideration in school.

Distinctions Between Concepts and Other Things

A child is supposed to know how: to read, to use logic, to use reference tools, to write to friends, to order a product, to recognize and respect certain pieces of literature, and to draw his values from a stack of approved traditions. It does not make much difference to most of us whether a child can conceptualize in an abstract sense, but he ought to be able to distinguish people from bears, laws from customs, and a good candidate for mayor from a bad candidate for mayor. He must be able to know a stop sign from a speed sign. He must be able to distinguish good literature from trash. To do all of these things he must be able to form concepts. Concepts, though, are not static. We use concepts to form other concepts. Eventually these other concepts, with greater refinement and data are likely to become generalizations; these generalizations we use to help us form other concepts.

"Language is a system," is a principle[12] which would be rather difficult to define as a concept, yet it probably is to a linguist. At the same time we can generate numerous examples operationally of how we can make specific distinctions among these various levels of learning, and of the various levels within them, for teaching purposes in schools. Blount et al. examined the presence of transformational grammar concepts among junior high students by examining the following behaviors: (a) recognition of concept example, given the concept name, (b) recognition of concept nonexample, given the concept name, (c) recognition of a concept name, given an example, (d) recognition of concept definition, given an example, (e) recognition of concept definition, given the name, (f) production of the concept name, given an example, (g) production of the concept name given the definition, (h) production of the concept definition, given the name, and (i) production of a concept example, given the name.[13]

---

[12]Elsewhere in this book a principle such as this would be called a generalization. Later on in this chapter the word *concept* is used for what others might define as a generalization. Wherever possible its differences will be noted. However, it seemed advisable at times to retain some of the ambiguity in terminology in order to maintain the integrity of the works described.

[13]N. S. Blount, et al., *The Effectiveness of Programmed Materials in English Syntax and the Relationship of Selected Variables to the Learning of Concepts*, Technical Report No. 17 (Madison, Wis.: Wisconsin Research and Development Center for Cognitive Learning, 1967). The testing examples, however, are provided in Dorothy A. Frayer, Wayne C. Fredrick and Herbert J. Klausmeier, *A Schema for Testing the Level of Concept Mastery*, Working Paper No. 16 (Madison, Wis.: Wisconsin Research and Development Center for Cognitive Learning, 1969), p. 17.

By examining the behavior list that Blount and his colleagues have developed, we can decide whether a child can demonstrate verbally his grasp of a concept. A child could easily have a concept at his command without being able to articulate it. Remember that children very often begin to use dialogue and direct quotes in their writing before they can do any of the above activities. We may mention in passing that the ability to name and recognize does not necessarily imply that the child with these abilities is conscious of these concepts when he reads, nor that he will choose to use them when he writes. Forming concepts as a process is distinct from re-quiring children to acquire a given set of concepts necessary for learning basic reading skills (such as recognizing letter shapes). Can we say that a child has a concept for each distinct letter in the al-phabet? Each letter can certainly be named, examples of each in different types and printing forms can be given. A child can recog-nize the nonexamples *b* and *c* when given the concept name *a;* he can name the letter when a written letter is pointed out, and so on. Given certain concepts of the alphabet, we can then generate many more concepts that the child must deal with: initial consonants, conso-nant digraphs, consonant blends, substitution, short vowel sounds, long vowel sounds, diphthongs, syllabication rules, prefixes, suffixes, and compound words among others. The permutations again become enor-mous. These might be handled on a *recognizes* or *does not recognize* basis. Yet even as we try to assess these skills, children would need to have an internalized habituated response that would allow them to distinguish the initial position in a word from the middle or last position. Much of this, though, could be learned at the level of signal learning or multiple discrimination learning (where children distinguish one ver-balization, in this case, from another).

Making these theoretical discriminations may help us define the universe, but it does not particularly help us define the communication arts. We are left with the questions: Where do we start? Where are we going? We might "suspect" that we could deal with spelling tasks this way as we move from phonemes to morphemes, to spelling generaliza-tions, to the need to spell, with a few minor side stops in the areas of historical linguistics, cultural differences, idiosyncratic behaviors and individual learning modes. Yet it would be difficult to push very far in prespecifying the concepts that one needs to read *Hamlet,* or even to define what a variety of people mean in vocabulary development. In the first place, one ought to read *Hamlet* only as a last resort. *Hamlet* was and is meant to be heard and seen. But if one were to read *Hamlet,* it seems difficult to specify the reading comprehension skills, the literary skills, the necessary age "wisdom," and the like that would be needed. (Some people argue that no one under thirty is able to understand *Hamlet* anyway).

When vocabulary development is considered, the prespecification becomes even more difficult. For example, family is a concept we presumably want kids to understand. We can denote family in one way with mothers, fathers, children; but what do we do when we come to extended family, nuclear family, a Mafia family, an animal family, a heavenly family, a family car, a commune family, a married couple, a business family? Sometimes the attributes that we use would be institutional, sometimes psychological. How we would choose to explore attributes of a family with children is even more difficult. Are *marriage, love, children, people under one roof,* and *role definition* all usable attributes for defining what a family is? Should we illustrate family relationships for young children by using cat families? Do the characteristics of cat habits, as children see them in real life, prohibit them from understanding "family" with "cat family" examples?

HOW WE CAN DETERMINE COMMUNICATIONS CONCEPTS

We will really get nowhere in determining the language-arts concepts most appropriate to children unless we can define a reasonable approach to selection of concepts. We need to start from a comprehensive approach to the selection of concepts (but not necessarily develop a comprehensive list of concepts) and then attend to the broad instructional strategies that help get the concepts across. To attempt to develop a complete collection of concepts would be to create an encyclopedia of witchcraft, with concepts relating to demonology, sabbats, incubi, poltergeists—authoritative and comprehensive, no doubt, but based upon a questionable premise. There can be no unique, universal compilation of required concepts. We can go to authorities to examine what has been determined, once we have decided what we want children to do. If we want children to read, then we might want to look at such items as Venezky, Calfee, and Chapman's *Skills Required for Learning to Read: A Preliminary Analysis.*[14] If we want students to be facile with information about the structure of English,

[14]Richard L. Venezky, Robert C. Calfee, and Robin C. Chapman, *Skills Required for Learning to Read: A Preliminary Analysis,* Working Paper No. 10 (Madison, Wis.: Wisconsin Research and Development Center for Cognitive Learning, 1968). In this paper the authors describe the task skills, oral language skills, and letter-sound decoding skills required in the initial stages of learning to read.

then we should consider such papers as Pooley and Golub's *Concepts and Objectives for Learning the Structure of English in Grades 7, 8, and 9.*[15] These researchers have developed extensive lists of concepts that pertain to learning to read and understanding the structure of the English language.

The words "preliminary" and "theoretical" really do define where we are with concept learning in the communication arts. But specifying the *tasks* that teachers and students might use for developing concepts to help students become more sophisticated users of language (and of other communication vehicles) is appropriate. Is it possible to generate questions from needs of students? What kinds of codes do we use in communicating? What is the influence of media upon our perceptions? What makes television different from the newspapers? How do poets develop their technical skill? What is the function of writing? What is rhetoric? How is rhetoric used? How do I use the camera to compose? How do I create a mood when I write or act? Such questions can and should be raised by the people who want to learn to identify the concepts which are needed and are most pertinent, and by the people most immediately responsible for helping them learn.

Any group wishing to determine the communications concepts appropriate to school learning might find it profitable to engage in the following time honored activities:

(a) Define the purposes of learning concepts.

(b) Generate (name) concepts that are known—brainstorming would be particularly appropriate to this activity. Brainstorming requires really that as many ideas as possible be produced without immediate regard to their utility, their political implications or whatever.

(c) Organize the concepts named into some kind of structure or cluster, i.e., find some way to catalogue all of the concepts generated. This practice will make holes or overlaps in the initial concept generation apparent. It is probably crucial to note the hierarchy mentioned earlier. Some concepts will in all likelihood look like generalizations or principles. The organizers may find that some concepts fall naturally into groups; other concepts may require more arbitrary fitting in order to group them with other concepts.

(d) Select concepts to be used in schooling. Presumably, at this point, enough concepts will have been named and organized to

---

[15]Robert C. Pooley and Lester S. Golub, *Concepts and Objectives for Learning the Structure of English in Grades 7, 8, and 9.* Theoretical Paper No. 22 (Madison, Wis.: Wisconsin Research and Development Center for Cognitive Learning, 1969).

force one to begin to make selections; if only because the number of concepts named will simply be more than can physically be handled. This process may involve setting priorities based on philosophy, or on assumptions about prerequisite concepts, i.e., which concepts are probably impossible to teach through any direct school intervention?

(e) Develop a rough plan for handling concepts in school situations. Presumably it would be useful in a school organization for committees to begin to determine concepts appropriate for the primary, intermediate (middle school or junior high areas) and senior high areas. These committees would then, after making selections, submit their proposals to a coordinating committee; this would help omit overlapping and show gaps in the total structure of concepts appropriate to the communications arts. (What hierarchy could be used?)

(f) Refine organized goals and objectives so that concepts can be fitted into school learning situations.

(g) Develop tentative strategies to help children learn the concepts. Here again it might be profitable to brainstorm the instructional strategies suitable to the concepts (deductive, inductive, etc.). What materials or media might help students understand concepts? Generally, what resources are available to help students learn concepts?

(h) Develop a total strategy to fit concepts and instructional strategies together.

(i) Develop evaluation techniques to determine whether concepts have been learned (informal and formal).

CONCEPTS IN COMMUNICATIONS ARTS AREAS

There has been built up over a period of years a *set of principles* or generalizations about language which appears crucial in order to make judgments about language, to understand relationships among people and ideas through language.[16] At different times these principles have been enunciated in different ways but basically, they are:

Language is a system.
Language is unique.
Language is arbitrary.
Language is tied to culture.
Language is to communicate.

[16]For further information see Stanley Kegler, "Toward a Definition of 'English'," in Herbert J. Klausmeier and Chester W. Harris, *Analysis of Concept Learning* (New York: Academic Press, Inc., 1966), pp. 263–264.

Language is primarily oral.

Language is a habit structure.

It is difficult to identify clearly whether we want to call these generalizations (principles), supraordinate concepts, or concepts. But I suspect that most of these statements would best fit the scheme as generalizations, although at one level of learning, they may indeed be conceived of as having observable attributes which would allow them to be called concepts. For example, we accept at the moment that language is systematic. In other words, we can say that words, their pronunciations, and the methods of combining them are interdependent and form a unified whole. Ordinarily, we add that this unified whole can be understood by a considerable number of people. We can shorten the definition and say that language is a systematic way of communicating. But there are certain basic attributes such as words and pronunciations; when specified these would enable us to look at any communication system and say that it is or is not a language. However, using ordinary devices to distinguish language would lead many people to say that underground slang is not a language but gibberish. The teacher might define it as a sublanguage; but in order to reduce cognitive dissonance, there is a tendency not to see the attributes of other people's language as meeting the requirements that we attribute to language. From a different viewpoint, we are still trying to find out what the characteristics of animal language are. We can make guesses; we assume, because we generalize from our statements about human language, that it must be systematic.

The situation will differ if we are trying to help someone look at all the attributes of language. All of the above-named generalizations can be described as attributes of language; taken together, they can differentiate a language from other forms of communication; other forms of communication can either complement language or exist without language—a child's tears, or sexual intercourse, or dancing.

Our problem here is that each component on a continuum of language data has some subordinate, coordinate or superordinate relationship to other components. Concepts may be generated from fact clusters which may be organized into generalizations to form theories. Actually concepts, generalizations, and fact clusters may all comprise the stuff of theories. To put it another way, a concept can presumably become a theory which becomes a concept for a generalization which forms the basis of a subordinate concept which becomes a theory. We may at one point in time call the statement "Language changes" a theory, and then after a sufficient period of observation call it an empirically validated concept; at some still later time it may be called a principle.

The understanding that language changes is a difficult one to grasp. We could demonstrate it by asking children to listen to recordings of old English, middle English, and modern English. We could also demonstrate it by reading children's books of the nineteenth century and comparing them with children's books today. We could demonstrate it by looking at a school English text of the 1940's and comparing it with current observations about people's language today. Or we could examine the semantic import of current words. To most men given to using "in" words, "chick" is a term of endearment for a woman, or at least a more picturesque word than "girl." The English use "bird." Within the last several years the term has been perceived by women as a sexist term blatantly reinforcing the inferior status of women. Other words, such as Negro and black have had a similar history. Even this example would leave lots of unanswered questions. The idea that language changes is tied to a lot of difficult concepts. We go from observation that language is changing every day to admonitions that a language item needs to have been in the language for a century or more to be considered good usage. How do we connect such statements?

If we approach these principles simply from the statements by linguists about them, we have another area of confusion. "Language is a habit structure" is a case in point. There are apparently different points of view about the principles of language. These differences are in themselves complex. Some language statements may be called assumptions—that is, they are outside the concept structure altogether. Chomsky made the point that language as a habit structure has no particular plausibility or a priori justification. As he states it,[17]

> Thus, it is taken for granted without argument or evidence (or is presented as true by definition) that a language is a "habit structure" or a network of associative connections, or that knowledge of language is merely a matter of "knowing how" a skill expressible, as a system of dispositions to respond. . . . There is no reason to react with uneasiness or disbelief if study of the knowledge of language and use of this knowledge should lead in an entirely different direction.

On the other hand, Allen in defining the principles listed above says that "they are all derived from observation and analysis of language, not from philosophizing about it."[18]

Smith, Goodman, and Meredith state "Concepts are never com-

---

[17]Noam Chomsky, *Language and Mind* (New York: Harcourt Brace Jovanovich, 1968), pp. 22–23.

[18]Harold Allen, "A Pharus for the Institute," in Robert F. Hogan (ed.), *The English Language in the School Program* (Champaign, Ill.: National Council of Teachers of English, 1966), p. 3.

pleted by any individual but are ever expanding and being altered. As new significant experience is incorporated into a person's symbolic structures, attributes are added and old ones are rearranged, some becoming prominent as others recede."[19] The implications of this information often go unrecognized in the press of living and working in schools. We are often guilty of retarding the conceptualizing process in children because we fail to recognize and deal with the attempts of children to build conceptual frameworks of their own. We tend to accept the empty-container notion; so much so that we often engage in some communication foibles of our own. The child tries to elaborate his understanding of the moon by describing it as reported on television, but we in our polite reinforcing style say, "But Johnny, the text says . . ." The child is trying to develop a concept of "advisor" including his understanding of that term covering American soldiers in Vietnam and we resort to the dictionary. The child is trying to formulate a meaning for love and we back off. The child is trying to understand violence and we stereotype it into "fighting the establishment" for him.

It is possible to aid the child in collecting and assigning attributes by engaging in a continual dialogue with him to help him confirm his conceptions. Smith, Goodman, and Meredith suggest "When the teacher asks children to talk about an object or picture brought to class, he is stimulating the process of selecting and rejecting attributes. If the teacher is aware of this process, he can lift the quality of ideating and can enhance the substance of such discussions by, for example, injecting negative attributes from other concept clusters into the talk in order to help children confirm their conceptions."[20] We may call this "show and tell" in the primary grades or sharing in the upper grades or reporting personal experiences in the high school. But the process is the same although handled in a more sophisticated manner as the child matures. The child, the young adult, needs help in refining his concepts, sometimes in confirming his concepts; but rarely does he really need to have them rejected out of hand as naive, childish, or "unworthy of a boy (girl) of your intelligence."

Language in this context may very well be the vehicle by which we describe attributes, but it is also a mediator that can separate experience from the brain. We can often feel or know without necessarily being able to describe; the abstraction of language does not necessarily provide the same referents for everyone. I am reminded of the poet

[19]E. Brooks Smith, Kenneth S. Goodman, and Robert Meredith, *Language and Thinking in the Elementary School* (New York: Holt, Rinehart & Winston, Inc., 1970), p. 80.
[20]*Ibid.*, p. 81.

who at a reading was asked "What does your poem mean?" and replied, "It means what I said." He could have added it means to you what it means to you, and to me what it means to me. What is important is that as teachers we try to convey what a poem means to us, while our students ought to be encouraged to convey what a poem means to them; and if perchance we come reasonably close in our interpretations, that's beautiful. But if we don't, the world is far better off for there being two interpretations instead of one.

Thus much of the conceptualizing that goes on when we work with students does not have to result in *taught* concepts. We can defend this on two bases: one, personal concepts are to be expected and even encouraged if children are to be able to think rather than recite; second, many concepts cannot be standardized enough for them to be treated as entities sacred enough to be inscribed on the memory tablets of children's minds. Most concepts are like guesses which we accept at the moment. They are subject to instant dismissal if new experiences or ideas make them obsolete, as for example, has happened with most of the concepts taught in earlier prescriptive grammars based on invalid generalizations from Latin grammar. We are nonetheless left with the necessity to interpret the world as we now find it while keeping in mind the arguments that go on outside the classroom about the nature of language, just as we rely on our own perceptions of poetry while remaining aware of the critics' interpretations.

Our attempt to describe concepts basic to learning the structure of the English language is that of Pooley and Golub. The sixteen "concepts" which they describe here are generalizations, not concepts, according to this book's frame of reference. However, they do provide one framework for examining what needs to be dealt with in language. Later in the paper concepts derived by Blount and his colleagues (in the same projects as Pooley and Golub) will be used specifically to illustrate concepts treated when studying the structure of language. It is significant that in the following list Pooley and Golub thought it important first to specify a teacher objective before detailing their concepts for students. Concept 1 emphasizes that language only very loosely conforms to any kind of natural laws as we now understand them, although the work on generative grammars may eventually lead to such laws becoming more clearly defined. But the point is that language is an arbitrary, culturally related phenomenon that is governed by the differences in human beings. Only loosely can we tie an attribute to language that would enable us to program children in the way one programs a computer—if for no other reason than that the child probably has internalized without our direction and intervention more programs than we will ever be able to generate for computers. The Pooley and Golub statements are[21]

1. Teachers recognize the assumption that language is human behavior.
2. Students learn that spoken English consists of sets of sounds forming words.
3. Students observe that English writing uses an alphabet.
4. Students learn that words have form and forms.
5. Students learn from sentence-building experience that words used in sentences may be classified into four *form classes* and several *function groups*.
6. Students learn that English language communication occurs by using words in sentences.
7. Students learn that sentences may be generated from the S = NP + VP kernel.
8. Students learn to identify and construct seven kernel sentence patterns.
9. Students learn that the verb in the VP may appear in many forms.
10. Students learn that sentences containing structural elements in addition to the elements of the seven-kernel sentence patterns are generated by transformations.
11. Students learn that transformations operating on the grammatical string of a single kernel are called single-base transformations.
12. Students learn that transformations operating on the grammatical strings of two or more kernels are called double-base transformations.
13. Students learn to employ transformations to achieve subordination of one sentence to another.
14. Students learn to employ transformation to achieve coordination of sentences or sentence elements.
15. Students learn how to make transformations that develop sentence modifiers, separated from the sentence they modify and identified in speech by falling juncture and in writing by a comma.
16. Students learn to analyze and create sentences of varied style and dense texture resulting from transformations and other stylistic treatments of grammatical structure.

The Pooley and Golub statement is not offered to present facts but to provide teachers with a series of structured concepts and related behavioral objectives. They include under their concepts (generalizations) statements which, within the framework we are using here,

---

[21]Pooley and Golub, *op. cit.*, p. 23.

would be treated as concepts. For example, under Concept 2 students learn that Spoken English consists of sets of sounds forming words.[22]

(a) The sounds that make words in English are called *phonemes.*
(b) English word sounds are calssified as consonants, vowels, and diphthongs.
(c) Changes of sound occurring within words may be called *phonemic changes.*
(d) Many phonemic changes are grammatical signals, e.g., we change fall to fell.

According to our earlier discussion we can talk about something as a concept when we can define the category (as Pooley and Golub have done), when we can show positive instances of it with exemplars, and when we can name it. We can say that one is learning a rule that may be applied to new instances. For example, we attempt to teach the concept "dialects." We set up opportunities for children to identify and relate the dialect attributes so that they can form genuine concepts about the features of language and dialect. We can clearly show positive instances of dialect. We can show instances of nondialect differences (beyond the idiolect). At different levels we can clearly help people distinguish what attributes actually distinguish dialects (sounds and words do; race and intelligence do not), albeit the presence of some dialect grouping which might lead one to believe dialect is tied to noncritical but highly visible phenomena such as skin color. Many nothern white civil rights workers in the South for the first time were exposed to a Southern dialect and found that ignorance and intelligence were not defining attributes of dialect.

Specific examples of the concepts that would be basic to our understanding of dialect are the following. They have been drawn from "unipac" type material developed by Swenson and colleagues for an in-service program for high school and middle school teachers. In their terms:[23]

Conceptualized Statement

A dialect is the set of shared language habits found among the members of a speech community.

Sub-Concepts

Grammar (syntax), vocabulary, and pronunciation are the three aspects of language which differentiate one dialect from another.

Historically, geographical and natural features, urban influences,

[22] *Ibid.,* pp. 3–4.
[23] Thomas L. Swenson, Karl Hesse, and Lee Hansen, *A Unipac on Dialect* (Madison, Wis.: Madison Public Schools, Title Three Language Arts Project, 1971), p. 2.

foreign influences, and population shifts are the factors that commonly influence formation of dialects.

Dialectical preferences are based on social preferences rather than on characteristics inherent in the language.

All persons speak a dialect of some sort.

In order that the teachers understand the concept they are dealing with, Swenson and his colleagues have designed a series of activities which ask teachers to read some material on dialects and respond to some questions about dialect. Then they are asked to engage in action research to make and test hypotheses about dialect differences, to design an instruction sequence intended to change a student's attitude about the dialects of others, and finally, on the basis of instruction in self-check feedback, to engage in further reading. The culminating activity is a posttest.[24]

This may seem like a lot of work to deal with since such simple statements could have been memorized. However, the project staff is operating under the philosophy that the concepts are instructionally useless, in essence nonsense, until one has had a chance to play with them and internalize them by operating on them. Dialect, syntax, cultural, and all other such items do not carry any weight unless they can be validated in practice rather than simply reproduced in a recall situation such as the paper-pencil test.

In a delightful little book called *Really Understanding Concepts or In Frumious Pursuit of the Jabberwock,* Markle and Tieman provide an example of a literature concept—*soliloquy.* To discover its relevant attributes, they give as an example a speech delivered by a character in a poem, play, or novel, a speech important to development of story, a speech delivered when a character is alone, a speech which reveals essential information. They then suggest some irrelevant attributes: prose or poetic form, the nature of the revelation, the importance of the character. They provide various teaching examples: Captain Ahab's "Sunset" (*Moby Dick,* Chapter 37); teaching nonexamples: a minor character remarks on the weather (*Moby Dick,* Chapter 122); testing examples: Starbuck's talk to himself when trying to decide whether to shoot Captain Ahab (*Moby Dick,* Chapter 123); and testing nonexamples: a narration by the author describing Ahab (*Moby Dick,* Chapter 132).[25]

Such defining of critical and noncritical attributes, with examples for teaching, does provide us with a basis to distinguish, and most of all

---

[24]*Ibid.,* pp. 1–9.
[25]Susan M. Markle and Philip W. Tieman, *Really Understanding Concepts or In Frumious Pursuit of the Jabberwock,* 3rd ed. (Champaign, Ill.: Stipes, 1970), p. 28.

to discuss, the phenomena in language which can be taught. We can define the attributes of a sonnet or a Haiku and distinguish between the two. A sonnet, for example, could be defined as a poem of 14 lines usually with 5-foot iambic meter with rhymes arranged according to one of certain definite schemes—the Italian, into a major group of 3 lines (the octave) followed by a minor group of 6 lines (the sestet) and in a common English form into 3 quatrains followed by a couplet. A Haiku could be defined as a poem of three lines usually with 19 syllables: seven in line 1, five in line 2, seven in line 3; it is usually about nature and sometimes develops a contrast among seemingly dissimilar things. For children seemingly different things might be icicles and walrus teeth. We certainly could provide examples and nonexamples of the two with sufficient skill to determine whether or not a child can distinguish sonnets or Haiku from other forms of writing. In any case, with these definitions it would seem fairly easy to make a distinction between these forms of poetry.

Of course, there remains the question of why one might want to do this. Knowing the difference between two poetry forms makes students more "knowing." As concepts though, these poetic distinctions with many others can give students a broader experience, might provide new possibilities for writing, and could encourage students to seek, cherish, and preserve the beauty in language. Or such concepts, at worst, might enable them to match some version of the knowledge one "must" have to enter college. However, there is nothing sacred or generically valid about including these two forms of poetry or any particular concepts in the school curriculum.

It seems far more important to share poetry with children than it does to conceptualize about it, particularly when the conceptualization deals with figures of speech and metre rather than meaning. Summerfield suggests that "one's questions should aim to extend insight rather than test vocabulary. . . . Meaning must be our first concern—not the extraction of demonstrable figures of speech . . ."[26] The most valid reason to include Haiku in the curriculum would be so that children could learn to write Haikulike poetry. I do not think I would include soliloquy for the same reason, although some budding writer might be delighted to understand the soliloquy for the purpose of reproducing it.

If we accept some of the more exciting ideas about writing programs today, learning to distinguish sonnets from Haiku, as an exercise in writing, may not be necessary (although one could use it for some-

[26]Geoffrey Summerfield, *Topics in English for the Secondary School* (London: Batsford, 1965), p. 23.

thing else). However, in order to develop language-art skills, students will have to examine and learn concepts of some type through one kind of experience or another. Koch has suggested that wishes, comparison, lies, metaphors and other poetry writing ideas all require that attention to given attributes of a form.[27] For example, he worked out a set of rules with children for a wish poem. ". . . every line should contain a color, a comic-strip character, and a city or a country; also the line should begin with the words 'I wish'."[28] The idea helped them to find that they could (write poetry), by giving them a form that would give their poem (a group poem) unity and that was easy and natural for them to use. . . .[29] Koch goes on to suggest the children not be forced to rhyme when writing poetry because it gets in their way. "The effort of finding rhymes stops the free flow of their feelings and associations, and poetry gives way to singsong."[30] Koch has here really suggested a concept that we don't need to teach. I doubt very much whether we could get agreement from many teachers about not teaching children to rhyme because it is such a standard expectation. But Koch's experiential poetic reasons for saying this certainly conform to many of the ideas that English education researchers have suggested over a number of years: various writing requirements often interfere with the child's conceptualizing/ideating process. Koch is primarily interested in a child's transforming his experiences to poetry in a sense, conceptualizing.

Clegg in his description of writing programs in the Infant, Junior, and Secondary Schools of Great Britain indicates similar kinds of input criteria, in his attempts to encourage children to find sensitive ways to draw on their own word stocks, and "to delight in setting down (their) own ideas in a way which is personal to (them) and stimulating to those who read what (they have) written."[31] He makes a distinction between personal writing and recording. "Personal" here would relate to what we call creative writing or writing about personal experiences, impressions, or imaginings. "Recording" refers to writing where much of the child's written work is based on books used and notes taken. In either Koch's or Clegg's descriptions the child needs to develop concepts which enable him to distinguish among the kinds of writing that he does. The child thus learns how to interpret and deal with the symbolic interpretation of others, but more importantly he learns how to use the art forms of writing to present his own ideas.

[27]Kenneth Koch, *Wishes, Lies, and Dreams: Teaching Children to Write Poetry* (New York: Chelsea House Publishers, 1970), p. 309.

[28]*Ibid.*, p. 5.

[29]*Ibid.*, p. 7

[30]*Ibid.*, p. 8.

[31]A. B. Clegg (ed.), *The Excitement of Writing* (London: Chatto and Windus, Ltd., 1965) p. 4.

More subtle or more complex concepts will need to be added as the children find reasons to expand and refine their linguistic presentation modes. They will need to develop ideas about points of view, audience conceptions, and speaker conceptions. For example, the images that we have of comedians and cartoonists seriously affect the judgments which we make about their speaking and writing, particularly when they attempt to move away from the image we have of them. Age, sex, physical appearance, observable behavior, education biases, interests, and status of the speaker or hearer affect how we give and receive messages. Our mood at the moment, our emotional relationship to the topic, our stereotypes, our relationship to authority are additional influencers of the way we receive and give messages. Although it is not particularly important that the child can produce in writing those factors that affect producer-receiver interactions, it is important that he attend to them in his production and in his receiving of language. In effect he is relating concepts to enable him to make generalizations about his own communication, and to analyze how he views the message of a speaker or writer within the context of all the other information that he uses.

CHANGING CONCEPTS IN ENGLISH EDUCATION

There are really several ways we can talk about changing concepts —helping children form concepts, helping children to deal with concepts that are changing, and revising the concepts that form the basis of the curriculum we are using in English education.

In education, experience counts for a great deal, and we have often failed to take into account that school is only a very limited learning experience. More learning goes on outside of school than in; this is a particularly important axiom to remember when attempting to teach concepts in the communication arts. We know that our functioning as literary critics depends heavily upon our accumulated experiences with literature and with the world. To any literature we read we bring all the other reading we have done. We examine, we appreciate, we refute, we describe, we define, we categorize on the basis of having read, seen, and viewed (whether *Batman*, the *Bible*, Edward Stratemeyer's *Nancy Drew*, Victor Appleton's *Tom Swift* series, Truman Capote's *In Cold Blood*, or Shakespeare's *A Midsummer-Night's Dream*).

On a concept level, our understanding, our definitional parameters, are altered with increased experiences and knowledge. We know a child of seven or eight has a more egocentric view of the concept of left and right than does the older child.[32] The younger child may correctly

[32]John H. Flavell, in collaboration with others, *The Development of Role-Taking and Communication Skills in Children* (New York: John Wiley, & Sons, Inc., 1968), p. 33.

specify his left hand or right foot but may not be able to generalize to other examples.

It seems reasonable to hypothesize a similar happening in a larger system, to us as we explore avenues of communication. In literature we move from American literature to English literature of the Western world, to Russian literature, to African literature, to Asian literature, to literature of the world (South American literature somehow undeservedly is often left out) with a profusion of political, social, geographical, and cultural boundaries that seem to defy any kind of a clean classification. I am reasonably sure that at this level our ethnocentrism is as great as that of the child trying to learn left from right. The problem is only partially solved when we consider literature, not nationalistically, but according to genres or types. Some confusion remains mainly because writers, playwrights, and others similarly disposed have in themselves a host of genres and types that they incorporate into their own products. Such confusion has left us in schools with obviously imperfect organizing structures for our program; these we tend to promulgate as if they were generic facts, without letting students in on the secret. Many students realize the fiction extant in our rhetoric. They often fail, however, to appreciate that most forms of intelligent communication are only approximations, only handles that help us relate to the real world; these communications do not and should not replace our aesthetic appreciation of that world.

At this point it seems appropriate to repeat that an unambiguous or "complete" attainment of such concepts as novel, fiction, confession, obscenity, adventure story, romance, tragedy, comedy, mystery, history, and so on are impossible, although we need such classifications to enable us to talk about and deal with the products of communication. It is not only appropriate that we treat communication concepts this way, but that we note that the complexity of meaning is really one of the semantic concepts we are trying to teach as we tie words and their uses to ambiguity, conventionality, vagueness, emotive meaning, simple meanings, multiple meanings (one name, several senses; one sense, several names), word formation, borrowing, why and how words, change meaning, logical classification, psychological classification, taboo and euphemisms, and deterioration.[33]

---

[33]Stephen Ullman treats these concepts in *Words and Their Use* (New York: Hawthorne Books, Inc., 1951). An excellent example of the complexity involved in concept building is provided by McCullough as she explores the possibilities in "What is an Apple?" Her explication leads her though sensory impressions, cognitive relationships, linguistic relationships, and cognitive and affective language. Constance M. McCullough, *Handbook for Teaching the Language Arts*, rev. ed. (Scranton, Pa.: Chandler Publishing Company, 1969).

Glaser has said that we have not as yet come to any hard position on what concept dimensions are or how they might differ as a function of societal norms, differing perceptual characteristics of the stimuli involved, or individual learner histories.[34]

There is another distinction here which applies to what children learn in communication. All literature is within the preserve of the communication arts; we attempt to expose children to a variety of literary experiences that appear to be good without any real grasp of either the nature of the literature being used or the cultural setting of the child as he uses the literature. Martorella gives an excellent example in Chapter 1 of the differences between conceptual and situational learning (in children's learning from literature) as he considers a child's response to reading or listening to nursery rhymes.[35]

Children often do not have the experiential base to assist in the assimilation of new data. A child asks: "What is a corner?" when hearing *Little Jack Horner;* another child wonders what curds and whey are when hearing Miss Muffit's tale. Here are examples of children expanding their understanding of various concepts when our intent was to offer them simply enjoyment. Do they really want to know what curds and whey are? Sometimes yes, sometimes no. Is it important to know? Analogous situations can be drawn through a whole series of folk tales, fairy tales, popular literature, and even the more sophisticated literature, to caution us about students' understanding of concepts. With adolescents we develop more serious concept discrimination tasks because of our failure to account for the human interpretation. We fail to account for what interests adolescents, whether magazines about true romance or cars or sex as opposed to journals and monthlies about world affairs.

Summerfield in his discussion of content states that "Poetry is concerned not so much with the extension of knowledge as with the improvement of knowledge; and we introduce poetry to our pupils not merely to excite and amuse them but in order to help them to know themselves better, to improve their knowledge, to know the 'known' world better."[36] Whether or not one agrees with this as the primary function of poetry (as opposed to preserving beauty), it is easy to lose sight of this: that one reason for all of our efforts in teaching is really to turn students on to literature because, potentially, literature enables us to respond more fully to other people.

---

[34]Robert Glaser, "Concept Learning and Concept Teaching," in Robert M. Gagné and William J. Gephart (eds.), *Learning Research and School Subject* (Itasca, Ill.: Peacock Press, 1969), p. 27.

[35]See p. 11.

[36]Summerfield, *op. cit.*, p. 25.

The question of what is good to read is a real question. Our response to the question may partially control how "turned on" to literature our students become. Carroll has suggested that "education is largely a process whereby the individual learns whether to attach societally standardized words and meanings to the concepts he has already formed or to form new concepts that properly correspond to societally standardized words and meanings."[37] Ironically enough much of the literature that is being called for in schools is designed to expose students to the African heritage, the Chicano heritage, and the Indian heritage. We have not thrown out the literature of yesterday, but tried instead to gain greater perspective by balancing it in different ways. Students would gain perspective by reading the *New England Primer* as well as modern literature.

But if we want our literary experiences to be readily transferable to life, we need to give greater attention to widening the stimuli that we tie literature concepts to. Lundsteen in her model for developing children's thinking during communication reinforces this statement. "The broader the base of a learned subcapacity or concept, the better the chance for transfer to a novel situation . . . teachers and pupils needed to move from the isolated literary selectives to other in-school and out-of-school activities for concept application."[38]

We can extend the relevance of concept learning well into other secondary schooling areas. We deal with "freedom of the press" in schools, we talk about freedom to express your ideas in print. We talk about individual responsibility, political ideas, respect for others' ideas just before we suspend the editor of the underground high school paper or remove *Love Story* from the library.

We have not even agreed on criteria for selection of literature, let alone given children an opportunity to come to some understanding of what literature is by increasing their opportunities to explore it and to make their own decisions about worth. Uppermost in our minds is: Do we encourage the reading of selected pieces so that children can infer about life from what they read or view, or, because the writers have so beautifully used language to describe life, do we assume their description is more "meaningful?" Is *Hamlet* more worthy than *Soul on Ice?* Is *Romeo and Juliet* more meaningful when read, or when viewed with all of the pathos, tragedy, and romance that a director and good actors can bring to it? The directors and actors in plays, the nature of the media

---

[37]Carroll, *op. cit.*, p. 187.
[38]Sara W. Lundsteen "A Model of the Teaching-Learning Process for Assisting Development of Children's Thinking During Communication," *Journal of Communication*, Vol. 18, No. 4 (December 1968), pp. 412–435.

(films vs. stage plays) and so on, all create problems because of the absolute criteria that we tend to attach to the statement we make. But maybe they create problems because we have not allowed time to explore the implications of the interactions, the relationships, that writers, actors, directors, cameramen and even printers have as they provide us with entertainment and information.

One can continue indefinitely with the conceptual problems inherent in the literature that children encounter. Is reading a more vicarious experience than live drama; or, in part, is viewing more vicarious than participation? We have data that suggests that people generally tend to learn through a variety of channels and modes. There are apparently dominances in the senses; some people touch, some look. Where does one draw the line?

When the argument is directed toward the media modes in another way, how do we approach a sophisticated sixteenth-century "Broadway" production like Shakespeare's work, meant for the people in the street, when we turn it into an academic experience? Sometimes one gets the feeling that Shakespeare's, Miller's, or Le Roi Jones' works, when used in school, are really vehicles to teach reading comprehension and the concepts which attend to that skill, rather than an attempt to understand the world through another human being's eyes. Perhaps the principle that ought to be dealt with is "accept the producer's media rather than the media of convenience." Many books are for storage of data until such time as people can recreate or create their own version of a piece of literature.

Perhaps our problem in teaching has been the attempted force-feeding of concepts. As pointed out earlier, one can appreciate or interpret most language at some level on the basis of his own experience. Vygotsky would go so far as to say that kids are not learning concepts if they are learning by imitation and definition as opposed to developing concepts spontaneously themselves.[39] They are instead learning pseudo-concepts.

RELATING CONCEPTS TO OBJECTIVES

If we would talk about language ideas as concepts, we must also consider the ways they are to be learned. What kind of strategies will we set up so that, in Gagné's terms, there will be a demonstration that the learner can generalize the concept to a variety of specific instances

---

[39]L. S. Vygotsky, *Thought and Language*, trans. and edited by Eugenia Hanfmann and Gertrude Vakar (Cambridge, Mass.: M.I.T. Press, 1962), pp. 75–77.

of the classes that have been used in learning?[40] Such a need then leads us to consideration of behavioral or performance objectives and the means by which we can make assessments about what has been learned.

In an attempt to elicit dialogue on the goals of the English language arts, Endres, Lamb, and Lazarus developed a set of objectives grouped under the headings of perceiving, listening, speaking, reading, and writing. Their objectives are developed under categories which range from consumer-assimilative to producer-creative.[41] From such objectives as these it is possible to begin to think about concepts which need to be available to handle the learning expected.

For example, one of their objectives under perceiving is

> To perceive motivations behind emotional appeals on billboards, radio, television, etc.; to be able to identify rationalizations and double talk.

These are supraordinate concepts explicit in the words of the objective as stated, but there are related concepts: exaggeration, personification, bandwagoning, color appeal, etc.; the recognition of these would appear necessary for students to work toward this kind of objective at all. At a more sophisticated level one could look at the concepts implicit here as they relate to sex appeal, status, intelligence, and so forth. At an even more advanced level students could examine this area as a subordinate concept in a study of indocrination or a study in values or the interpretation of the good life, or of the power of persuasion.

But the key to all of these would be basically examining the phenomenon itself either in its natural setting (e.g., ads on television programs), or pulled from its natural setting (e.g., film clips of ads in class). In any case the ads would be studied for their similarities, information load, deception, truthfulness, and so on to enable students to become critical consumers of these types of communications. Unfortunately, the objectives/goals of Endres, Lamb, and Lazarus do not readily translate into appropriate concepts for our use, although they provide a reasonable basis for discussing the goals of communications arts.[42]

More explicitly stated objectives have been developed from the work of teachers and other experts in the field. Two specific examples will be provided here. One comes from Project PLAN, a system of

[40]Robert M. Gagné, *The Conditions of Learning*, 2nd ed. (New York: Holt, Reinhart & Winston, Inc., 1970).

[41]Mary Endres, Pose Lamb, and Arnold Lazarus, "Selected Objectives in the English Language Arts (Pre-K through 12)," *Elementary English*, Vol. XLVI (April 1969), pp. 418–462.

[42]It should be noted that one of these authors has also written a more in-depth treatment of behavioral objectives that have utility at the secondary level: Arnold Lazarus and Rozanne Knudson, *Selected Objectives for the English Language Arts* (Grades 7–12) (Boston: Houghton Mifflin Company, 1967).

individualized education for elementary and secondary students in the areas of language arts, mathematics, science, and social studies. The other comes from the Instructional objectives, as well as a center for collecting and developing measuring techniques for assessing the attainment of objectives.[43]

Flanagan, Mager, and Shenner in Project PLAN have developed behavioral objectives for primary, intermediate, and secondary levels which are more amenable to examination for appropriate concepts.[44]

> Listening skills
> Speaking skills
> Writing skills
> Grammar skills
> Study skills
> Personal communication and development skills
> History and dialectology
> Classification, interpretation and analysis of literary forms
> Original writing
> Oral and dramatic interpretation
> Critical analysis of media

Let us look at the more specific objective that appears to bear a relationship to the example from Endres, Lamb, and Lazarus. [45]

> Given examples of common propaganda devices, classify them as being associated with 1) name-calling, 2) glittering generalities, 3) transfer, 4) testimonial, 5) plain folks, 6) card stacking and 7) bandwagon.

Each of the classifications can be treated as a concept for which we can find excellent examples to help students make sense of the task defined. (Again, examination of the devices themselves will help students become more aware of the ambiguities in language and the extremely slipshod way language is often used.)

It is here that we might refer back to admonitions about the easy path of pseudo-concepts and to the relational nature of many concepts like these.

From these kinds of concepts we can set up the relationships to build generalizations and theories, in this case about propaganda. But we can also slip into the problems associated with "fake" learning,

---

[43]The compilers of all of these objectives stress their tentative nature, their function as stimulators to developing objectives at the local level to meet the educational needs of *local* situations and of individual students. My position is that "adopting" them at the local level would be dereliction of duty.

[44]John C. Flanagan, Robert F. Mager, William M. Shanner, *Behavioral Objectives; A Guide to Individualized Learning: Language Arts* (Palo Alto, Calif.: Westinghouse Learning Press, 1971).

[45]*Ibid.*, p. 105.

better known as "give the teacher the response that the teacher wants."

The compilers of the PLAN objectives have also provided objectives which are "do" objectives. These would allow for informal evaluation of whether or not the requisite concepts noted above were understood by students, whether they could articulate their understanding or not.

The final objective in the PLAN scheme provides an opportunity for students to demonstrate their ability to combine concepts, principles, and generalizations considered as synonymous here; for the category *critical analysis of media* the objective is: in a working group, produce a brief film of a commercial or a parody of a commercial. Many teachers and students might wish to start with such a product, not only because it is an excellent vehicle for developing composition skills, but because it would provide a stimulating inductive beginning to the study of media.

The Instructional Objectives Exchange has pushed its specifications a little differently by providing a collection of objectives with sample test items. For instance, in Grades 7–9 Language Arts under the Major category "Mass Media," Subcategory "Advertising Appeals," they would state the objective: "Given an advertisement, the student will identify the propaganda device used in the advertisement and state reasons for his identification." There follows a sample test item: "Read this advertisement (a copy of an ad is shown with the item). What type of propaganda device is used? Give reasons for your choice."[46] A sample response is also provided.

EVALUATION OF CONCEPT LEARNING

Although our discussion of the objective above entailed some attention to evaluation an additional discussion of that topic seems warranted. Frayer, Fredrick, and Klausmeier have developed a schema for paper and pencil testing of the level of concept mastery.[47] "(The) schema includes both verbal aspects of concept learning, differentiates qualitatively different behavioral objectives, and is adaptable to concepts of various types."[48] From their schema they have listed the kinds

[46]Instructional Objectives Exchange, *Language Arts 7–9* (Los Angeles: Instructional Objectives Exchange (IOX), 1970), p. 230. Similar objectives and items in reading and other language arts areas for all grade levels have been developed and are available from IOX.

[47]Dorothy A. Frayer, Wayne C. Fredrick, and Herbert J. Klausmeier, *A Schema for Testing the Level of Concept Mastery*, Working Paper No. 16 (Madison, Wis.: Wisconsin Research and Development Center for Cognitive Learning, 1969), p. 9.

[48]*Ibid.*, p. 9.

of information an item writer should have in order to test concept mastery and these are discussed in Chapter 8.

Other examples of tests which seem in fact, to measure concepts and related learnings are the Illinois Test of Psycholinguistic Abilities,[49] The Linguistic Ability Test,[50] and possibly even the NCTE and Educational Testing Services' *A Look at Literature.*[51] The latter is intended to measure interpretive responses to imaginative prose and poetry of upper elementary children, but bears a heavy conceptual load. (For example, one item from this test: "The writer speaks of fire flies as though they are people. Which pair of lines show this best?" This item tests not only interpretation but reading comprehension and personification understanding, and could be placed under concept examples and concept attributes.)

Obviously, paper-and-pencil devices are not the only way to arrive at an assessment of concept mastery. Indeed, many concepts cannot be mastered in the absolute sense, their meaning can only be refined. Writing so that you persuade people or make people laugh indicates "mastery" of concepts basic to writing. Performing does indicate a satisfactory understanding of concepts for living although apparently this is seldom believed to be true in schools.

Borton states "students should know *how* (not what)—how to use a syllogism, coordinate three variables, see themselves from someone else's point of view, fantasize at will, perform systems analysis, read precisely and at high speeds, generate a range of actions to express degrees of any emotion, etc., etc., . . . each [process] should specify what we want the child to be able to *do* by the end of an educational experience."[52]

As we examine the range of objectives available, and attempt to relate them to how we structure schooling, at present, in the language arts it is possible to develop a very myopic view of where we need to go to help young people learn concepts. We systematize schooling through the development of performance specifications. These specifications will make sense only if they develop from childrens' needs, from what they want and need to find out. Objectives of the kind we envision

[49] *Illinois Test of Psycholinguistic Abilities* (Urbana, Ill.: University of Illinois Press, 1969).

[50] Wayne C. Fredrick, Lester F. Golub, and Shelby L. Johnson, "Analysis of the Linguistic Ability Test, Grades 4 and 6," Technical Report No. 121 (Madison, Wis.: Wisconsin Research and Development Center for Cognitive Learning, 1970).

[51] Research Foundation of the National Council of Teachers of English and Educational Testing Service, *A Look at Literature: The NCTE Cooperative Test of Critical Reading and Appreciation* (Princeton, N.J.: Educational Testing Service, 1969).

[52] Terry Borton, *Reach, Touch, and Teach: Student Concerns and Process Education* (New York: McGraw-Hill Book Company, 1970), p. 169.

relate to competence, competence which I believe we must have if we as people are going to function effectively. It is time to attend to the wisdom in McLuhan's *Verbi-Voco-Visual Explorations:* "Instead of the inward gaze of Minerva's owl there rises from the collective couch of bureaucratic inquisition a discordant howl".[53]

It is possible that shifting more to performance objectives will indeed cost us dearly in terms of our hopes and desires for children.[54] This fear is amply demonstrated by the very appropriate questions raised at the annual business meeting of the National Council of Teachers of English in Atlanta, Georgia, November 1970. In the form of a resolution the following position was officially adopted by the council:

> *Resolved*, That when members of the National Council of Teachers of English are put in the position to use or develop behavioral objectives, they assert their right to have satisfactory answers supported by adequate evidence to the following questions, among others:
>
> 1. Do changes of surface behavior constitute real changes in the language competence of learners?
> 2. Does performance on test items adequately measure cognitive and affective growth in the areas of literature and composition?
> 3. Does the concern to control short-term, easily measured objectives work against the attainment of basic long-range goals?
> 4. Are behavioral objectives relevant to and modifiable by students in planning curriculum?
> 5. Are behavioral objectives and their sequencing based on sound theory and research on the processes, competencies, and behaviors being developed?
> 6. Are behavioral objectives, the methods of their presentation, and the system of intrinsic and extrinsic reinforcement likely to cause any unintentional learning, emotional strain, or other unplanned outcomes detrimental to the well-being of the learners? Be it further
>
> *Resolved*, That concerned teachers ask: Who has the professional and moral right to predetermine and control what shall or shall not be the limits of acceptable behavior of young people? In short, do we help students grow or shape them into a mold?

Certainly we must begin to find answers to these questions to avoid wasting the time of students. But the only way we are going to find out is to try to develop and take value stances about what is to be learned, to use the objectives and procedures as one alternative in education. All

[53]Marshall McLuhan, *Verbi-Voco-Visual Explorations* (New York: Something Else Press, 1967), n. p.

[54]An excellent discussion of the place of behavioral objectives is provided in John Maxwell and Anthony Tavatt (eds.), *On Writing Behavioral Objectives for English* (Champaign, Ill.: National Council of Teachers of English, 1970).

educational objectives imply value choices. Behavior objectives are just as much a judgment item as other, presumably more open stances, in the conduct of education. In the main, such other approaches provide more hidden behavioral objectives than do performance based programs. (Unions, womens' liberation groups, and black militant groups are aware of this. It is difficult to see why teachers are not.)

What is more likely, however, is that in our attempts to develop behavioral objectives for concept learning we will forget much that it has taken us a long time to realize. Raths reminds us that behavioral objectives can not be justified through data.[55] I would add *at the moment* we simply do not know what the ramifications of performance objectives are. We must find out. Ironically, we will have to use Raths' own criteria for trying them. In his extremely provocative list of twelve criteria for determining activities for children he includes: "All other things being equal, one activity is more worthwhile than another if it involves students and faculty members in 'risk' taking—not a risk of life or limb, but a risk of success or failure." I have taken his statement totally out of the context in which he uses it. Nonetheless, it seems that pushing ahead with behavioral objectives and exploring completely free environments are risks which we must take. Raths also reminds us of Whitehead's dictum that in terms of the rhythm of education, many more of the tasks assigned to younger children should be justified on noninstrumental values than those assigned at the upper levels which might reasonably contain more performance-related activities.[56]

Tying concepts to behavioral objectives is only a way of processing information and organizing. In effect, organizing concepts and objectives help us explain and order subject matter; they do not explain and order children. As we organize and test we can find which concepts have more explanatory power than others, i.e., are more effective in aiding concept development in children.

For younger children, Widmer has summarized our understanding of concepts for school purposes. "They (concepts) represent *his* [the child's] attempts to organize *his* own *personal* environmental experiences into relationships invested with meaning for *him.*" [Italics added.] However, she goes on to add that concepts can be formed, clarified and extended by provision for direct experiences, multisensory impressions, motor manipulation, problem solving, creating, and questioning.[57]

[55]James D. Raths, "Teaching without Specific Objectives," *Educational Leadership*, Vol. 28 (April 1971), pp. 714–720; quote on p. 718.
[56]Alfred N. Whitehead, *The Aims of Education* (New York: Mentor Books, 1929), pp. 27–28.
[57]Emmy Louise Widmer, *The Critical Years: Early Childhood Education at the Crossroads* (Scranton, Pa.: Intext Educational Publishers, 1970), p. 33.

We provide experiences, not the concepts; we can aid in the definitional, clarification, and exemplary process when children appear to be ready to clarify and make the appropriate distinctions among certain concepts.

Vygotsky says, "Direct teaching of concepts is impossible and fruitless. A teacher who tries to do this usually accomplishes nothing but empty verbalism, a parrotlike repetition of words by the child, simulating a knowledge of the corresponding concepts but actually covering up a vacuum."[58]

Vygotsky's comment is undoubtedly a justified skepticism that ought to be kept in mind. But such direct teaching can and does go on in school whether we are using the techniques suggested earlier in this chapter or those elsewhere in the text. It goes on from the small child's asking "What is a people?" to the adult's questions about the drug culture. Concepts are necessary for literacy and they are necessary for finding ways to improve our relationships with other people. Good intentions, a kind heart, and undirected experience do not necessarily provide us with the appropriate techniques to put a person at ease or to engage in nondirective therapy. We often attend more to children's concept attainment rather than to their concept formation—what Jones calls *invention*.[59] Children need to invent, need to be creative.

Moffett in his discourse on rhetoric further cautions us about the nature of our activities with concepts. He defines rhetoric as "the ways one person attempts to act on another, to make him laugh or think, squirm or shiver, hate or mate ,"[60] explicating his definition by suggesting that since one of our major influencing devices with the words is logic, "the categories and logical relations the child uses must gradually approximate universal ones."[61] The childs' logic is subjective, unconscious, unsystematic. "Primitive thought tends toward very broad categories and propositions (wild generalizations, if you like) so that the use of words and sentences having a large extension or range of applicability may indicate undeveloped rather than sophisticated thought. I'm afraid we teachers are often taken in by pseudo-concepts and pseudo-abstraction, which incidentally, the too early assigning of exposition naturally invites. Real advances in verbal growth should be measured not only by the extension of the concepts and propositions but by

[58]L. S. Vygotsky, *op. cit.*, p. 8.

[59]Richard M. Jones, *Fantasy and Feeling In Education* (New York: New York University Press, 1968) provides an involved statement of the differences between concept attainment and concept formation; particularly relating to more emotional input into the curriculum.

[60]Moffett, *op. cit.*, p. 14.

[61]*Ibid.*, p. 117.

whether they are ranged in a hierarchy of subordinates and superordinates."[62]

CONCLUSION

In concluding this chapter on communications concepts we are faced with several questions. Do we understand or have any better grasp of concepts from having studied it? Does it help us define our schooling tasks any more clearly? What is the nature of the schooling tasks it does help us define? How can we validate these tasks? What are the consequences of thinking about concepts in the ways this chapter suggests? What restrictions are imposed on us if we ask these questions? These are all questions involved in attaining concepts. They may be asked again if we consider ways to aid in concept attainment. Moffett has perhaps best summarized our concerns: "choosing spring algae or scum is a conceptual option entailing different ways of classifying the same physical phenomenon—but it is of great theoretical importance because of the difference in effect on the audience".[63] Likewise, our choices for concept development and concept development tasks will make a great difference to our scholastic audience.

SUGGESTED READINGS

Blount, N. S., H. J. Klausmeier, S. L. Johnson, W. C. Fredrick, and J. G. Ramsay, *The Effectiveness of Programmed Materials in English Syntax and the Relationship of Selected Variables to the Learning of Concepts,* Technical Report No. 17 (Madison, Wis.: Wisconsin Research and Development Center for Cognitive Learning, 1967).

This report provides the results of field testing and suggests ways for improving instructional materials in structural and transformational grammar.

Borton, Terry, *Reach, Touch and Teach: Student Concerns and Process Education* (New York: McGraw-Hill Book Company, 1970).

Describes the author's attempt to *reach* students at basic personality levels, *touch* them as individuals, and yet *teach* them in an organized fashion.

Carroll, John B., "Words, Meanings, and Concepts," *Harvard Educational Review,* Vol. 34, No. 2 (Spring 1964), pp. 178–202.

This thesis relates psychological and psycholinguistic theory to some of the problems in the teaching of concepts. This whole issue of the HER is devoted to language and learning.

[62] *Ibid.*
[63] *Ibid.*, p. 115.

Chomsky, Noam, *Language and Mind* (New York: Harcourt Brace Jovanovich, Inc., 1968).

Three essays on the study of mind and the nature of language. The first deals with the past, the second, current development, and the third with speculation on the future.

Clegg, A. B. (ed.), *The Excitement of Writing* (London: Chatto and Windus, Ltd., 1965).

Although primarily an anthology of children's writings, the editor describes the writing program and the circumstances in which the writing selections were produced.

Endres, Mary, Pose Lamb, and Arnold Lazarus, "Selected Objectives in the English Language Arts (Pre-K through 12)," *Elementary English*, Vol. XLVI (April 1969), pp. 418–462.

This article describes broad objectives for language arts and tries to suggest emphasis according to age groups.

Flanagan, John C., Robert F. Mager, and William M. Shanner, *Behavioral Objectives: A Guide to Individualized Learning—Language Arts* (Palo Alto, Calif.: Westinghouse Learning Press, 1971).

This volume indexes, states, and classifies, according to *Taxonomy of Educational Objectives, Cognitive Domain*, language arts objectives at all levels. One of a series; the other three volumes deal with mathematics, science, and social studies.

Flavell, John H., in collaboration with others, *The Development of Role-Taking and Communication Skills in Children* (New York: John Wiley & Sons, Inc., 1968).

This volume consists of a series of related studies illustrating the child's developing ability to infer psychological processes in others (role-taking), and to make use of this information in devising and transmitting effective messages to others (communication).

Ford, G. W., and L. Pugno (eds.), *The Structure of Knowledge and the Curriculum* (Chicago: Rand McNally, 1964).

Scholars in education and natural sciences, mathematics, English, and the social sciences have analyzed each discipline, examining its proper domain and concepts and methods of inquiry.

Gorrell, Robert M., (ed.), *Rhetoric: Theories for Application* (Champaign, Ill.: National Council of Teachers of English, 1967).

The fifteen essays in this NCTE monograph reevaluate definitions of rhetoric and the teaching of rhetoric.

Gray, Susan, et al., *Before First Grade* (New York: Teachers College Press, 1966).

This report describes an early training project designed for disadvantaged children. It includes sections on attitude development, aptitude, activities and materials used in the program, schedule and lesson plans, and procedures on working with parents.

Hogan, Robert F. (ed.), *The English Language in the School Program* (Champaign, Ill.: National Council of Teachers of English, 1966).

The twenty-two papers in this publication, drawn from the 1963 and 1964 NCTE Spring Institutes on Language, Linguistics, and School Programs, concentrate on the relevance of recent scholarship for English language programs in elementary and secondary programs.

Instructional Objectives Exchange: *Language Arts 7–9* (Los Angeles: Instructional Objectives Exchange (IOX), 1970).

The IOX has a series of collections of objectives in most areas of the communications arts. The objectives have been collected and rewritten to fit a standard format. Objectives and evidence items are provided.

Jones, Richard M., *Fantasy and Feeling in Education* (New York: New York University Press, 1968).

Jones emphasizes the need to coordinate cognitive approaches in school with emotional and imaginal ones. He develops his own theory of instruction and suggests guides for teachers—a psychotherapeutic orientation.

Klausmeier, Herbert J., and Chester W. Harris (eds.), *Analysis of Concept Learning* (New York: Academic Press, 1966).

The sixteen papers in this publication, drawn from the 1965 Conference on Analysis of Concept Learning, concentrate on classifying and relating concepts, learning of concepts, learning-teaching processes, and concepts in mathematics, science, and English. The paper on English concepts, though worth reading, does not deal with concepts so much as generalizations.

Koch, Kenneth, *Wishes, Lies, and Dreams: Teaching Children to Write Poetry* (New York: Chelsea House, 1970).

There are really two books in one: a collection of children's poetry and a long informal essay in which Koch describes his experience in teaching poetry and how it can be used by others.

Lazarus, Arnold, and Rozanne Knudson, *Selected Objectives for the English Language Arts*, (Grades 7–12) (Boston: Houghton Mifflin Company, 1967).

The book begins with a discussion of the function of objectives. It is followed by a selected list of objectives that the authors believe to be relevant.

Lundsteen, Sara W., "A Model of the Teaching-Learning Process for Assisting Development of Children's Thinking During Communication," *Journal of Communication*, Vol. 18, No. 4 (December 1968), pp. 412–435.

This theoretical discussion presents the base for a series of experimental studies designed to develop thinking processes in elementary school children. Illustrative pupil and teacher verbalizations are provided.

Markle, Susan M., and Philip W. Tiemann, *Really Understanding Concepts or In Frumious Pursuit of the Jabberwock*, 3rd ed. (Champaign, Ill.: Stipes Publishing Company, 1970).

This is a text workbook designed to enable the user to analyze basic concepts in order to design instructions enabling students to avoid predictable errors, and to evaluate the extent of conceptual understanding of students.

Maxwell, John, and Anthony Tavatt (eds.), *On Writing Behavioral Objectives for English* (Champaign, Ill.: National Council of Teachers of English, 1970).

The twelve statements in this monograph developed under the guidance of the NCTE Commission on the English Curriculum discuss the prospects and problems of using behavioral objectives in the English program.

McLuhan, Marshall, *Verbi-Voco-Visual Explorations* (New York: Something Else Press, Inc., 1967).

A different relationship between man and his environment is advanced in this book. McLuhan and others describe different ways to examine people, language, media and a host of other phenomena. It is a different way to explore concepts.

Moffett, James, *A Student-Centered Language Arts Curriculum, Grades K–13* (Boston: Houghton Mifflin Company 1968).

The main thesis of the book is that students should use language more than they do. The curriculum is based on a "naturalistic approach" whereby students learn essentially by doing and receiving feedback.

Pooley, Robert C., and Lester S. Golub, *Concepts and Objectives for Learning the Structure of English in Grades 7, 8 and 9*, Technical Report No. 22 (Madison, Wis.: Wisconsin Research and Development Center for Cognitive Learning, 1969).

The report outlines concepts for learning the structure of English, provides lists of descriptive statements and behavioral objectives. It stresses both behavioral and social aspects of language.

Raths, James D., "Teaching without Specific Objectives," *Educational Leadership*, Vol. 23 (April 1971), pp. 714–720.

This article presents 12 criteria for worthwhile activities in schools. His argument is that the major focus in schools should be away from activities to bring about specific behavioral changes in students.

Smith, E. Brooks, Kenneth S. Goodman, and Robert Meredith, *Language and Thinking in the Elementary School* (New York: Holt, Rinehart & Winston, Inc., 1970).

This book presents a language-centered view of teaching and learning. It synthesizes modern and earlier views of language and linguistics, literature and symbolism, and thinking and knowing.

Summerfield, Geoffrey, *Topics in English for the Secondary School* (London: B. T. Batsford, Ltd., 1965).

An extended discussion of the nature and scope of English with 30 illustrations of topics with which to engage students.

Ullman, Stephen, *Words and Their Use* (New York: Hawthorne Books, Inc., 1951).

The writer shows how words acquire and change their meanings, how new terms are introduced and how old ones disappear. The use of synonyms, the nature of figurative speech, and other aspects of style are fully discussed including the misuse of language by the propagandist and salesman.

Venezky, Richard L., Robert C. Calfee, and Robin C. Chapman, *Skills Required for Learning to Read: A Preliminary Analysis*, Working Paper No. 10 (Madison, Wis.: Wisconsin Research and Development Center for Cognitive Learning, 1968).

This speculative analysis of selected component skills presumably related to reading is a good example of how one might go about generating a list of concepts for school learning.

Vygotsky, L. S., *Thought and Language*, trans. and edited by Eugenia Haufmann and Gertrude Vakar (Cambridge, Mass.: M.I.T. Press, 1962).

The theoretical discussions of Vygotsky are based on concept formation studies. He describes sequenced stages in word meaning development, genesis and function of inner speech, the nature of written speech, and the role of school instruction in the development of higher mental operations.

Widmer, Emmy Louise, *The Critical Years: Early Childhood Education at the Crossroads* (Scranton, Pa.: Intext Educational Publishers, 1970).

The major theme of this book is the development of understanding about young children and effective early childhood programs. Concept learning is treated in various places throughout the book.

Alan Voelker

CHAPTER 6

Concept Learning in the Science Curriculum, K–12: Issues and Approaches

The importance of science concept learning as a curricular and an instructional objective has never been more crucial than at the present time. Further, there is no indication that the relative importance of learning science concepts is going to lessen in the future. Conceptual knowledge in the various science disciplines is being accumulated and generated at a phenomenal rate. The time span for doubling the amount of conceptual knowledge in science has been estimated as between eight and ten years. In any event there is no doubt that the amount of conceptual knowledge for an individual in today's society will increase two to three times during the period it takes a child to reach adulthood.

As a result of this phenomenal rate of knowledge growth, it is mandatory that concept learning receive more emphasis than traditional approaches to learning such as acquisition of factual knowledge. The learner can be more efficient and what he learns will have greater survival value in terms of society, the respective scientific disciplines, and the interests of the learner. Thus from the standpoint of learning efficiency, concept learning is indispensable because, unfortunately, the rate of increase of the learner's ability to learn and the rate of growth of knowledge are not proportional. Fortunately, this desirability to make concept learning in the sciences more efficient is not incompatible with the nature of the scientific enterprise nor with a current philosophy of science teaching.

SCIENCE IS CONCEPT FORMATION

Both concept formation and the scientific enterprise are intellectual activities of mankind. The initial step in both enterprises is to make observations. These concrete experiences provide facts and percepts, to serve as the raw materials for processing. Both activities rely heavily on perception, inductive reasoning, and inventiveness. Through the utilization of these processes to "operate" on facts and percepts, descriptions and "lesser" concepts result. As these simpler ideas are related to each other and more experiences are added, the processing produces more refined concepts and tentative theoretical conceptual structures. Through refinement, modification proceeds in a manner which permits the incorporation of new data in the absence of many of the facts used to create the original concepts. The simpler concepts are merged into more complex forms; yet the expressed forms become even more simplified. The net result is an efficient way to acquire understanding and accomplish learning.

An oversimplified example of this refining process occurs in the evolution of a concept, *living thing*. Young children develop concepts of *tree* and *dog* at an early age. At that point in time, they apply the concept label to a specific example of the concept rather than referring to a class of trees or dogs. Encounter with other trees or dogs that "differ" from their tree or dog results in application of the concept label to classes rather than single instances of these concepts. As plants and animals other than than trees and dogs are experienced, the more complex concepts of plant and animal are developed. Relating these concepts produces another concept, *living thing*. Each successive concept is more complex than that preceding because of the vast amount of data processing involved in its formation, yet it is simpler in that previously unencountered examples of the concepts can be identified. And all the "lesser" concepts have been subsumed under a general class.

Concept formation in the scientific enterprise is a system of organizing knowledge (imposing order) based on observation and experiment. It provides for economy of effort and freedom of thought, and eventually frees us from concrete experiences. The participants in the enterprise can then operate at the theory level, theory being the most sophisticated form of conceptual knowledge.

Because theories in science are creations of the mind having their first origin in encountered experiences, we can teach efficiently from the psychological standpoint, covering content and nature of science simultaneously by teaching the science concepts.

In addition, inadequately developed or incorrect concepts and theories have similar origins. These result from a limited opportunity to experience, inadequate and insufficient perceptions, incorrect prior assumptions, incorrect deductions, and the state of the individual involved in the formulation.

To teach concepts, then, is fruitful in terms of both the processes and the products of science. The processes of concept formation are analogous to those of scientific inquiry and discovery, and possession of the concepts represents the knowledge of the theories of science.

Not only is concept learning advantageous in reference to the nature of science, but it will also do a more complete job of meeting the need of the child to belong and identify. The need to understand the environment will be met by proper selection of experiences to use as the stimuli for formation of concepts. The learning of concepts is thus seen to be of value by the student if he can be shown how they can be utilized to explain what he has experienced and what he will encounter.

Gagné has stated that "acquiring the ability to generalize distinguishes concept learning from all types of learning."[1] In light of the exponential rate at which scientific knowledge (facts and concepts) is being accumulated, we desperately need a powerful educational tool of this type; it is mandatory that we adopt a "model" for structuring the science curriculum that will assist us in keeping pace with knowledge growth while we learn that of value from the past and prepare to deal with the future.

CLASSES OF SCIENCE CONCEPTS

The model of the scientific enterprise whereby man engages in the gathering, formulating, and evaluation of knowledge produces two major types of concepts which can be utilized as the focal point for developing the K–12 science curriculum. There are those concepts concerning the precedures and techniques for gathering, formulating, and evaluating knowledge. Through the utilization of these procedures and techniques there are accumulated bits of knowledge—facts—which are organized in various patterns to produce the conceptual knowledge of the enterprise. Those concepts which are employed to carry on investigations, i.e., the knowledge-forming activities, become what are known as the *process concepts,* while those concepts which evolve out of the processing of factual data are known as the *product concepts.* The process concepts are those that evolve and develop out

[1] R. M. Gagné, *Conditions of Learning* (New York: Holt, Rinehart & Winston, Inc., 1965).

of the generation of knowledge, and the product concepts are those that are generated.

Process Concepts

Historically, models for developing school science curricula have been concerned with the product concepts of science. Such models are based on the notion that the easiest and most appropriate way to structure the school curriculum is to have students learn those science concepts already generated by the scientific enterprise. More recently, however, much emphasis has been devoted to testing models for science-curriculum development focused around the process concepts of science. Much effort has gone into identifying and defining these process concepts and hypothesizing whether or not there is a learning hierarchy inherent in the way in which these process concepts are used.

Although there is some variance in the number and nature of the process concepts listed on respective lists, some process concepts appear on all such lists. These are observation, classification, inference, prediction, measurement, communicating, data interpretation, operational definition, hypothesis and question formulation, experimentation, and model formulation. Some data have been collected which indicate that there may be a type of general hierarchy involved in their formulation. However, the notion of a hierarchy of process concepts appears to be based on a model of the scientific enterprise having its roots in the "scientific method"—formulating a problem and proceeding through a series of logical steps in completing the investigation. Unfortunately this procedure is more apt to have been deduced from the manner in which research reports are presented rather than from the way an actual investigation is conducted.

Each of the processes of science is itself a major concept to be developed through concept-learning methodologies. Each is extremely critical to the perpetuation and improvement of the scientific enterprise and a well-developed concept of each of these concepts is critical to understanding how the other class of concepts—the product concepts—are developed. The learner attempting to learn product concepts without an adequate understanding of the process concepts learns primarily by rote and sees little connection between the concepts that are developed and the manner in which they are used.

Product Concepts

An examination of "dictionary definitions" of science often reveals science defined as an accumulated body of knowledge. But this is only one aspect of the scientific enterprise—certainly not the least of its components. However, the notion of knowledge accumulation leaves a false impression about the nature of the scientific enterprise. For it is the conceptual knowledge derived through the organization of the factual knowledge, not the bits themselves, that is the real outcome.

As one studies the aspects of the respective scientific enterprises, there appear to be three types of activities that scientists engage in to organize the factual and conceptual knowledge they accumulate. One major activity of the enterprise has always been to organize knowledge by classifying, an activity tied very closely to the observation and description of objects and things. Out of this kind of activity evolves a whole class of knowledge, a class of concepts commonly referred to as *classificatory* concepts. They develop from a concern for organizing observations and descriptions into groups and subgroups. Examples of concepts evolving from activity of this nature are heavily represented in the biological sciences. They include concepts such as *mammal, insect, living thing, animal,* and the like.

A second major organizational activity of the scientific enterprise is an attempt to formulate explanations for a variety of observed phenomona. Whereas in the previous kind of activity the concern was for taking various animate and inanimate objects and things and grouping them to acquire conceptual understanding of the nature of a class, this activity is more concerned with observing classes of phenomena rather than classes of objects and things. An attempt is made to formulate an explanation for "why" something took place rather than accepting it as it is and trying to group and regroup on the basis of similarities and differences. The set of concepts which evolves from this kind of activity is commonly referred to as a set of *correlational* or *relational* concepts. These concepts usually evolve from directly observable phenomena and the attempt to relate what is observed in a cause-and-effect relationship. Many of the concepts which develop as the result of this activity are common to the physical sciences and earth sciences. Examples include *force, evaporation, condensation, velocity, acceleration,* and *momentum.*

The third type of product concept which evolves from the processing of accumulated factual and conceptual knowledge is referred to as a *theoretical concept.* Theoretical concepts have the least connection with directly observable phenomena. Their abstractness is a function of the way they are formed and the learner's difficulty in understanding them is also a function of this abstract quality. Examples of these theoretical concepts include *atom, ion, electron,* and *evolution.*

All the above-mentioned classes of concepts, as indicated earlier, are creations of mankind. The range of this creation and the amount of ingenuity involved in formulating the concepts is a function of the amount of direct evidence that can be acquired. At the level of the classificatory concept practically all evidence is directly attributable to the characteristics and properties of objects and things. At the correlational or relational level there is a lessening concern for the actual properties and particular characteristics of the objects and things, and a shift to a concern for how these objects and things behave when they interact with other objects and things. The concepts that result are concerned with the relationships observed as a function of various interactions. As one proceeds to the theoretical level there is less concern for actual description of the objects and things, less concern for the actual nature of the interactions themselves. There is a much increased concern for explaining why the object or thing has the properties or characteristics it has, and why the phenomenon occurred rather than a concern for what was actually noted.

MODELS FOR CONCEPT SELECTION—GENERAL CHARACTERISTICS

Theoretically, the conceptual content of a curricular area such as science is selected with some degree of consideration for one of three curricular dimensions, namely, the child, the society, and the discipline. The resulting curricular model should lie somewhere along a continuum between the concern for the child and the concern for the discipline that provides a vehicle upon which to build the model. Characteristically, however, the content—conceptual ideas—of the science curriculum has been selected from the standpoint of discipline respectability rather than from an emphasis on the child and/or society.

At present there is still less emphasis on the child than either society or the discipline because of an absence of research on science concept learning. While research in this area is beginning to develop, as will be indicated later, it is still at a minimum. There is no solid research based on science concept learning available to draw on in developing a K–12 science curriculum.

Other models for selecting the content of the science curriculum were based almost entirely on a concern for the discipline. Granted that over the years as a science emphasis was developing in the school curriculum there had been a concern for the practical aspects of science as well as the basic science aspects concerned with the development of knowledge. However, with increased emphasis on improved content preparation for the prospective science teacher the school science curriculum placed the bulk of its emphasis on either pure or applied science (technology) aspects of science. There was little emphasis on understanding the role that science plays in society or the manner in which society dictates the growth and the directions of growth of science and its bridesmaid technology. The concern for an emphasis on pure science aspects for determining the conceptual content of the curriculum has been evidenced by the National Science Foundation supported Course Content Improvement Projects which have been so much in evidence during the 1960's.

During the same period in which the development of science curriculum via mass team effort was being carried on, committees of National Science Teachers organizations and basic research groups in science education at various universities were engaged in activities devoted to bringing some order to school science curriculum efforts, particularly a concern for what should be the conceptual content of that curriculum. These committees and research groups have produced a set of excellent models to serve as organizing centers for concept selection for the K–12 science curriculum.

The development of these models has been characterized by at least two major factors. The science disciplines for many years have striven to develop a set of schemas that could be used to organize accumulated knowledge as well as to focus present and future knowledge production activities. Contrary to the position taken in the early part of the twentieth century—a time, for example, when many considered that the research in physics had produced the ultimate in knowledge and that it only remained for the physicists to clean up bits and pieces—there has developed a recognition that while there are lull periods in the development of knowledge new breakthroughs occur and initiate new research efforts. Historically, these breakthroughs usually stem from working around some central focusing theme. For example, since the early 1800's there has been in existence the fundamental notion of matter being composed of small particles. Work in this area produced concepts such as atom and molecule. Witness how the past 150 years has been an evolution of the concepts of atom and molecule but the fundamental notion of matter being composed of small particles is still with us.

Thus present attempts to organize science and formulate those fundamental ideas of the past most apt to have survival value have resulted in a concern for developing science curricula around a few basic themes. Concepts are selected concepts which help to emphasize these themes from the point at which a child begins to "study" science in an informal sense until he proceeds to the formal stage—in other words, from the beginning to the termination of the K–12 science curriculum.

The concern for having a limited number of basic conceptual ideas, much less in number than in earlier eras of science-curriculum development, has been one of the major aspects for developing models for structuring science curricula. A second major aspect of newer models for science-curriculum development is for the concern given to methods employed in generating knowledge (the processes) as well as the conceptual knowledge which develops (the products). While there has been a weighting factor in emphasizing process over product in some models while the reverse is true in others, it is readily discernible that newer models do given considerable concern for both the knowledge-generating aspects of the scientific enterprise as well as the knowledge generated.

Recent models for selecting concepts for inclusion in the science curriculum are also characterized by two other aspects, not so obvious as the process-product aspects, but either directly or indirectly implied. While model developers specifically set forth their conceptual schemes and explicitly state that these schemes should be the focusing device for the curriculum, they also note that there can be and should be a great deal of local autonomy in selecting the particular concepts that serve to develop a basic understanding of these broader schemes. In most instances the schemes proposed allow a selection of concepts from the biological, earth, and/or physical science areas and permit these to be organized in a variety of conceptual development patterns. This aspect of the models should serve to bring the advocates of national curricula more in harmony with the advocates of total local autonomy science curriculum development. For even though there might be a generally agreed-upon set of schemes, they can be developed in a variety of ways according to the strengths and limitations of the local situation.

The second aspect that seems to be coming to the fore in the newer models is that the student must learn of the interrelationships between science and society. As indicated earlier, the concepts selected to be learned via the science curriculum should be those that help a student understand the role science plays in society and the role that society dictates to science. For with the present state of affairs science too often receives the blame for what "it" produces, the blamers failing to recognize that it is they who initially made the demand for product development. This attitude is prevalent with our current environmental crisis. There is little if any concern for the role that self plays in environmental degradation. Rather the polluter dons the hat of the accuser and thus removes himself from any blame.

Another potential of recent models is the opportunity to make the science curriculum a problem-oriented curriculum. While not expressly stated in the background for many of the science-curriculum models, there is much to be said for the opportunity for the problem-centered curriculum. A science curriculum which derives its concepts from a select number of schemes permits a wide variety of concepts to be learned and allows concept learning to occur via a problem-solving situation. In essence, it shifts the organization of the science curriculum from learning concepts in a deductive fashion to one where one learns concepts inductively—a fundamental component of the scientific enterprise.

The remaining sections of this part of the chapter will be devoted to a general discussion of the nature of several recent models for developing science curricula. A general orientation to the nature of the criteria for selecting the models will be provided, as will samples of the conceptual schemes advanced by the developers. In instances where it is quite obvious what some of the sample concepts embodied in the schemes would be, they will be listed. Examples will be provided from the biological, earth, and/or physical science areas.

SELECTION OF CONCEPTS FOR INCLUSION IN THE SCIENCE CURRICULUM

As indicated earlier, there have been many good models developed in recent years to guide curriculum developers and instructional personnel in selecting concepts for inclusion in the K–12 science curriculum. The positions range from priority emphasis on understanding a discipline or disciplines, to studying science for the sake of understanding society. Models for description have been chosen to represent several different orientations toward science curriculum development.

Of particular note in the discussion of the models for the structuring the K–12 science curriculum and the selection of the concepts and their relationships is that they have a common curricular goal. That goal is to establish a pattern for selecting of concepts which emphasizes organization rather than coverage. All concepts and relationships are to be used to further develop a limited number of ideas, rather than acquaint students with a brief introduction to the "total" realm of the accumulated knowledge of the scientific enterprise. Also of note is that basically any one of these approaches to developing a science curriculum will ultimately expose the bulk of the students to a common set of basic concepts that are important to society and the individual.

Referents for Scientific Literacy

This model was developed at the Wisconsin Scientific Literacy Center.[2] It evolved as a consequence of seeking meaning for the term scientific literacy.

[2]M. O. Pella, G. T. O'Hearn, and L. J. Stiles, *Scientific Literacy*, Technical Report No. 1 (Madison, Wis.: Scientific Literacy Research Center, University of Wisconsin, 1966).

A survey of literature in science, science education, sociology of science, history and philosophy of science, and the like was conducted to determine what was being specified as the characteristics of the scientifically literate. There were found six commonly stated characteristics of the scientifically literate individual. A scientifically literate individual was one who possessed an understanding of

1. The interrelationships between science and society.
2. An understanding of the ethics of science.
3. The nature of the scientific enterprise.
4. Some of the conceptual knowledge of science.
5. The differences between science and technology.
6. The interrelationships between science and the humanities.

An elaboration of these understandings follows to illustrate how they can provide a framework for selecting process and product concepts for inclusion in the science curriculum.

Science and Society. (1) Development of new scientific knowledge is necessary to a sound and vigorous economy, and (2) our present society is powered by science. To understand the nature of science and its role in society, process concepts such as model formation, observation and classification, related to the development of new knowledge, and product concepts such as matter and energy need to be developed.

Ethics of Science. Statements characteristic of an understanding of the ethics of science include

1. The aim of pure science is to increase man's knowledge of the physical and biological world without respect to any present or future good or evil.
2. Scientific knowledge requires some encompassing understanding of the whole, some appreciation of causes and connections and of conceptual models and their relationships to observable reality.

The first statement would necessitate dealing with the concepts of morality and amorality as against the responsibilities of the scientist to his profession and society. Concepts for developing and refining physical, mental, or mathematical models such as DNA and the particulate nature of matter also need to be included.

Nature of Science. A statement characteristic of an understanding of the nature of science is: The citizen must have an improved understanding of how (science) operates. Statements of this nature lend credibility to the place of the process concepts in the science curriculum—those used in generating, formulating, and evaluating knowledge.

Conceptual Knowledge. Statements which lend support to including specific product concepts in the curriculum are

1. Key concepts or conceptual schemes are the only answers to the layman's understanding of mushrooming scientific and technological knowledge.
2. The study of scientific facts and concepts relative to certain controversial topics may produce desirable changes in attitudes with regard to these topics.

These statements are a strong endorsement for selecting concepts so students learn the more important concepts, those at the forefront of work in the discipline, those which have the greatest probability of survival value for the future, and those most closely related to what society is and what it might become.

Science and Technology. Key statements that will help curriculum developers select concepts pertinent to helping children understand the distinction between science and technology include

1. Public understanding of the differences between the short- and long-run purpose of science and technology are essential to advancing our science and society.
2. The educated layman must understand that science is not technology; it is not gadgetry; it is not some mysterious cult; it is not a great mechanical monster; science is an adventure of the human spirit.

Science and Humanities. Broad ideas joined to the interrelationships between science and the humanities that could be used by concept selectors in planning a science curriculum include

1. The study of science in our schools is carried out without regard for the humanities, and the study of the humanities carried on without regard to science; yet each is complementary to the other.
2. Society requires wisdom and concensus for policy decisions which in turn necessitate communication between scientist and humanist.

Statements of this kind indicate that the concepts selected for inclusion in the science curriculum should be those having meaning to man as a member of society rather than to man as a professional discipline.

If a major concern for selecting science concepts is to help the learner understand the role of science in society as well as the influence that society has on science, this model provides an appropriate framework. It becomes even more appropriate when one realizes that it does not eliminate *learning* conceptual-knowledge concepts or process concepts, but rather gives direction to *selecting* these concepts. For it is only through learning of the conceptual knowledge of science and how this conceptual knowledge is generated, formulated, and evaluated that the learner can understand the role of science in society and see that science is an integral part of our culture. Further, a model such as this has the advantage of permitting a great deal of flexibility in determining which concepts are included.

Environmental Resources Management

The environmental resources management model for structuring the science curriculum also stresses the role of science in society.[3] A desirable feature of this model is that concept-selection criteria must consider the implications for interdisciplinary curriculum efforts between science and the social studies as well as other curricular areas such as art and music.

A literature survey of environmentally related areas including science, political science, economics, ecology, and the like produced a list of environmental resource management themes. Professionals from over forty disciplines having some relationship to environmental resources management rated the themes as essential, desirable, highly desirable, or satisfactory for inclusion in the curriculum. Sample themes from arbitrary subgroupings follow.

The theme which connects all subject-matter disciplines of environmental resources management is, *Living things are interdependent with one another and their environment.*

Sample schemes from the other areas include the following.

Environmental Management
Man has been a factor affecting plant and animal succession and environmental processes.

Management Techniques
Increased population mobility is changing the nature of the demands upon some resources.

Economics
Ready transportation, growing interest, money surpluses, and increased leisure time combine to create heavy pressures on existing recreation facilities and demands more new ones.

Environmental Problems
Safe waste disposal, including the reduction of harmful and cumulative effects of various solids, liquids, gases, radioactive wastes and heat is

[3]R. E. Roth, M. O. Pella, and C. A. Schoenfeld, *Environmental Management Concepts—a List*, Technical Report No. 126 (Madison, Wis.: Wisconsin Research and Development Center for Cognitive Learning, 1970).

important if the well-being of man and the environment is to be preserved.

Environmental Ecology

Natural resources are interdependent and the use or misuse of one will
affect others.

Adaptation and Evolution

An organism is the product of its heredity and environment.

Natural Resources

Water supplies, both in quantity and quality, are important to all levels
of living.

The Sociocultural Environment

Man has a responsibility to develop an appreciation of and respect for the
rights of others.

Culture

The culture of a group is its learned behavior in the form of customs,
habits, attitudes, institutions, and life ways that are transmitted to its
progeny.

Politics

Individual citizens should be stimulated to become active in the political
processes.

The Family

Family planning and the limiting of family size are important if over-
population is to be avoided and a reasonable standard of living assured
for successive generations.

The Individual

An individual must develop his ability to perceive if he is to increase his
awareness and develop environmental perspective.

Psychological Aspects

Opportunities to experience and enjoy nature are psychologically re-
warding to many and are important to mental health.

Examples of particular concepts for inclusion in the K–12 science
program include: *man, environment, natural resources, population,
individual, change, management, energy, mineral, plant, water, animal, interaction, organism, species, living levels,* and the like. These
concepts are not new to the science curriculum, but because of the rate
of growth of scientific knowledge and the increasing need for that
scientific knowledge to be put into context it is necessary to select
particular concepts and develop them more thoroughly than in the
past. It is especially critical to develop them in an interdisciplinary
context which promotes an understanding of man and the environment.

Key Concepts. Over a period of generating and refining concepts,
seeking relationships between and among concepts, seeking to formu-

late new concepts by relating relationships and striving to formulate concepts which relate many lesser concepts and many relationships, some extremely powerful science concepts are developed. These concepts can be identified with one word. A curricular model which uses this approach has been developed by the Wisconsin Department of Public Instruction.[4] They have selected six encompassing science concepts, identified with one word, based on the premise that other relationships and lesser concepts should serve to further an understanding of these broader concepts. (The aspect of the model to be discussed here is related to an approach for selecting conceptual knowledge concepts; however, it should be noted that the model has as a heavy societal emphasis as did the two previous models.) There is concern for concepts of science, science processes, the nature of the scientific enterprise, the cultural implications of science, and interrelating the science disciplines.

The six concepts selected for structuring the total K–12 science curriculum are *diversity, change, continuity, interaction, organization* and *limitation*. Using this model for structuring science curriculum, it is possible to select concepts and themes from the biological, earth, and physical sciences which tend to further the development of these broader science concepts. Likewise, it is comparatively easy to select different levels of concepts and relationships to build across the curriculum from the beginning level to a higher level. At a less refined level of concept development, an individual's understanding of these concepts could be represented by the following conceptual ideas from the earth-sciences area.

Diversity. There is variety in the natural materials of the earth. There are identifiable similarities and differences in these materials.

Change. Wind and water are agents of change which act on the earth's surface.

Continuity. Events on earth often occur with dependable regularity. Day and night and the seasons occur now as they have for eons.

Interaction. Without energy from the sun, the earth would become a cold, dark, lifeless body.

Organization. The earth's surface is made up of the atmosphere, the seas and the solid land. The atmosphere has no definite outer boundary.

Limitation. The earth and other observable bodies in the universe are approximately spherical.

[4]Wisconsin Department of Public Instruction, *A Guide to Science Curriculum Development*, Bulletin No. 161 (Madison, Wis.: Wisconsin Department of Public Instruction, 1968).

Note that these statements include many simpler concepts to be related to one another in many ways. Examples are *material, earth, wind, water, day, night, seasons, energy, sun, atmosphere, sea,* and *land.* Note that these concepts are traditionally found in the content-oriented science curricula for the early elementary school years.

At a more refined or complex level, these same concepts could be further developed as indicated by the following statements.

Diversity. Form and composition are indications of the environment in which materials were formed. Under different conditions the same materials may form different minerals.

Change. Gravity, energy from the sun, and diastrophism are primary factors causing the earth's surface to change.

Continuity. Composition, structure, orientation and relationships between strata of rocks can be used to interpret the earth's history.

Interaction. The atmosphere is always moving. Gains and losses in heat cause local vertical movement. Rotation of the earth causes massive horizontal movement.

Organization. The earth and other planets move in the same direction around the sun in roughly the same plane.

Limitation. The period of revolution of the planets varies directly with their distance from the sun.

Note that several of the previous concepts such as energy, earth, and atmosphere are still present and being further refined. But in addition, new concepts such as mineral, environment, gravity, and rocks are now being developed.

At a very sophisticated (abstract) level the key concepts in the model might be expressed as

Diversity. The galaxies of the universe exhibit a variety of forms, compositions and organizations.

Change. Stars and galaxies evolve through a series of stages which are irreversible.

Continuity. Although the exact nature of the universe cannot be determined, present evidence indicates that the universe is systematic.

Interaction. The observation that all galaxies are moving away from the Milky Way at velocities proportional to their distances from it indicates that all galaxies in the universe may be interrelated.

Organization. Matter in the universe exists in a hierarchy of organizational systems from atoms to galaxies.

Limitation. Observations of the universe are limited by the distances separating stars and galaxies and by the maximum relativistic velocity.

Use of a model of this nature for structuring the K–12 science curriculum allows for continual refinement of concepts, introduction of new concepts and relationships, and exercising control over the rate of increase of the abstractness of concepts and the sophistication of relationships between and among them.

Another example illustrates levels of development of the concepts across disciplines. Consider the concept *change*.

CHANGE

Biological	Physical	Earth
As living things grow and age they change in form and activity. Some also change in habitat.	Whenever a force acts on an object to change its position or motion, energy is exchanged.	The earth, moon, and sun are continuously changing position with respect to each other. No one of these three bodies can be considered to be at rest with respect to the other two.
Evolution is the result of chance changes in the inherited characteristics of an individual of a species which makes the individual better able to adapt to a changing environment than was the parent or its predecessor.	Changes in all position and motion of particles of all sizes which bring about different relationships between particles without changing the composition of matter are called physical changes.	Many earth changes are repeated periodically in cycles. Other changes occur without regularity and are often irreversible.
When an individual develops characteristics which differ from its parent generation, the change is due to a difference in the chemical composition of the genetic substance of the cells.	The wavelength of radiant energy can be changed by changing the density of the medium through which the energy passes. The frequency of radiant energy can be changed only if it is absorbed by matter and reradiated.	The energy emitted by the sun, as well as by other stars, is a product of nuclear changes which are taking place.

As in the previous examples there are lesser concepts and relationships to be developed to facilitate continual advancement of the understanding of the major focusing concept. Nothing is included in the curriculum unless it contributes to furthering an understanding of the central themes. Concepts from any and all disciplines can and should be included.

A Process Approach

Another model for structuring science curriculum that has been used extensively and has probably had more quality verification with school children than most others is the one that served as the developmental base for the National Science Foundation Curriculum Improvement Project, *Science: A Process Approach.*[5] This model is predicated on the philosophy that once an individual learner has developed concepts of the science processes and utilizes them, he is in a position to apply these processes to learning the conceptual knowledge of science. Those utilizing this model infer that elementary school children, for example, could best be served by learning the process concepts of science. Then by the time they reach higher levels of the school curriculum they would be in a better position to learn how knowledge concepts are generated, formulated, and evaluated.

In this model the conceptual knowledge concepts included are of lesser importance than the process concepts. In fact they need not come from the domain of science. The model is also based on the premise that the psychological development of the child parallels a hierarchy in which the process concepts are purported to be learned. For example, possession of a concept of observation would be prerequisite to learning all other process concepts, the psychological development of the child being such that it would be at the bottom of the learning hierarchy. The lower-level process concepts would also include classification and inference, and higher-level concepts would include the building of models. This model for selecting the particular concepts to be included in the science curriculum places more emphasis on the ability of the children to learn as a function of maturation and the development of mental abilities.

This model concerns itself more with a discipline orientation, whereas the former models placed more emphasis on learning science concepts in relationship to the role of science in society. It treats science as a discipline unto itself—one learns science concepts, products, and processes for their own sake rather than in order to better relate science to society. A great deal of emphasis is placed on performance skills and hierarchical approaches based on prerequisite knowledge and learning levels.

The major weakness of the model is that it is based on an unwarranted assumption that process concepts are knowledge-free. For ex-

[5]Commission on Science Education, *Science—A Process Approach* (Washington, D.C.: American Association for the Advancement of Science, 1964).

ample, knowledge of many physics concepts is necessary to adequately develop the respective process concepts.

Conceptual Schemes

Another curricular model which places emphasis on learning science for its own sake is that developed by the National Science Teachers Association.[6] The components consist of some broad conceptual themes divided into two groups. The first group is primarily oriented toward the conceptual knowledge aspect of science—the *product* concepts, while the other group is primarily oriented toward the *process* concepts of science. The developers state that this model is appropriate for selecting concepts and their relationships from the biological, earth, and physical sciences. In this way it is similar to the model in the Wisconsin Curriculum Guide, except instead of the major conceptual ideas being stated as one-word concepts they are stated in relationships among concepts—in other words, in sentence form. Focusing themes for selecting concepts and relationships follow.

Major Items in the Process of Science

1. Science proceeds on the assumption, based on centuries of experience, that the universe is not capricious.
2. Scientific knowledge is based on observations of samples of matter that are accessible to public investigation in contrast to purely private inspection.
3. Science proceeds in a piecemeal manner, even though it also aims at achieving a systematic and comprehensive understanding of various sectors of aspects of nature.
4. Science is not and will probably never be a finished enterprise, and there remains very much more to be discovered about how things in the universe behave and how they are interrelated.
5. Measurement is an important feature of most branches of modern science because the formulation as well as the establishment of laws are facilitated through the development of quantitative distinctions.

Conceptual Schemes

1. All matter is composed of units called *fundamental particles;* under certain conditions these particles can be transformed into energy, and vice versa.

[6]National Science Teachers Association, *Theory into Action* (Washington, D.C.: National Science Teachers Association, 1964).

2. Matter exists in the form of units which can be classified into hieraracies of organizational levels.
3. The behavior of matter in the universe can be described on a statistical basis.
4. Units of matter interact. The bases of all ordinary interactions are electromagnetic, gravitational, and nuclear forces.
5. All interacting units of matter tend toward equilibrium states in which energy content (enthalpy) is a minimum and the energy distribution (entropy) is most random. In the process of attaining equilibrium, energy transformations or matter transformations or matter-energy transformations occur. Nevertheless, the sum of energy and matter in the universe remains constant.
6. One of the forms of energy is the motion of units of matter. Such motion is responsible for heat and temperature and for the three states of matter: solid, liquid, and gaseous.
7. All matter exists in time and space and, since interactions occur among its units, matter is subject in some degree to changes with time. Such changes may occur at various rates and in various patterns.

Structure of the Discipline

Another model for structuring the school science curriculum is more oriented toward a single discipline than science itself. One that has been developed recently is specific to the biological sciences.[7] Decisions concerning what is important for inclusion in the K–12 curriculum were made by professionals in the various areas of study related to the biological sciences. The result of this initial generation, plus a series of refinements and validation by a national panel resulted in the production of a group of themes that one who had completed the K–12 science curriculum should understand. These, as were the themes for environmental resource management (Model 2), were rated as satisfactory, desirable, highly desirable, or essential for inclusion in the curriculum.

1. With minor exceptions, living things obtain their energy directly or indirectly from the sun through the process of photosynthesis.
2. To meet future needs, the use of biological resources must be governed by the role these resources play in the ecosystem.

---

[7]B. E. Thompson, *A List of Currently Credible Biology Concepts Judged by a National Panel to Be Important for Inclusion in K–12 Curricula*, Technical Report No. 145 (Madison, Wis.: Wisconsin Research and Development Center for Cognitive Learning, 1970).

3. Living things tend to increase in numbers to the level the environment will permit. Man's ability to modify his environment does not make him an exception. His success in bypassing some environmental barriers is now challenged by new barriers.
4. All living things are interdependent with one another and with their environment.
5. The natural environment is being so altered through the effects of technology and the rapid expansion of wealth and population that man must make drastic changes in his behavior or consider his extinction probable.
6. By and large living things are composed of a fundamental unit of structure and function known as the cell.
7. No one major ecological factor but a combination of them determines the environment; soil, water, air, energy, plants, and animals (including man) all contribute.
8. The earth's carrying capacity is finite for one and all species. Its space, materials, and available energy are limited mainly by surface area, the rate of cycling of water, gases, and materials, and the efficiency of photosynthesis.
9. In a biochemical reaction there is no loss or gain of energy, only a transformation of energy from one form to another.
10. The phenomenon of heredity in all living things thus far investigated is attributable to the replication and transmission of the genetic materials DNA or RNA.

Using a set of themes such as these to select concepts from the biological sciences areas would ultimately permit the identification of key concepts for inclusion in the curriculum; these concepts could be developed at various levels of understanding. Samples of some of the more important concepts needed for inclusion would be *organism, animal, cell, environment, life, plant, population, man, species, system, energy, evolution, reproduction, survival, change, individual, interaction, living things,* and *water*. Of particular note is that these concepts are the same concepts that are included in most instructional materials for science programs, either printed or otherwise. The uniqueness of this kind of approach is that the concepts are taught in relationship to some broader conceptual idea rather than being taught in isolation. They give continuity to the vertical structuring of the K–12 curriculum.

ORGANIZING INSTRUCTIONAL SEQUENCES

The organization of instructional sequences for facilitating concept learning in the K–12 curriculum is in essence a reflection of the expectation of the kinds of concepts for students to learn, and the level of sophistication of the concepts to be obtained. Likewise, there are expectations for the nature of the relationships and interrelationships between and among concepts. This problem of expectations has been a major one in science-concept placement, particularly since about 1955. It seems that every new model for structuring science curriculum development has had a tendency to move concepts downward in a vertical curriculum structure. The result has been that a great deal of inappropriate content in terms of both the concepts themselves and the desired level of sophistication has been jammed down the throats of children because the child as an individual learner has been ignored. The content of the discipline has taken precedence over all else and produced some problems in organizing instructional sequences.

Those persons in the disciplines are not wholly at fault, however, for the results are derived from their concern for improvement of the content of the science curriculum. The lack of concern for the learner has come partly if not largely from the lack of a basis for decision making concerning the concepts to include in the science curriculum and setting expectations for the level of understanding of a particular concept at various periods of time in the curriculum. With a lack of knowledge about the kinds of concepts that children can learn, either by class or by individual concept, it is no wonder that a conflict has arisen between those concerned with relevant and current content and those concerned with the life, interests, and abilities of the learner. Part of this problem of imposing irrelevant concept development on students is the notion that children learn concepts in the same inductive manner in which concepts can be analyzed. In other words, the child is still being buffeted by the content specialists on one hand and the learning specialists on the other. The points of departure between these two groups has a tendency to push the learner back in the corner so that he has no vote on what will be imposed upon him. Some of this difficulty is based on the fact that much of the results of laboratory learning studies is assumed to be translatable to the learner in school situations. Theory about science-concept learning has been developed in the laboratory with young adults and mature adults and corresponding learning structures are imposed indiscriminately on young children—another form of imposition of adult structures and thinking processes on younger learners.

This has produced some major difficulties because most of the concept teaching in schools is done in a deductive manner. Again this may be a reflection of a lack of concern for the learner in selecting concepts for inclusion and organizing instruction to bring the student to a certain level of concept attainment. Emphasis on closure and immediate attainment takes precedence over most else. Little if any concern is given to the nature of the learner and to what is pertinent to him at a particular time in his development. In any case, one means of alleviating these major problems from the standpoint of learning theorists and the content-oriented person is to develop a system of concept analysis that can be utilized to organize for instruction and determine what children can learn against what someone from the external world "wants" them to learn. Concept analysis can provide a basis for selecting classes of concepts to be included in a curriculum at a respective level, the nature of the individual concepts and relationships between items. More important than anything else is the setting of reasonable learning expectations for the child at his age or stage of development.

Whether a deductive approach to science-concept learning or an inductive approach to science-concept learning is superior to the other is a secondary issue to whether children can learn what is expected of them in terms of the concept and the desired level of sophistication. The major concern should be for what can be learned over time—the total amount of concept development rather than the amount of immediate attainment. Without the analysis of concepts prior to their inclusion in the curriculum and organizing for instruction there is no basis for establishing and/or confirming a learning hierarchy consistent with the child's development. Without concept analysis there can be no means of gathering organized data to serve as a basis for making decisions about the content of the science curriculum. Concept analysis becomes a means of gathering and checking off relevant data and provides a vehicle for making decisions about what is to be expected of a child, cutting down on adult impositions on younger learners.

By setting up an analysis procedure and gathering data regarding instruction, learning sequences, evaluation, and the like, decisions can be made whether the arbitary frameworks for science-curriculum development which were initially used because of a lack of data are in fact the appropriate ones for children and learners of given characteristics. A structure is then available for making decisions about the inclusion of a concept and its supraordinate, coordinate, and subordinate concepts. Decisions can be made about the nature of the instructional approach for teaching concepts.

For example, it is often assumed that young children cannot learn science concepts of an abstract or theoretical nature. Yet a study conducted by Pella and Ziegler indicated that young children with proper instruction could be taught to utilize static and dynamic models as a means of developing abstract concepts about the particle nature of matter.[8] However, without a formal means of concept analysis the data

[8]M. O. Pella and R. E. Ziegler, *The Use of Static and Dynamic Models in Teaching Aspects of the Theoretical Concept, the Particle Nature of Matter,* Technical Report No. 20 (Madison, Wis.: Wisconsin Research and Development Center for Cognitive Learning, 1967).

collected in studies of this nature or in a less formal, observational sense by classroom teachers cannot be effectively utilized to make decisions about curricular content. With such as these it is possible to establish reasonable expectations for the learner based on the amount of abstractness a concept possesses and the ability to represent the concept and its examples and nonexamples in some physical model representation. If models can be constructed to help children understand what their data means, then it may be possible to include theoretical concepts in the elementary science curriculum. At this point the absence of concept analysis produces a serious hindrance to making decisions of this kind.

CONCEPT ANALYSIS SYSTEMS

A major deficiency in organizing for science-concept learning—planning instructional sequences and selecting appropriate evaluation techniques—has been the absence of concept analysis. Without concept analysis, decisions cannot be made as to what aspects of a concept are appropriate for younger children or older children, what aspects of a concept lend themselves to concrete experience rather than something more abstract. Likewise it is not possible to establish an initial sequence of possible learning levels. Although arbitrarily set learning sequences may require much modification after being tested with children, it is still necessary to perform concept analyses. Patterns of the concept development can be derived from the information provided by such analyses.

Two useful techniques for concept analysis have been developed in recent years. One of these approaches—the Klausmeier-Frayer scheme—has been found to be of particular value in analyzing classificatory concepts. With modification the general model holds promise for the analysis of other classes of concepts. The Klausmeier-Frayer scheme yields the following kinds of information.[9]

1. A list of attributes—criterial, relevant, and irrelevant.
2. Supraordinate, coordinate, and subordinate concepts.
3. A definition.
4. Examples and nonexamples.
5. Relationships of the concepts to other concepts.

[9]D. A. Frayer, W. D. Fredrick, and H. J. Klausmeier, *A Schema for Testing the Level of Concept Mastery,* Working Paper No. 16 (Madison, Wis.: Wisconsin Research and Development Center for Cognitive Learning, 1967).

Information of this kind serves as a vehicle for making curricular and instructional decisions. For if the concern is only that the learner be able to distinguish concept examples from nonexamples of the concept the analysis procedure has provided appropriate examples and nonexamples for utilization in instruction. Likewise, research on the nature of learning that transpires for respective science concepts and classes of science concepts allows the establishment of reasonable learning expectations. Two examples of the information produced by concept analysis of this variety are presented. (Note that the analysis was done pertinent to children in the intermediate grades and would necessarily include more sophisticated aspects for more advanced learners.)

The significant advantage of the concept-analysis procedure is that there is a basis for making decisions about the assessment of levels of concept learning. In addition to the information for use in selecting examples and nonexamples, relevant and irrelevant attributes etc., for use in instructional decision making, there is additional information that can be used in devising evaluation procedures of a paper-and-pencil variety or of a performance variety. A set of questions that could be employed in whole or in part to measure concept attainment is presented for the concept *mammal* in Chapter 8.

CONCEPT ANALYSES[10]

Area: Biological science

Target Concept Label: MAMMAL

Definition that gives the name of the supraordinate concept and the criterial attributes of the target concept. (If there is no supraordinate concept, then all attributes of the target concept should be given.)

A mammal is a warm-blooded animal that has hair and feeds its young on the mother's milk.

(*Definition tested:* A mammal is a warm-blooded animal that feeds its young on the mother's milk.)

---

[10]A. M. Voelker and J. S. Sorenson, *An Analysis of Selected Classificatory Science Concepts in Preparation for Writing Tests of Concept Attainment,* Working Paper No. 57 (Madison, Wis.: Wisconsin Research and Development Center for Cognitive Learning, 1971).

Supraordinate concept(s): vertebrate, animal

Coordinate concept(s): fish, reptiles, birds, amphibians

Subordinate concept(s): dog, cat, squirrel, lion, rabbit

Criterial attributes that differentiate the target concept from the supraordinate
  concept (or coordinate concepts if a supraordinate has not been identified).
    Mammals:
    1. Feed their young on the mother's milk.
    2. Have hair.

Other attributes that are relevant but not criterial for the target concept. (The
  attributes of the supraordinate need not be specified.)
    Other attributes relevant to mammal are those of its supraordinates, verte-
    brates and warm-blooded animals, such as:
    1. Having a backbone (vertebrate).
    2. Maintaining a constant body temperature (warm-blooded animals).
Irrelevant attributes of the target concept (attributes which vary among instances of the target concept) include the following:
    Irrelevant attributes of mammal include:
    1. Color: black, brown, yellow
    2. Pattern of coat: plain, striped, spotted
    3. Habitat: lives on land, lives in water
    4. Eating habits: eats other animals, eats plants

Relationship with at least one other concept. (This relationship should prefera-
  bly be a principle. It should definitely *not* be a direct supraordinate-subordinate relationship, a relationship involving a criterial attribute, or a relationship involving an example.)
    Mammals use *lungs* for breathing.
Concept examples include:
    dog, cat, squirrel, rabbit, horse, cow, camel

Concept nonexamples include:
    frog, alligator, chicken, snake, salamander

Another concept-analysis system developed simultaneously but independently from the Klausmeier-Frayer scheme is that of Markle and Tieman.[11] There is a great deal of similarity in the two schemes in that both deal with the basic analysis of concepts as a means of designing instructional sequences and making decisions about the degree of a student's understanding of the respective concepts. Major emphasis is placed on identifying attributes of a concept and designing and selecting examples and nonexamples. The major distinction from the Klausmeier-Frayer scheme appears to be that the Klausmeier-Frayer scheme was developed as a research tool to assess the relative degree of understanding of concepts whereas the Markle-Tieman scheme is more oriented toward designing specific instructional sequences.

The basic approach is as follows. (The concept selected for illustrative purposes is *solid*.) The various attributes of the concept such as three-dimensional, resistance to flow, etc., are identified and classified as critical or irrelevant. The criterial attributes are those common to all examples of the concept. Following the identification of the respective critical and irrelevant attributes a large number of examples and nonexamples of the concept are selected. These examples and nonexamples then are grouped into examples to be used in teaching and examples to be used in testing. At all times the examples and nonexamples are selected to be appropriate to the age level of the child who will receive instruction. All teaching is done by presentation of examples and nonexamples of the concept. In the presentation of the examples one critical attribute is missing at a given time. While the absence of the critical attribute is manipulated, changes are also made in the irrelevant attributes.

Both of these concept-analysis schemes are best utilized with the kinds of concepts which are identified as classificatory concepts. However, they appear to be sufficiently flexible that they can be extended to use with some relational and theoretical concepts. This is not as easily done with the Tieman-Markle analysis scheme.

Although both analysis systems have been developed primarily in terms of planning for instruction and conducting appropriate evaluation activities, they are structured in a way that the information obtained by utilizing them can help make instructional decisions about the kinds of science concepts and particular science concepts that can be included at various curricular levels. Decisions can be made about the level of concept attainment that can be expected, the classes of

[11]S. M. Markle and P. W. Tiemann, *Really Understanding Concepts: or In Frumious Pursuit of the Jabberwock* (Champaign, Ill.: Stipes Publishing Company, 1969).

Science concept: SOLIDS (elementary)
Next higher category: Matter

Attributes	Critical	Irrelevant
Three-dimensional	X	
Resistance to external force	X	
Inability to flow *(at room temperature)**	X	
Weight		X
Shape		X
Size		X
Color		X
Texture		X
Hollowness		X

	Examples	*Nonexamples*
Teaching	Windows (glass)	Water
	Books	Air
	Cooking seasonings	Maple syrup
	Light bulb	Elmer's glue
	Toothpaste	Liquid detergent
	Tree bark	Milk
	Swiss cheese	Vinegar
Testing	Sponge	Raw egg (without shell)
	Ice	Steam
	Snow	Paint
	Drinking straw	Cake batter

*Analyst indicated the examples and nonexamples to be appropriate for third- or fourth-grade students. Notice the implicit value judgment (italics added by authors) with respect to the attribute "inability to flow." The example of toothpaste, which more sophisticated learners recognize as a suspension, has been classed as "solid" by the analyst to locate a concept boundary and avoid the complex issues raised by emulsions, suspensions, and so forth.

concepts that might be included at a respective curriculum level, and the nature of the evaluation techniques that might be employed in testing situations.

EVALUATION

Much of the recent research and evaluation work on concept attainment has implications for developing models for structuring the science curriculum. Research studies conducted by generalists in concept learning as well as science subject-matter specialists indicate that science-concept learning not only *can* be measured with both verbal and nonverbal approaches but that the level of concept attainment *should* be measured both ways. If decisions on the nature of science concepts to be included in the curriculum is based only on children's ability to verbalize, then many concepts deemed appropriate for the curriculum may be excluded. Likewise many concepts that children may give evidence of understanding based on nonverbal approaches might be excluded from the curriculum. A study conducted by Voelker gives evidence that when young children are given an opportunity to *demonstrate* their understanding of concepts they do statistically as well as older children.[12] The significance is that those kinds of concepts should be included in the science curriculum where instructional sequences can be organized around a great deal of data gathering and manipulative experiences. It follows that the evaluation and testing procedures should be organized in the same manner. Those concepts that do not lend themselves well to instructional sequences based on an activity approach as well as testing situations where children can demonstrate their understandings by manipulating materials may not have a place in the science curriculum. This would be especially true for younger children. The tendency in recent years to move away from the "concrete" kinds of concepts in science-curriculum development toward more abstract content is contradicted by research data.

The analysis systems previously described can provide a framework for determining the kinds of tasks that children and learners can perform verbally and nonverbally. The nature of the tasks that learners might perform compared to the kinds of tasks that curriculum developers would want learners to achieve can be a set of criteria for structuring the science curriculum. By analyzing the concepts, decisions can be made about the concepts to be included—for example, whether they are too theoretical to be adequately represented by physical models for learners who need this kind of representation. Decisions can also be made about the order of inclusion in the curriculum and establishing relationships between and among the respective concepts. Most important of all, a framework of this kind can be utilized to strike a balance between the expectations of a content specialist in the discipline and the capabilities of the learner. Far too often compromise between these two groups has been ignored.

If testing and evaluation is conducted along a pattern which permits *specific* kinds of data to be collected, then judgments can be made about the level of sophistication that can be achieved by learners of given characteristics. Data collected in this manner can be used in preassessment activities as well as in evaluation and formal research

[12]A. M. Voelker, *The Relative Effectiveness of Two Methods of Instruction in Teaching the Classificational Concepts of Physical and Chemical Change to Elementary School Children*, Technical Report No. 39 (Madison, Wis.: Wisconsin Research and Development Center for Cognitive Learning, 1968).

study. If tests of this nature give consistent patterns of attainment across concepts sampled from a class of concepts, then the data collected may approach a form that can be used to generate a model for particular class of concepts for inclusion in the curriculum.

One means of constructing useful concept attainment tests is to write items which parallel the Klausmeier-Frayer schema.[13] (See Chapter 8 for sample test items constructed along these lines.)

Concept-attainment tests of this nature readily permit the generation of types of information about the attainment of the respective concept. The ability to answer each one of the questions on the concept attainment test is a measure of an individual's attainment of the concept. If different kinds of data of this kind are obtained relative to concept attainment, then decisions can be made about the level of expectation for a learner. In a general sense decisions can be made whether concept *should* be included in the science curriculum. Note also that the schema permits gathering data through both verbal and nonverbal kinds of measures. In addition to the commonly employed paper-and-pencil format, there is no reason why a child could not be given an opportunity to demonstrate his understanding through a performance test or through a teacher observational system. If the learner can do none else but identify examples and nonexamples, and if more than this ability is considered to be necessary to meet the expectations for concept attainment, then there is a means for determining whether to delay the inclusion of a concept in the curriculum and/or return to it at some later point in time. Information on whether or not learners can identify nonexamples and examples may be a critical factor in determining whether appropriate relationships can be understood. If those learners who do not understand the relationships are also those who cannot identify examples and nonexamples, then there is an associative type of base for making curricular and instructional decisions. Likewise if the learners do not seem to understand the attributes of the concept, there is additional justification for delaying the inclusion of a particular concept in the curriculum or possibly even omitting it from any consideration. Often attributes of concepts or the learners' language development, generally, could also be a deterrent to concept learning. If relationships between or among concepts is the desirable outcome of the learning experience, and if learners are not able to attain these relationships, then there is reason to delay or omit the concept from consideration or revise the expectation for the level of

[13]A. M. Voelker and J. S. Sorenson, *Items for Measuring the Level of Attainment of Selected Classificatory Science Concepts by Intermediate Grade Children*, Working Paper No. 58 (Madison, Wis.: Wisconsin Research and Development Center for Cognitive Learning, 1971).

concept attainment. If one has an analysis of all concepts involved in the relationship and if the learners apparently understand one concept quite well but not the other, then there is evidence for making decisions about the deficiencies. If the deficiencies are due to the sophistication of the concept or inadequate abilities of the learner at the time, there is cause to omit the concepts from the curriculum.

Thus the concept-analysis approach provides a supporting basis for developing models for structuring the science content of the science curriculum. If an analysis model of this type is utilized on a regular basis to analyze concepts and to make plans for curriculum development within sciences and in conjunction with other subject-matter disciplines, there will be more sophistication and organization in selecting and/or developing a science curriculum model. A model of this kind places emphases on what the learner can learn in conjunction with what is desired for him to learn always placing first priority on the learner rather than on the discipline.

APPROACHES FOR THE FUTURE

As indicated throughout this chapter, the best model for developing a science curriculum is the one that places priority focus on the learner and his abilities. The discipline and society are to be supportive to the needs of the learner. It is necessary, however, when considering the discipline portion of any model for science curriculum that the concepts to be included in the curriculum are not only appropriate for the learner but that they also have a high degree of probability for current credibility within the discipline itself.

Selecting content for the science curriculum has often been done by analyzing existing curricular materials and surveying various professionals, scholars in the disciplines, science educators, classroom teachers, or collections of these groups for an assessment of the current credibility of the particular content. More recently, however, an approach that appears to have much merit is to go directly to the content specialists. Such specialists are asked for the basic concepts in their subject-matter areas or its subdivisions which are not only important to them in facilitating their research and teaching but also which they think are the kinds of ideas that a learner completing the K–12 curriculum should understand. This latter approach for generating a concept list with current credibility appears to be more appropriate for determining science curricular content than to review a content framework which was originally derived from older materials and which in most instances was reviewed in a restrictive. Once the list has been generated and edited to remove duplications it should be analyzed and rated by the science educators, those persons who have substantial content expertise in their field as well as expertise as teachers and teacher educators. Another group which should review such lists for the appropriateness to the learner is the classroom teacher. A list which was generated by professionals in the discipline and which has been reviewed by the two major groups involved in making assessment about instruction should maintain a current science curriculum respectable to the discipline as well as appropriate to the learner. Ideally those concepts which would be included in the curriculum would be those in which there is a high degree of agreement between all reviewers, in terms of their credibility and their appropriateness to the learners.

In those instances where a decision has to be made about whether a concept or set of concepts is to be included in the curriculum the first criterion should be their appropriateness for the learner and the second major criterion should be whether an understanding of these concepts better helps the learner to understand the nature of the scientific enterprise. The notion of learning the science concept for its own sake should have lesser priority than either of the other two previously mentioned criteria.

In order to keep the content of the curriculum current and to insure that appropriate decisions are being made in regard to the learner, as soon as a list is completed and made available for curriculum developers those persons engaged in the business of producing lists should begin planning for repetition. For the period of time it takes to prepare curricular materials based on that list is lengthy. By the time revision of those materials is deemed appropriate the curricular content should have also been updated so that the revision is based on current data rather than arbitrary judgments.

SUGGESTED READINGS

Commission on Science Education. *Science—a Process Approach* (Washington, D.C.: American Association for the Advancement of Science, 1964).

This program is a K–8 science program based on a model for developing the process concepts of science. The major thesis is that a child is not ready to learn product-oriented conceptual knowledge concepts until he has learned the process concepts that are used in gathering and processing data. The process concepts—observation, measurement, etc.—are arranged in a hierarchal structure, criterion referencing used for determining levels of concept attainment.

Haney, R. E., "The Development of a Nonverbal Test of Children's Concepts of Animals," *Journal of Research in Science Teaching,* Vol. 3, No. 3 (1965), 198–203.

The need for measuring concept attainment by means other than standard paper and pencil tests is discussed. The development of a picture test for measuring children's understanding of selected life science concepts is presented, and the results of the subsequent research study in which they were employed are reported.

Helgeson, S. L., *The Relationship Between Concepts of Force Attained and Maturity as Indicated by Grade Levels,* Technical Report No. 42 (Madison, Wis.: Wisconsin Research and Development Center for Cognitive Learning, 1968).

The results of research conducted to determine elementary school children's ability to learn selected subordinate concepts and relationships concerned with the key concept *force.*

Novak, J. D., "A Model for the Interpretation and Analysis of Concept Formation," *Journal of Research in Science Teaching,* Vol. 3, No. 1 (1965), 72–83.

Professor Novak proposes a model for concept attainment based on his and other research studies, in which the recall of factual information is related to concept formation. A biochemical model for learning is hypothesized.

National Science Teachers Association, *Theory into Action* (Washington, D.C.: National Science Teachers Association, 1964).

This report summarizes the thoughts of a National Science Teachers Association Committee charged with examining science curriculum development. Five major themes from the processes of science are put forth as a structure for developing science curricula, as are seven major themes from the product dimension of science.

Pella, M. O., "Concept Learning," *The Science Teacher,* Vol. 33 (1966), 31–34.

Professor Pella reiterates the difficulty in deriving a generally acceptable definition of a concept. Rather than attempt to formulate a specific definition of a concept, the approach taken is to identify characteristics of concepts; examples are listed. In addition he discusses the grouping of science concepts into three categories based on the major activities that scientists engage in. Examples of conceptual ideas fitting each of these categories are presented.

Pella, M. O., G. T. O'Hearn, and L. J. Stiles, *Scientific Literacy,* Technical Report No. 1 (Madison, Wis.: Scientific Literacy Research Center, University of Wisconsin, 1966).

This study reports the results of a literature survey designed to determine the characteristics of a scientifically literate individual. Six referents for scientific literacy (characteristics of the scientifically literate) are identified. Statements indicative of a level of understanding of each referent are cited.

The generalizations stated are sources of process and product concepts to include in the K–12 science curriculum. The approach taken is that the conceptual knowledge aspects of a science curriculum should be developed within the framework of a broad concept of scientific literacy.

Pella, M. O., and R. E. Ziegler, *The Use of Static and Dynamic Models in Teaching Aspects of the Theoretical Concept, the Particle Nature of Matter,* Technical Report No. 20 (Madison, Wis.: Wisconsin Research and Development Center for Cognitive Learning, 1967).

This research details the role that static and dynamic mechanical models can play in instructional strategies for helping children formulate concepts. The vehicle used for facilitating this methodological study was the particle nature of matter.

Phenix, P. H., "Key Concepts and the Crisis in Learning," *Teacher's College Record,* Vol. 58 (1956), 137–143.

Professor Phenix discusses the crisis in learning which has been produced by the increasing void between man's ability to learn and the rate at which knowledge is developed. Justification is given for identifying key concepts for inclusion in a curriculum, those which will insure the necessary general understanding for the public. These key concepts are to be used as a base for organizing and teaching the respective subjects.

"Piaget Rediscovered: Selected Papers from a Report of the Conference on Cognitive Studies and Curriculum Development," *Journal of Research in Science Teaching,* Vol. 2, No. 3 (March 1964), 168–252.

An entire issue of the *Journal of Research in Science Teaching* was devoted to reporting selected results of a conference relating cognitive studies ala Piaget to curriculum development. The papers were expressly chosen to relate to science teaching. There are three groups of papers: (1) cognitive development in children, two papers written by Piaget; (2) cognitive development in children, selected psychological reports—several authors discuss basic notions of concept learning in relationship to Piagetian ideas and the implications for teaching science concepts; (3) reports from science curriculum projects that have utilized Piagetian ideas in preparing their development schemes for producing science curriculum materials.

Raven, R. J., "The Development of the Concept of Momentum in Primary School Children," *Journal of Research in Science Teaching,* Vol. 5, No. 3 (1967–68), 216–223.

The major thesis of this article is that there is often incompatibility between the hierarchy of learning concepts drawn from the structure of the discipline in contrast to the psychological development of the child. The results of Raven's research on the concept "momentum" indicate that the development of the concept via the child is not consistent with an a priori discipline model.

Roth, R. E., M. O. Pella, and C. A. Schoenfeld, *Environmental Management Concepts—a List,* Technical Report No. 126 (Madison, Wis.: Wisconsin Research and Development Center for Cognitive Learning, 1970).

The results of a study designed to identify environmental education themes for inclusion in the K–16 curriculum are presented. These themes, judged to be currently credible by scholars in many fields related to environmental education, are sources of concepts and relationships among concepts that can be utilized for designing interdisciplinary social-science studies curricula. An excellent source of a unifying framework for selecting concepts when a concern for the environment is a major factor in determining curricular content.

Scott, N., "Strategy of Inquiry and Styles of Categorization: a Three-Year Exploratory Study," *Journal of Research in Science Teaching,* Vol. 7, No. 2 (1970), 95–102.

This summary of several studies concerns itself with the relationship between concept attainment and the cognitive style of the learner. A major outcome of the study is the implication for the method(s) of assessing concept attainment. Both verbal and nonverbal measures of concept attainment must be utilized because children of different ages have unique characteristics, depending on the particular method of assessing cognitive function.

Stauss, N. G., *An Investigation into the Relationship Between Concept Attainment and Level of Maturity,* Technical Report No. 40 (Madison, Wis.: Wisconsin Research and Development Center for Cognitive Learning, 1968).

This study describes the results of research related to elementary school children's understanding of selected concepts and ideas related to the key concept *biological cell.* Concept attainment was measured by using the Bloom categories of knowledge, comprehension, and application.

Thompson, B. E., *A List of Currently Credible Biology Concepts Judged by a National Panel to Be Important for Inclusion in K–12 Curricula,* Technical Report No. 145 (Madison, Wis.: Wisconsin Research and Development Center for Cognitive Learning, 1970).

A set of currently credible biological themes judged appropriate for inclusion in the K–12 science curriculum was the major outcome of this study. These serve as a framework for organizing a biological science curriculum and selecting concepts for inclusion in that curriculum.

Triezenberg, H. J., *The Use of An Advance Organizer in Teaching Selected Concepts of Ecological Systems,* Technical Report No. 42 (Madison, Wis.: Wisconsin Research and Development Center for Cognitive Learning, 1968).

This study was designed to measure middle-school and junior high school children's understanding of concepts and relationships connected with the key concept *ecological homeostasis*.

U.S. Department of Health, Education, and Welfare, *Strategies and Cognitive Processes in Concept Learning,* Final Report, Project No. 2850, Contract No. OE 5–10–143, Department of Educational Psychology (Madison, Wis.: University of Wisconsin, March 1968).

This document summarizes the results of nineteen research studies on concept learning. The conclusions drawn are in regard to the nature of concepts, the strategies and cognitive processes in concept learning and the relationship of various stimulus and instructions variables to concept learning. The implications are outlined for each set of conclusions.

Voelker, A. M., "Concept Teaching and the Nature of the Scientific Enterprise," *School Science and Mathematics,* Vol. 69 (1969), 3–8.

A discussion of the parallel between concept formation from the standpoint of the learner and the development of concepts through the scientific enterprise is presented. The major thesis is that science is a concept forming activity and that much can be learned about organizing instructional sequences based on the ways science concepts are formulated. An analogy is drawn between concept formation in general and theory formation in science.

Voelker, A. M., *The Relative Effectiveness of Two Methods of Instruction in Teaching the Classificational Concepts of Physical and Chemical Change to Elementary School Children,* Technical Report No. 39 (Madison, Wis.: Wisconsin Research and Development Center for Cognitive Learning, 1968).

The need for measuring concept attainment by both verbal and nonverbal means is illustrated by the results of this study. It is indicated that young children perform statistically as well as older children when they are given an opportunity to demonstrate their learnings rather than only verbalize them.

Voelker, A. M., and J. S. Sorenson, *An Analysis of Selected Classificatory Science Concepts in Preparation for Writing Tests of Concept Attainment,* Working Paper No. 57 (Madison, Wis.: Wisconsin Research and Development Center for Cognitive Learning, 1970).

The rational and procedures for analyzing concepts in preparation for organizing instructional strategies and developing corresponding concept attainment tests are described. A total of 30 concept analyses are presented, 10 each from the biological, earth, and physical science areas.

Voelker, A. M., and J. S. Sorenson, *Items for Measuring the Level of Attainment of Selected Classificatory Science Concepts by Intermediate Grade Chil-*

dren, Working Paper No. 58 (Madison, Wis.: Wisconsin Research and Development Center for Cognitive Learning, 1970).

Procedures for developing and refining paper and pencil tests for measuring concept attainment via the Klausmeier-Frayer scheme of concept analysis and corresponding item construction are described. A total of 30 concept attainment tests are included, 10 each from the biological, earth, and physical science areas.

Wisconsin Department of Public Instruction, *A Guide to Science Curriculum Development*, Bulletin No. 161 (Madison, Wis.: Wisconsin Department of Public Instruction, 1968).

In this guide, six concepts purported to serve as unifying concepts for the total K–12 curriculum are presented. They serve to interrelate the biological, earth, and physical sciences. Generalizations which illustrate advancing levels of development of each concept are listed, examples being chosen from the biological, earth, and physical science areas.

CHAPTER 7

Concept Learning in the Social-Studies Curriculum, K–12: Issues and Approaches

Within the current climate of social concern over the direction of our society, the perennial controversy over educational objectives has taken on a new importance. Particularly is this traditional issue a significant and sensitive one in the domain of the social studies, whose important goals must of necessity intersect with the pulse of social concerns.

Historically, social-studies educators have differed in their opinions concerning appropriate goals for the social studies. Edwin Fenton has indicated that "There are three popular conceptions of the purposes of social studies. Social studies prepare children to be good citizens; social studies teach children how to think; social studies pass on the cultural heritage."[1] Hunt and Metcalf, in a major work, have argued that "The foremost aim of instruction in high school social studies is to help students reflectively examine issues in the problematic areas of American culture."[2]

In a succinct essay, *Alternative Directions for the Social Studies*,[3] Dale Brubaker has reflected the continuum of opinions within the profession on the issue of what goals are appropriate for the social studies. His suggestion, however, is that the spectrum of views may be bifurcated into the fundamental categories of "citizenship education"

[1]Edwin Fenton, *The New Social Studies* (New York: Holt, Rinehart & Winston, Inc., 1967), p. 1.

[2]Maurice P. Hunt and Lawrence E. Metcalf, *Teaching High School Social Studies: Problems in Reflective Thinking and Social Understanding*, 2nd. ed. (New York: Harper & Row, Publishers, 1968), p. 288.

[3]Dale Brubaker, *Alternative Directions for the Social Studies* (Scranton, Pa.: Intext Educational Publishers, 1967).

and "social-science inquiry"[4] In the former group are the "majority" of social studies educators, according to Brubaker.

Paradoxically, the associated products of the various social-studies projects across the United States since the early 1960's have both resolved and created problems for social-studies teachers. Not the least of the new problems is the issue of how selection of subject matter from the wealth of materials available is to be made, and how the various social-science disciplines are to be represented efficiently in the curriculum, K–12. Clearly, it is impossible to incorporate all the social sciences at all grade levels in the degree and scope recommended by project authors, even if this plan were deemed desirable. A focus upon concepts rather than disciplines or topics, however, provides at least some measure for selection of relevant subject matter. A key criterion of "relevancy" in subject matter selection becomes the degree to which it has potential for teaching a concept, regardless of its discipline identification. The historian Edwin Saveth has made a similar point.[5]

> Current efforts to cope with curricula, especially in the high schools, generally result in a tug of war between teachers of history and teachers of the social sciences themselves, as to how much of the subject matter of history and the disciplines is to be included. The premises of this argument are false once the concept is understood as being, by its nature, interdisciplinary and having a theoretical development in more than one social science."

In recent years concept learning as an objective for the social studies has received considerable attention among social-studies educators.[6]

"One of the functions of education and of school learning," Fancett and her associates have written, "is to transmit relatively definitive meanings of certain concepts, and at the same time transmit the ability to reorganize instances of experience into newly discovered or personally held concepts."[7] Reflecting this pattern, myriad curriculum materials have been advertised as being designed to teach significant social-science concepts.

---

[4]*Ibid.*, Chapters 1 and 2.

[5]Edward N. Saveth, "The Conceptualization of American History," in Edward N. Saveth (ed.), *American History and the Social Sciences* (New York: The Free Press, 1965), p. 16.

[6]See, for example, Hunt and Metcalf, *op. cit.;* Verna S. Fancett et al., *Social Science Concepts and the Classroom* (Syracuse, N.Y.: Social Studies Curriculum Center, 1968); Hilda Taba, *Teaching Strategies and Cognitive Functioning in Elementary School Children*, Cooperative Research Project No. 2404 (Washington, D.C: U.S. Office of Education, 1966); Marlin L. Tanck, "Teaching Concepts, Generalizations, and Constructs," in Dorothy McClure Fraser (ed.), *Social Studies Curriculum Development: Prospects and Problems, 39th Yearbook* (Washington, D.C.: National Council for the Social Studies, 1969); and Edith West, "Concepts, Generalizations, and Theories: Background Paper No. 3," unpublished paper, Project Social Studies, University of Minnesota, n. d.

[7]Fancett et al., *op. cit.*, p. 3.

This apparent consensus on the importance of concept learning is deceptive, however, as a careful analysis of the literature will reveal. Terminology is at best fuzzy, and definitions usually are absent or lack precision. In many respects, the term *concept* has become a catch-all category for cognitive operations, and frequently is used synonomously with "idea," "generalization," "structure," "topic," or "labels." Massialas observed this point in a 1962 report:[8]

> One could read several curriculum guides and social studies essays and texts and find as many different usages of the term "concept," a term which is fundamental to all learning and instruction in this particular area (social studies). In addition to this many people refer to concepts on a very abstract level, with no effort whatever to provide some illustrative examples. It is often true that in committee meetings and lectures persons repeatedly use words such as "concepts," "ideas," "generalizations," "conclusions," and "hypotheses," but fail to suggest specific and relevant examples of each.

What the dialog concerning concept learning has lacked, then, are common referrents. Education in general, and social studies in particular, has lacked a precise terminology through which practitioners could communicate effectively, and progress in understanding the nature of concept learning has suffered from this general malaise. Social-studies educator Alan Griffin in 1942[9] sounded a warning which still has a contemporary ring, concerning "fuzzy and ungrounded verbalizing," which he saw as "one of the most serious handicaps now impeding the professionalization of education."

A second dimension of difficulty has stemmed from the failure of curriculum designers to match concept-learning objectives, however stated, with curricular materials. Little empirical or even logical evidence has been adduced to indicate that curricular materials labeled as "concept oriented" do in fact produce the outcomes specified. The arrangement of content within textbooks and related material (usually in chronological or topological fashion), furthermore, bears in most cases little resemblance to that predicated by general principles of concept learning reflected in the experimental literature. Since this match between objectives, learning principles, subject-matter structure, and organization has not been made in most textual materials, subject matter must be "taken out of context" to make it contribute systematically to concept learning. Selakovich has made this point in, *Problems in Secondary Social Studies*, in a general commentary upon

[8]Byron G. Massialas, "Research Prospects in the Social Studies," *Indiana University School of Education Bulletin*, Vol. 38 (January 1962), p. 4.

[9]Alan Griffin, "A Philosophical Approach to the Subject-Matter Preparation of Teachers of History," unpublished doctoral dissertation, Ohio State University, Columbus, Ohio, 1942.

the failure of authors to use principles of learning theory in designing curricular materials.[10]

> Learning principles widely accepted in educational psychology have not yet been widely applied to curriculum organization and content in the social studies. . . . The materials which constitute the social studies have yet to incorporate the ideas. Because social studies texts make little effort to organize content on the basis of principles of learning, such organization becomes the responsibility of the classroom teacher—and the extent to which learning principles are applied to teaching depends largely on the teacher's ability to apply them.

A final related problem that has been associated with social-studies objectives concerns the failure of textual material designers to recognize adequately the need for designing their products in structurally different ways for differing objectives. A variety of factors, many of them economic, account for this situation. The fact remains, however, that materials conventionally have been designed to achieve a range of objectives, explicit or implicit, with differing subject matter generally correlated in some narrative fashion with these objectives. The *structural* or *organizational* form of such subject matter, however, generally has been held *constant* across objectives. Thus curricular materials for teaching "generalizations" structurally resemble those used for teaching "concepts," even though the author may explicity discriminate the two categories of objectives.

STUDIES OF CONCEPT LEARNING IN THE SOCIAL STUDIES

Gilbert Sax, in a recent review of the research literature, has noted,[11]

> From the period 1960 to the present, there has been an almost complete lack of research interest in concept formation in areas other than mathematics and science. . . . Generally, the published material on concept formation in the social studies . . . has tended to be vague or weak in experimental design or has included suggestions for innovations without evidence to support them.

While no systematic body of empirical information exists relating to *social-science* concept learning specifically, several relevant studies have been conducted over the past decade. Using the concepts of "lobbying" and subsidizing." sixth-grade students were presented with

---

[10]Daniel Selakovich, *Problems in Secondary Social Studies* (Englewood Cliffs, N.J.: Prentice-Hall, Inc., 1965), p. 6.

[11]Gilbert Sax, "Concept Formation," in Robert L. Ebel (ed.), *Encyclopedia of Educational Research*, 4th ed. (New York: The Macmillan Company, 1969), p. 201.

case-study positive and negative exemplars in a study by Grannis.[12] Analyzed were the effects of additional information, "learning exercises," and a requirement to write a definition of the concept. While the author did not find that these were significant variables, approximately 15 percent of the students were able to demonstrate mastery in recognizing new cases as positive or negative instances of the concept and to correctly change such instances from positive to negative or vice versa.

Concerned with different variables, Newton and Hickey examined the effects of prior instruction and the learning of subconcepts upon the learning-rate of the concept "gross national product."[13] Their conclusion was that performance was faster when the advance information was given first and when the subconcepts of "consumption" and "investment spending" were learned together rather than discretely.

A comparison of alternative strategies for teaching concepts was analyzed by Nuthall in a study involving 432 tenth- and eleventh-grade students.[14] Four operationally discrete strategies were used to teach the concept of "cultural symbosis" and "ethnocentrism" through the medium of programmed-text materials. Six statements for each of the two concepts determined their parameters for the teaching strategies. Other variables examined were the students' level of knowledge related to the concepts and the content of instruction immediately preceding the strategies. Nuthall found that differences in teaching strategy (as defined in the study) could be related to differences in student performance on open-ended and multiple-choice criterion tests used in the study.

A recent study by Martorella and Wood analyzed the relative effects of two categories of variables upon the learning of a basic social-science concept by a preschool population.[15] Independent variables were variations of irrelevant data and of positive-negative exemplar ratios. Subjects were kindergarteners in a large urban school system. Each subject was assigned to one of nine different treatment groups.

The learning task was the conjunctive concept *island* with the rule "land surrounded by water." Slides, tapes, and pictures were used to administer and measure treatments and their effects. The students were tested immediately and then retested one week later over seven criteria measures. Contrary to the findings of other investigators work-

[12]Joseph C. Grannis, "An Experimental Study of the Inductive Learning of Abstract Social Concepts," unpublished doctoral dissertation, Washington University, St. Louis, Mo., 1965.

[13]John M. Newton and Albert E. Hickey, "Sequence Effects in Programmed Learning of a Verbal Concept," *Journal of Educational Psychology*, Vol. 56 (1965), pp. 140–147.

[14]Graham Nuthall, "An Experimental Comparison of Alternative Strategies for Teaching Concepts," *American Educational Research Journal*, Vol. 5 (1968), pp. 561–584.

[15]Peter H. Martorella and Roger Wood, "Variable Affecting a Geographic Concept-Learning Task for Pre-School Children," *Journal of Geography*, Vol. 70 (December, 1971).

ing with nonsocial-science concepts and older subjects, increasing irrelevant detail did not produce a significant decremental effect on learning.[16] Likewise, decreasing contrast did not significantly influence learning efficiency.[17]

The Relevancy of Piaget's Ideas for the Social Studies

One of Piaget's most widely cited contributions to the development of instructional procedures in the elementary grades has been his analysis of the stages of cognitive development in children. These stages, as indicated in an earlier chapter, present a basic variable to be considered in instruction by establishing the theory that children normally are best prepared to learn certain propositions at maturational levels that generally correspond to chronological ages. Children at the *concrete operational* stage that Piaget outlined must have concrete empirical props illustrating the criterial attributes of the concept they are to learn, rather than purely verbal or abstract illustrations. Thus kindergarten and first-grade students tend to be more literal-minded. Children in this period will learn to develop the ability to add, multiply, divide, compare, or enlarge classes or categories. Items, persons, events, and memories are grouped and sorted according to their attributes. Categorization may be predicated on the basis of a variety of different criteria including size, smell, shape, texture, hue, site, composition, function, or sound. Consequently, concepts like *democracy, government,* and *legislature,* while commonly found in curricula for children at the concrete operational stage, normally would be inappropriate to teach in their abstract form.

While most of the direct applications to classroom subjects of Piaget's research are in the areas of science and math, E. A. Peel has speculated on the implications of Piaget's findings for social studies and the problems inherent in translating his ideas.[18] He notes that, unlike science, the data of history, for example, consists essentially of the intentions behind the actions of people in the past.[19]

> The first bridge, therefore, the teacher of history has to cross is that between present and past. He accounts for the past by whatever knowledge he can use from the child's present experience and by whatever concrete historical material he has available. In this way he builds up the right historical data. . . . But there is more to history than

[16] *Ibid.*

[17] *Ibid.*

[18] E. A. Peel, "Learning and Thinking in the School Situation," in Richard E. Ripple and Verne N. Rockcastle (eds.), *Piaget Rediscovered,* Cooperative Research Project, No. F-040 (Washington, D.C.: U. S. Office of Education, 1964), pp. 103–104.

[19] *Ibid.*

this. Its course can be viewed as a series of equilibria and disequilibria between the acts and intentions of men. The mature student of history is sensitive to the fine interplays and balance in such situations as the events in 1939 leading up to the Second World War. . . .

The balance of powers, physical or human, involves the two important principles of cancellation and compensation which forms an essential part of Piaget's account of adolescent thinking. Some investigations carried out recently using short passages of history demonstrated that this sensitivity is under present educational circumstances, a characteristic of mid-adolescence.

Another equation between Piagetian ideas and social-studies curriculum has been developed by Frank Hooper. He indicates a corresponding relationship between certain dimensions of social-science learning and Piaget's notions of classification, multiple causation, and conservation of invariants.[20]

Piagetian Principles	*Social-Science Learnings*
Probabilistic reasoning—the notion that combinations of insufficient causes can render a conclusion more likely to occur—is a cognitive prerequisite for learning.	The basic uncertainty about the accuracy of historical predictions of conclusions. The conception of outcomes as the product of identifiable determinants plus chance elements
Multiple classification—the notion of multiple rationality and hierarchical groupings—is a cognitive prerequisite for learning.	Data such as government tables of organizations, authority relations, and taxonomic classifications and role-hierarchies.
Multiple causation—the ability to think in terms of natural causes and to conceive of a variety of types of causes; the ability to regard an event or series of events as being generated by a prior event or series of events—is a cognitive prerequisite for learning.	The causal relationship of historical phenomena, a notion of multiple-causality, and the notion of causes continuously operating across extended time periods.
Conservation of invariants—the idea that certain things stand still or remain constant even though some of their characteristics may be altered—is a cognitive prerequisite for learning.	The possibility of generalizations about historical processes that are applicable to a variety of different events.

[20]Frank H. Hooper, "Piagetian Research and Education," in Irving E. Sigel and Frank H. Hooper (eds.), *Logical Thinking in Children* (New York: Holt, Rinehart & Winston, Inc., 1968), pp. 426–429.

Probably the best-known application of some of Piaget's findings to social-studies instruction and curriculum design has been that of the late Hilda Taba and her associates, whose work has already been discussed in our presentation of generic models of concept learning in chapter 3. Their conclusions relating to concept learning in the social studies have been reported in two studies, *Thinking in Elementary School Children*[21] and *Teaching Strategies and Cognitive Functioning in Elementary School Children.*[22] One of the more provocative relevant findings of their studies was that "slow learners" were capable of abstract thinking under a program of instruction that regulates assimilation according to student needs and that allowed ample opportunities for concrete operations before making a transition to abstract operations and symbolic content.[23]

Taba, Levine, and Elzey, in *Thinking in Elementary School Children*, summarized their conclusions concerning the structuring of learning experiences for concept development in the social studies, as follows.[24]

> There should also be a sequence in learning experiences so that each preceding step develops the skills which are prerequisite for the next step. For example, because the transition from concrete to operational thinking is of especial importance for school-age children, the sequence of school experiences should begin with experiences with concrete objects, materials to facilitate description, analysis, and differentiation. The early years of school may need to concentrate on providing abundant experience in manipulation and combining, matching, and grouping objects in order to facilitate the mastery of concrete thinking. Opportunities for the active processing of information may provide the necessary conditions for the evolution and organization of abstract conceptual schemes. This preparation lays the groundwork for formal thinking, for manipulation of abstract symbols, and for the capacity to discover relationships between objects and events.

Irving Sigel has suggested that Piaget's contributions to social-studies curriculum may come more from his conceptions of mental operations than in his description of development in specific areas.[25]

---

[21]Hilda Taba, Samuel Levine, and Freeman Elzey, *Thinking in Elementary School Children*, Cooperative Research Project No. 1574 (Washington, D.C.: U.S. Office of Education, 1964).

[22]Hilda Taba, *Teaching Strategies and Cognitive Functioning in Elementary School Children*, Cooperative Research Project, No. 2404 (Washington, D.C.: U.S. Office of Education), 1966.

[23]Taba, Levine, and Elzey, *op. cit.*, p. 176.

[24]*Ibid.*, p. 22.

[25]Irving E. Sigel, "The Piagetian System and the World of Education," in David Elkind and John H. Flavell (eds.), *Studies in Cognitive Development: Essays in Honor of Jean Piaget* (New York: Oxford University Press, 1969), p. 486.

According to Piaget, when a youngster is able to master multiple classes, he is now able to grasp the important principle of conservation —namely, the phenomenon whereby an item may be transformed and yet retain its initial basic characteristics. At this stage of development children normally also acquire the capability of performing the mental operations of reversibility and reciprocity which are prerequisite to the ability to deal with multiple class. Reciprocity includes the ability to deal with *relational* concepts and reversibility includes the capacity to see items as reorganized or reconstructed to their original state.

Sigel provides an illustration of multiple classification related to the social studies.[26]

> An awareness of the range of attributes or aspects of any instance is a crucial prerequisite for the development of more complex classification behaviors. If we are able to specify many labels, we can classify instances in many categories. Thus, for example, . . . we could categorize the American Revolution under the class "revolution," or "independence," or "anti-British," or "war," and so on.
>
> The number and kind of instances that can be brought under a particular heading depends on the criterial attribute selected. Thus, for the class "fruit," we could include such objects as pears and oranges; but if our criterial attribute were the class "red," we would select additional instances possessing the attribute "red." Similarly, we could construct a class, "wars on the American continent," including the American Revolution, the Civil War and the War of 1812; and we could construct a class, "British-American wars," including the American Revolution and the War of 1812, but excluding the Civil War. . . .
>
> The ability to combine two or more attributes is a very significant one in the logical development of thought; it is a prototype of complex thinking, in which classes are combined and recombined as the needs of the problem dictate. In the process of combining and recombining a group of items, a child has to shift his criteria; flexibility is required in the manipulation of multiple criteria.

Sigel goes on to note how, in order to deal with problems of multiple classification and interdependence of attributes, a youngster must be capable of performing two-mental operations—reversibility and reciprocity.[27]

> Reversibility is a mental operation in which materials or ideas are reorganized so as to reconstruct the original state or class. . . .

[26]Irving E. Sigel, *Child Development and Social Science Education: A Teaching Strategy Derived from Some Piagetian Concepts, Part IV*, Publication No. 113 (Lafayette, Ind.: Social Science Education Consortium, 1966), pp. 5–6.
    [27]*Ibid.*, pp. 8–9.

A social science illustration of reversibility is the case of dollars which can be changed into British pounds, and then converted back into dollars. The value of the dollar, or the value of the money in question, has been conserved even though it appears in a different form. Also if the money is changed into other denominations, such as smaller coins or smaller bills, the amount is still the same.

Reciprocity connotes an interaction between things. For example, in economics, reciprocal relationships are evident when one country reduces tariffs and the other country involved sells it more goods. As applied to this specific case, the principle is that tariffs are related to the amount of goods bought and sold. An increase in tariffs causes a decrease in trade, while a decrease in tariffs leads to an increase in trade. There is a reciprocal relationship between trade and tariffs. . . .

Sigel has concluded from his research that children are not able to use two separate attributes *simultaneously* as the basis for classification normally until the *fourth* grade.[28] He does suggest, however, that with certain concepts and under appropriate instructional conditions, kindergarten–first-grade children may be capable of multiple classification. He found, for example, that certain material presented to young children in a three-dimensional visual format elicited multiple-classification.

These experiences have led him to surmise that procedures to expand styles of categorization could be initiated in the primary grades.[29] He notes that, "Content would have to be selected which could visibly present to the child the possible alternative classification responses; later, use could be made of more symbolic representational material, such as pictures; and eventually, words."[30]

Some important considerations for organizing concept learning, as inferred from Sigel's writings, are summarized as follows.[31]

1. Objects, persons and events have many discrete attributes.
2. These attributes, individually or in clusters, can be used as the bases for forming classifications, and hence, for organizing content for a concept-learning task.
3. Classifications on the basis of an individual attribute is easier for students than classification on the basis of multiple attributes. For younger children, therefore, single-attribute items are easier to deal with.
4. With an appropriate instructional sequence and demonstrations, children can learn that individual attributes can be clustered to generate new subclasses through the combination of two or more attributes.

[28] *Ibid.*, p. 2.
[29] *Ibid.*, p. 18.
[30] *Ibid.*,
[31] *Ibid.*, p. 19.

5. The intellectual operations of reciprocity and reversibility are cognitive prerequisites for multiple classification.
6. When students have acquired the operations of reciprocity and reversibility and are capable of multiple classifications, they are capable of conservation.
7. The use of discovery or inductive procedures can expedite students integration, or coordination of attributes.

One may see Sigel's considerations systematically applied in his example of how a social-studies unit might be taught. He uses the illustration of a unit study on the pioneers,[32] a topic commonly found in the curriculum, with the general objective being "to show something about the white man and the Indian in early colonial days." He suggests first the alternate development of the concepts of *tepee* and *log cabin* by identifying their respective attributes, discussing their respective functions as domiciles, their portability, their shapes, and the materials from which they were constructed, and illustrating to students how these respective attributes apply to the tepee and to the log cabin. At a second level, the similarities between tepee and log cabin would be discussed, such as their similarities in functions and materials. Then differences would be analyzed, such as differences in construction and shape. Having examined similarities and differences, students would be ready to examine these items and discuss or reflect upon the significance of each of their attributes.

He suggests some typical interactions that might be directed toward, for example, the attribute of shape: "Why is a tepee conical? What function does this shape serve? It is related to fire; a simple way to make smoke escape is to leave a hole in the top of a conical structure. Why is a log cabin rectangular? This is a simple way to build with logs."[33]

To this point, his suggested procedures have focused upon how two discrete items may be shown to have similarities and differences, but with an emphasis on single attributes. Sigel notes that a teacher might now include in the discussion other types of dwellings prevalent in pioneer communties, such as lean-tos and clapboard houses; similarly, forts and other types of buildings, "all of which have the common attributes of domicile, but which also have the other qualities which permit subclassifications."[34] A next step would be to locate in one category those buildings which were wooden and permanent domiciles, and in another category to place those dwellings that were portable.

[32] *Ibid.*, pp. 12–13.
[33] *Ibid.*, p. 13.
[34] *Ibid.*

Sigel notes that these procedures require students to discover the attributes relevant for discussion, along with their relationships.[35]

> From our research efforts it has become clear that letting the child provide the labels and discover the similarities and differences enables him to assimilate this information more readily, and to achieve an awareness of the complexity of items before him. This conclusion is consistent with the Piagetian theory, which holds that assimilation of information leads to alterations in the point of view. Thus, as these new bits of information become categorized in appropriate cognitive schemas, the schemas increase in content. The act of the child searching and labeling, uttering and hearing himself say "wood," "big," "small," and so forth, provides the context within which he acquires significant bits of information with which to identify environmental phenomena.

Charlotte Crabtree offers yet another illustration of social-studies instruction with children at the stage of concrete operations. Her project was concerned with the effects of instruction related to geographic concepts on primary grade children.[36] In her observations she reports how questions were raised concerning how a city could meet its vastly expanding construction needs and generally about certain locational relationships.[37] Visits were made to new freeways under construction and a new mall nearing completion. Also observed were new apartments and the city's public works programs, including street repairs, and rail facilities where gravel rock products were arriving daily. Specifically, questions focused on the sources of the supply of gravel, cement, and concrete for the construction, since local resources in the community were nearly exhausted.

In the next stage, a terrain model was introduced representing the topography of the Los Angeles lowlands, the mountain rim, and the deserts to the north and southeast. Through the placement of small red houses on the model children were asked to indicate where they thought rock products might be found. Then through data on the range, a soil box, and a simulation of water washing gravel down the mountains to the lowland, students were able to evaluate their location-hypotheses and then to revise them.

At this point, an acetate overlay unit was used to indicate rivers, a map legend, and mining sites. Children then formulated statements about the relationship of sites to geographic features. Crabtree interprets: "At a 'concrete' level their statements incorporated relationships

---

[35] Ibid.

[36] Charlotte Crabtree, "Supporting Reflective Thinking in the Classroom," in Jean Fair and Fannie R. Shaftel (eds.), *Effective Thinking in the Social Studies, 37th Yearbook* (Washington, D.C.: National Council for the Social Studies, 1967).

[37] Ibid., p. 95.

between granitic mountains, rock products, and the downhill flow of streams. At a more abstract level, their statements indentified an areal relationship between the resource and the mining site."[38]

INDIVIDUALIZATION OF LEARNING

It should be noted that little empirical data exist concerning the scope and variety of concepts that students bring with them to school.[39] DeCecco has made this point succinctly: "As yet we have no studies of the concepts and principles with which most American children enter school and of the concepts they should learn first and those they should learn later."[40]

Also, it should be underscored that the unique emotional make-up of each individual student itself presents a highly significant affective variable in concept-learning tasks. It is possible, in fact, that one's degree of affective involvement with a concept will overshadow and color his cognitive attachments. Carroll relates the case of the youngster who fears and rejects the barber because his white coat and scissors make him resemble the doctor, whom the child has learned to fear.[41] Carroll observes that "My concept of 'stone' may reflect, let us say, my positive delight in collecting new varieties of minerals, whereas your concept may reflect the fact that you had unpleasant experiences with stones—having them thrown at you in a riot, or finding lots of them in your garden."[42]

The task of providing an instructional program for concept learning *uniquely* tailored to an individual's cognitive and affective state would of course be an impossible one. Such a program would not only take into account an individual's past experiences and current motivational state but would provide for variables such as reading levels, topical preferences, and learning-style preferences, just to cite a few items. Although manipulating all of these variables simultaneously is impossible for an instructor, certain dimensions of the task, given set parameters, would be possible for a computer.

What would be required in developing such a computer-related instructional system is a listing of the constraints imposed and the parameters that will be set; for example, the range of differences that

---

[38] *Ibid.*, p. 96.

[39] See the following document for a listing of available studies: Irving Sigel and Elinor Waters, *Child Development and Social Science Education, Part III: Abstracts of Relevant Literature* (Lafayette, Ind.: Social Science Education Consortium, 1966).

[40] John P. De Cecco, *The Psychology of Learning and Instruction* (Englewood Cliffs, N.J.: Prentice-Hall, Inc.), 1968, p. 400.

[41] John B. Carroll, "Words, Meanings and Concepts," *Harvard Educational Review*, Vol. 34 (Spring 1964), p. 184.

[42] *Ibid.*

will be allowed in categorizing profiles, the variety and types of subject-matter outputs that will be used, the number of alternative instructional sequences that will be permitted, and the degree of sophistication in the pretests employed. Such a system if made operational would allow for a wider latitude of learning options than most schema for individualization that are operative today. An illustration of how such a system might be organized is provided in Table 7-1, and then is discussed below.[43]

TABLE 7-1
A Computer-Assisted-Instruction Individualization Model

Sequence of Operations

1. Developmental Stage

    1.1 Develop or acquire testing instruments.
    1.2 Select student population.
    1.3 Pretesting.
    1.4 Develop student profiles from pretests.
    1.5 Organize data for interdisciplinary concepts selected and student profiles.
    1.6 Develop varied positive and negative instances of concepts in sequenced fashion.
    1.7 Develop questions concerning concepts.
    1.8 Develop reviews for instructional sequences.

2. Programming Operations

    2.1 Introductory instructions for all students concerning use of the system.
    2.2 Correlate episode sequences with limited range of student profiles, plus develop additional alternative bank of varied positive and negative content episodes for students who wish to call them up.
        2.21 Upon identification, student is provided with a sequence of instruction based upon his profile.
        2.22 Allow for responses to provide direction for future routines.
        2.23 Make provisions for students requesting parallel less complex or more complex examples by signaling at any point.
        2.24 Make provisions for students to request additional data during an instructional sequence. Such data would be called up by a "Key-Word in Context" (KWIC) sorting mechanism.
        2.25 Make provisions for students to request printouts for further exploration of data related to any episode which will be coordinated with individual profiles.
        2.26 Keep records of student interface with the computer.

[43]For a more detailed analysis and an illustration of this system, see Peter H. Martorella, *Concept Learning in the Social Studies: Models for Structuring Curriculum* (Scranton, Pa.: Intext Educational Publishers, 1971), pp. 82–83, 96–101.

Developmental Stage

In the initial stages, potential users of the instructional system would be pretested to develop individual "profiles." Profiles would include indices on such features as reading-ability levels, areas of particular interest, knowledge of subordinate and coordinate concepts, knowledge of critical attributes of the concept to be learned, and possibily attitudinal orientations toward the general subject matter to be studied.

In turn, profiles would provide general indicators for constructing varied instructional episodes including exemplars and nonexemplars of the concept to be learned, along with corresponding questions. The format of such episodes could also be varied: written (computer print-outs, computer instructions to consult short handouts adjacent to the computer terminal, or cathode-ray tube or television-screen messages), oral (tape or records), visual (computer-generated graphics—such as charts and graphs or simple drawings, still pictures, slides, films, or transparencies), or a combination of the preceding. A *basic* series of episodes for a narrow range of similar profiles might be constructed, and then additional *supplementary* episodes which could function in reviews and/or reinforcement or exploratory sessions. Additionally, data relating to subordinate or coordinate concepts would be prepared, correlated with reading ability levels and interests, for students' retrieval, if they desire them.

Programming Operations

In the programming phase, provisions would be made for providing all users of the system with a common introduction to the use of the system, including its objectives, capabilities, and limitations. As students identify themselves to the computer, they would be equated with their profile indices and provided with the appropriate individualized instructional sequence. Provisions would be included for allowing students to switch to supplementary instructional series correlated with their profiles, if they should wish; or to request less difficult sequences, with respect to profile indices. In effect, when a student requests a less complex instructional sequence, he would be routed to another sequence based upon a profile with lower proficiency scores, as the hypothetical rating in Table 7-2 illustrates.

A Key-Word in Context (KWIC) sorting mechanism would provide for retrieval of data relating to coordinate and subordinate concepts and correlated with some dimensions individual profiles. "Follow-up" work for students, upon request would be provided through references

TABLE 7-2

A Hypothetical Case, Illustrating a Computer-Assisted-Instructional Sequence When a Less Difficult Sequence Is Requested

	Assumed Elements of a User's Profile			
	Reading Ability Level	Knowledge of Critical Attributes Inventory	Knowledge of Selected Subordinate and Coordinate Concepts Inventory	Interest Categories
User's profile index	9.1	1, 2, 4, 6	1.1, 8.3, 9.8, 11.5, 12.1, 12.4, 12.6	20, 23, 27 29, 31, 38
Sequence provided initially	9.0	1, 2, 4, 6	1.1, 8.3, 9.8, 12.6	20, 23, 38
Some alternative instructional sequences (1)	8.5	1, 2, 3, 5	1.1, 11.5, 12.6	20, 23
(2)	8.5	3, 4, 5, 6	11.5, 12.1, 12.4	27, 29
(3)	9.0	1, 2, 3, 4, 5, 6	1.1	31, 38

NOTE: The concept involved has six attributes, and difficulty is reduced by reevaluating and subsequently decreasing the assumptions made concerning a user's reading-ability level, knowledge of the concept's critical attributes, knowledge of selected subordinate and coordinate concepts, and interest areas. Correspondingly, the user then is provided with additional and/or different information that was supplied in the initial instructional sequence.

to sources that the student might consult. References would be based upon dimensions of the individual profiles, and perhaps, the rate of success in the computer-assisted instruction system.

Finally, students would be evaluated in terms of their ability to discriminate new exemplars from nonexemplars, differentiate the concept rule from a nonrule, and discriminate relevant attributes from nonrelevant attributes. Provisions would be made for keeping records of students' interfacing with the computer and these would provide feedback for modification of the system.

CONCEPTS IN THE CURRICULUM

As noted earlier, in recent years a number of curricular materials —for example, the Greater Cleveland Social Studies Project curriculum,[44] the University of Minnesota, Project Social Studies materials, the Harcourt Brace Jovanovich *Concepts and Values* series, to cite just a few—have been promoted as being designed to teach significant social-studies concepts. Edith West, Director of the University of Minnesota Project, has offered some guidelines that curriculum developers should consider with respect to *concepts*.[45]

> First, curriculum builders must provide many direct and vicarious experiences for those concepts which are difficult. Second, the curriculum builder should limit the number of difficult concepts introduced within a brief period of time. Third, the curriculum builder must decide how many concepts of narrower scope must be understood prior to teaching a higher-level concept which relates them. How many concepts must the pupil learn, for example, before he can be taught the concepts of "mountain pass," "harbor," or "region" in geography? Of "stratification" or "self" in sociology? Of "market" or "real income" in economics? Of "century" or "generation" in history? Of "interest group" or "constitution" in political science? Of "enculturation" or "modal personality" in anthropology? Finally, the curriculum builder must decide whether or not a difficult concept is significant enough to warrant teaching it in early grades when it might be taught more quickly at a higher grade level because of the types of experiences which most American children have had by the time they reach that grade.

Marlin Tanck, in a National Council for the Social Studies 1969 Yearbook chapter entitled "Teaching Concepts, Generalizations, and

---

[44]The project materials now are being marketed commercially by Allyn & Bacon, Inc., Boston, Mass.

[45]West, *op. cit.*, p. 7.

Constructs," developed a model of the structure of knowledge as a basis for curricular organization.[46] His schema entails a four-tiered hierarchy of knowledge, moving from facts and attributes to concepts to generalizations to constructs. Within concept learning, the focus of this chapter, Tanck has differentiated three different instructional strategies that may be used: *concept attainment,* consisting of "leading students to develop their own knowledge by associating related kinds of knowledge in context;"[47] *concept augmentation,* which is "to expand and deepen students understanding of a concept of which they already have some knowledge;"[48] and *concept demonstration,* which "involves initial expansion of knowledge, followed by association of related parts of knowledge in appropriate contexts."[49] Abstracted models of the instructional steps Tanck suggests for each of these three processes are provided in Tables 7-3,[50] 7-4,[51] and 7-5.[52]

TABLE 7-3
CONCEPT-ATTAINMENT MODEL

Sequence of Operations

1. Identify the symbol, major attributes, examples, and nonexamples of the concept.
2. Present students with the examples, identified by their concept name, and with nonexamples, and have them identify the critical attributes of the concept.
3. As an optional but desirable step, have the students define the concept by listing its major attributes.
4. Introduce more examples and nonexamples, and have students identify whether they are positive or negative instances and give reasons why or why not.
5. Have the students locate and label new examples.
6. Evaluate learning by ascertaining whether students can identify examples and nonexamples, and can locate new ones.

Of the steps in Table 7-3, the *concept-attainment* model, Tanck remarks,[53]

> These steps need not be precisely as described or follow this exact order. Identification of the cognitive elements, for example, might be

[46]Tanck, *op. cit.*
[47]*Ibid.,* p. 117.
[48]*Ibid.,* p. 121.
[49]*Ibid.,* p. 117.
[50]*Ibid.,* pp. 117–118.
[51]*Ibid.,* 121–122.
[52]*Ibid.,* pp. 120–121.
[53]*Ibid.,* p. 118.

TABLE 7-4
CONCEPT-DEMONSTRATION MODEL

Sequence of Operations

1. Identify the symbol, major attributes, and examples and nonexamples of the concept.
2. Name and define the concept and note its major attributes. Optionally, it may be compared with other known concepts.
3. Provide examples and nonexamples of the concept through a variety of instructional formats. Initially, more examples than nonexamples should be used, and the examples should be simple and familiar. There should be progression to more complex and remote illustrations, with increasing use of nonexamples. With the concept symbol prominently featured, the major attributes of examples and nonexamples should be illustrated.
4. Provide students with practice in selecting and creating examples of the concept.
5. Evaluate learning by ascertaining whether students can identify examples and nonexamples, and can locate new ones.
6. Reinforce the concept periodically in repeating Step 4 above.

followed first by definition of the concept and then by distinguishing examples and nonexamples, in effect reversing the second and third steps.

Tanck provides the reader with three clear applications of each of the models to social-studies classroom instruction. In the illustration of "concept attainment" Tanck is concerned with "associating related kinds of knowledge in context,"[54] Whereas, with his "concept demon-

TABLE 7-5
CONCEPT-AUGMENTATION MODEL

Sequence of Operations

1. Identify the concept symbol, attributes and examples already known, attributes and corresponding examples yet to be learned, and the nonexamples.
2. Have students compare examples with the new attributes and with those attributes and examples already known.
3. Include the new attributes in the concept's rule.
4. Provide practice in locating and classifying examples from new materials.
5. Evaluate learning of the new attributes and more complex examples by ascertaining whether students can identify examples and nonexamples, and can locate new one.

[54] *Ibid.*, p. 117.

stration" example, he is involved with an initial explanation of facts. Finally, with the illustration of "concept augmentation," he shows how new elements may be added to one's existing cognitive structure.

Concept-Attainment Illustration[55]

Selecting the concepts of *land, labor,* and *capital,* Tanck defines their attributes and suggests some contexts. Attributes are then associated with the concept symbol. Students in studying about New England, for example, may read about lobster fishing and deep-sea fishing, and then be shown pictures dealing with these activities, while being questioned about the major attributes. For example, a teacher may show a picture of a lobster trap, indicate that it is "capital" and ask, "Is this used in the fishing industry?"

Following these activities, nonexamples such as children playing on a beach are introduced and discussed. At the conclusion of the example and nonexample presentations, the concepts are defined by listing their attributes. Tanck suggests "The teacher might simply ask students to tell what they think land, labor, or capital is or he may use a 'gimmick' like giving students cards with pairs of attributes on each and asking whether land, labor, capital, or none of these is described."[56]

Subsequently, additional exemplars and nonexemplars are presented in varied contexts such as Pennsylvania coal mining and Florida fruit production, and students are asked whether specific incidents illustrate the three concepts and why.

In the next stage, students are required, through reading, sorting data, viewing films, and the like, concerning, for example, cotton cultivation, to find new examples of land, labor, and capital. Or they may be asked to *create* examples through stories.

As a concluding step, students would be evaluated on their attainment by being asked to indicate whether a new set of pictures may be classified as either of the three concepts in question.

Concept Demonstration[57]

For this dimension of concept learning Tanck uses the illustration of the concept *culture.* He suggests the teacher initially have students read and discuss "a short written explanation" of culture. As a follow-up,

[55] *Ibid.,* pp. 118–119.
[56] *Ibid.,* p. 119.
[57] *Ibid.,* p. 121.

the students are given lists of familiar objects and are instructed to discuss why one list characterizes elements of culture while the other does not. In the "cultural" list might be artifacts such as houses, electric motors, and lawns, and in the noncultural list swamps, lightning, and sparrows.

Subsequently, more complex examples are provided in new lists, and the preceding level of discussion is repeated. These lists might be: reading, smoking, and believing in democracy versus color of the skin, amount of body hair, and digestion.

Tanck suggests that students then be asked to list ten cultural and ten noncultural phenomena in the school neighborhood, and to collect corresponding pictures. Evaluation is accomplished through an assignment whereby students are to sort given items into cultural and noncultural categories.

Reinforcement of these processes are to follow. Tanck recommends: "For example, as the students study ancient Egypt, they discuss which things influencing Egyptian life were cultural and which were natural. As they read in language arts, they sometimes discuss which portions of character's environments and behaviors were cultural and which were not."[58]

Concept Augmentation[59]

Returning to the concept *labor,* Tanck uses as his data contexts the professions of doctor, teacher, and clergyman, and the tourist industry. Augmentation of the concept revolves about the new attributes: labor is used in the production of services, and it may involve physical, mental or emotional effort.

After reading about a doctor's work, for example, students might be asked:[60]

How is the doctor like the fisherman?

How is the doctor different from the fisherman?

Is the doctor labor?

Does the doctor produce goods, as the fisherman does?

Does the doctor work more with his muscles, brains, or feelings? Related discussions could compare attributes of other professions, concluding with discussion of how students can tell if someone is an example of labor or what labor is like.

Practice follows, with students working with subclasses designated

[58] *Ibid.,*
[59] *Ibid.,* pp. 122–123.
[60] *Ibid.,* p. 122.

by different attributes of labor, or by having students collect pictures of examples of nonphysical labor. Students might be shown pictures of workers, professional people, and nonlaborers and then be asked to discriminate between the producers of goods, the producers of services, those who do physical labor, those who do mental work, those who do emotional work, and the nonproducers.

Evaluation is accomplished by two methods: for example, by describing a mother in various activities such as paying bills, soothing a crying child, and sweeping the floor and asking students to indicate whether she is and is not an example of labor. A second approach would be to read a story relating to a "community in another culture," and requesting students to list all examples of labor. "If they include persons who produce services and who do mental and emotional work, they are probably aware of the new attributes and the new types of examples."[61]

CONCLUSION

Although a variety of studies systematically relating principles of concept learning to social studies instruction do not exist, some evidence has been accumulated, and it suggests important curriculum considerations. The studies of Piaget, as interpreted and applied to the social studies by Taba, Sigel, Peel, and others, are particularly fertile sources of information. Apart from the generic models for instruction and learning considerations outlined and illustrated in earlier chapters, several additional schema for the social studies were presented.

Certainly the area of the social studies is fraught with complexity with respect to concept learning due to the nature of the concepts it embraces. "Concepts like *family* and *legislature*, of the type that make up the disciplines of the social sciences," Gagné has stated, are the most difficult of all.[62] As teachers of social studies are sensitized to this and similar realities and instructional suggestions from the literature, they should be able to improve students' learning efficiency.

SUGGESTED READINGS

Brubaker, Dale, *Alternative Directions for the Social Studies* (Scranton, Pa.: Intext Educational Publishers, 1967).

---

[61] *Ibid.,* p. 123.
[62] Robert M. Gagné, *The Conditions of Learning*, 2nd ed. (New York: Holt, Rinehart & Winston, Inc., 1970), p. 187.

A brief, basic categorization of the divergent views concerning the objectives of social studies teaching.

Crabtree, Charlotte, "Supporting Reflective Thinking in the Classroom," in Jean Fair and Fannie R. Shaftel (eds.), *Effective Thinking in the Social Studies, 37th Yearbook* (Washington, D.C.: National Council for the Social Studies, 1967).

Presents an illustration from the primary grades of how a complex concept-learning model may be applied.

Fancett, Verna S., et al., *Social Science Concepts and the Classroom* (Syracuse, N.Y.: Social Studies Curriculum Center, 1968).

A short general overview of selected literature relating to instructional precedures and issues concerning social-science concept learning.

Griffin, Alan, "A Philosophical Approach to the Subject-Matter Preparation of Teachers of History," Unpublished Ph.D. dissertation (Columbus: Ohio State University, 1942).

One of the truly seminal pieces of social-studies education literature relating to rationale, objectives, and methodology.

Hooper Frank H., "Piagetian Research and Education," in Irving E. Siegel and Frank H. Hooper (eds.), *Logical Thinking in Children* (New York: Holt, Rinehart & Winston, Inc., 1968).

Summarizes instruction-related research concerning Piaget's theories, with a special section dealing with the social studies.

Hunt, Maurice P., and Lawrence E. Metcalf, *Teaching High School Studies: Problems in Reflective Thinking and Social Understanding* (New York: Harper & Row, Publishers, 1968), Chaps. 4 and 5.

Excellent, brief discussions of the distinctions in instructional procedures for teaching concepts and for generalizations.

Martorella, Peter H., *Concept Learning in the Social Studies: Models for Structuring Curriculum* (Scranton, Pa.: Intext Educational Publishers, 1971).

An in-depth analysis of concept learning applied to the social studies.

Sigel, Irving, *Child Development and Social Science Education. Part IV: A Teaching Strategy Derived from Some Piagetian Concepts* (Lafayette, Ind.: Social Science Education Consortium, 1966).

Suggests some possible applications of selected aspects of Piaget's work.

Taba, Hilda, *Teaching Strategies and Cognitive Functioning in Elementary School Children*, Cooperative Research Project No. 2404 (Washington, D.C.: U.S. Office of Education, 1966).

This and the earlier project report presents an instructional model based upon three cognitive tasks with specific hierarchical procedures.

Tanck, Marlin L., "Teaching Concepts, Generalizations, and Constructs," in Dorothy McClure Fraser (ed.), *Social Studies Curriculum Development: Prospects and Problems, 39th Yearbook* (Washington, D.C.: National Council for the Social Studies, 1969).

Presents a three-phase model for concept learning that outlines procedures for teaching new concepts as well as augmenting old ones.

West, Edith, "Concepts, Generalizations, and Theories: Background Paper # 3," unpublished paper, Project Social Studies, University of Minnesota, no date.

Perhaps the only theoretical discussion by a major social-studies project of the distinctions between concepts and other cognitive processes, and their implications for classroom instruction.

CHAPTER 8

Measuring Concept Learning

A variety of materials already exist concerning different dimensions of evaluation, and certainly much of this applies equally well to concept learning as to other intellectual phenomena. It is not the purpose of this chapter to summarize or critique the existing evaluation literature, although several new exciting developments in the field, such as "mastery learning" well warrant the serious attention of those concerned with concept learning.[1] Rather, the intent is to provide the reader with an in-depth explanation and illustration of a schema for measuring concept learning that has been developed and tested at the Wisconsin Research and Development Center for Cognitive Learning.[2] Modified illustrations will be drawn from the Center's work in the areas of mathematics, communications arts, science, and social studies.

A SCHEMA FOR MEASURING CONCEPT LEARNING

The schema, as initially developed by Frayer, Fredrick, and Klausmeier, consisted of thirteen behaviors from which concept learning may be inferred.[3] In turn, a system for *analyzing* concepts was generated, and a modified version of it will be used for sample illustrations throughout this chapter. Finally, sample *test items* for each of the thir-

---

[1]See for example James H. Block (ed.), *Mastery Learning: Theory and Practice* (New York: Holt, Rinehart & Winston, Inc., 1971) and M. C. Wittrock and David E. Wiley (eds.), *The Evaluation of Instruction: Issues and Problems* (New York: Holt, Rinehart & Winston, Inc., 1970).

[2]Dorothy A. Frayer, Wayne C. Fredrick, and Herbert J. Klausmeier, *A Schema for Testing the Level of Concept Mastery*, Working Paper No. 16 (Madison, Wis.: Wisconsin Research and Development Center for Cognitive Learning, April 1969).

[3]*Ibid.*, p. vii.

teen dimensions of concept learning are given. Subsequent versions of the schema, as applied by the Research and Development Center investigators, have used only twelve of the items, omitting the item relating to "problem solving."[4] Consequently, this later pattern will be followed in our discussions, and *twelve* items will be used in illustrations.

The schema is applicable to all types of concepts, and reflects a logical analysis of the varied dimensions of concepts. The following type of information is required for appropriate use of the twelve test items in the schema:[5] (a) names of the attributes which make up the concept examples, and which of these are relevant and which are irrelevant to the concept, (b) examples and nonexamples of the attribute values, (c) the concept name, (d) examples and nonexamples of the concept, (e) the definition or rule of concept, (f) the names of supraordinate, coordinate, and subordinate concepts, and (g) generalizations or principles containing the concept. Both verbal and nonverbal aspects of concept learning may be tested.

Prototype Learning Tasks

The twelve prototype learning tasks in the schema are listed below.[6] These comprise the *nonverbal* mode for measuring learning.

1. Given the name of an attribute value, the student can select the example of the attribute value.
2. Given an example of an attribute value, the student can select the name of the attribute value.
3. Given the name of a concept, the student can select the example of the concept.
4. Given the name of a concept, the student can select the nonexample of the concept.
5. Given an example of a concept, the student can select the name of the concept.
6. Given the name of a concept, the student can select the names of the relevant attribute values of the concept.
7. Given the name of a concept, the student can select the names of the irrelevant attributes of the concept.
8. Given the definition of a concept, the student can select the name for the concept.
9. Given the name of a concept, the student can select the correct definition of the concept.

[4]See for example the papers relating to science and the social sciences discussed later in this chapter.
[5]Frayer, Fredrick, and Klausmeier, *op. cit.*, p. 10.
[6]*Ibid.*, pp. 13–21.

10. Given the name of a concept, the student can select the name of a concept supraordinate to it.
11. Given the name of a concept, the student can select the name of a concept subordinate to it.
12. Given the name of two concepts, the student can select the principle which relates them.

The alternative mode for measuring dimensions of concept learning requires students to *verbalize* or construct responses, as the prototypes below indicate.[7]

1. Given the name of an attribute value, the student can supply an example of the attribute value.
2. Given examples of an attribute value, the student can supply the name of the attribute value.
3. Given the name of a concept, the student can supply an example of the concept.
4. Given the name of a concept, the student can supply a nonexample of the concept.
5. Given an example of a concept, the student can supply the name of the concept.
6. Given the name of a concept, the student can supply the names of the relevant attribute values of the concept.
7. Given the name of a concept, the student can supply the names of the irrelevant attributes of the concept.
8. Given the definition of a concept, the student can supply the name of the concept.
9. Given the name of a concept, the student can supply the correct definition of the concept.
10. Given the name of a concept and a concept coordinate to it, the student can supply the supraordinate concept to which they belong.
11. Given the name of a concept, the student can supply the name of a concept subordinate to it.
12. Given the name of two concepts, the student can supply the principle which relates them.

ANALYZING AND MEASURING THE LEARNING OF MATHEMATICAL CONCEPTS[8]

A sample concept from the field of mathematics is included to illustrate application of the schema. The concept *quadrilateral* will first

[7] *Ibid.*, pp. 23–27.
[8] *Ibid.*, pp. 12–16.

be analyzed, and then measurement items for each of the twelve prototype learning tasks will be presented in a nonverbal mode.

Concept Analysis

Concept label: *quadrilateral*
Criterial attributes: closed figure, plane figure, simple figure, 4 sides
   (4 angles).
Irrelevant attributes: relative length of sides, relative size of angles,
   parallelness of sides, size of figure, orientation of figure.
Concept Examples:

Concept Nonexamples:

Concept definition: A plane closed figure with 4 sides.
Supraordinate concept(s): *polygon.*
Coordinate concept(s): *triangle, pentagon, hexagon.*
Subordinate concept(s): *trapezoid, kite, parallelogram, rectangle,
   rhombus, square.*
Principle: The perimeter is the distance around a quadrilateral.

Sample Items

1. Which drawing is a *closed* figure?

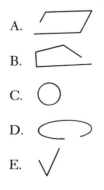

2. 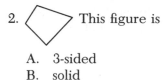 This figure is

    A. 3-sided
    B. solid
    C. closed
    D. open
    E. parallel-sided

3. Which figure is a quadrilateral?

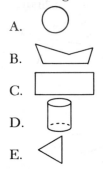

    A.
    B.
    C.
    D.
    E.

4. Which figure is *not* a quadrilateral?

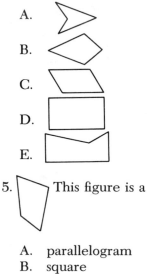

    A.
    B.
    C.
    D.
    E.

5. This figure is a

    A. parallelogram
    B. square
    C. rhombus
    D. quadrilateral
    E. rectangle

6. *All* quadrilaterals have
   A. 4 sides
   B. all sides equal
   C. 2 sides equal
   D. 5 sides
   E. opposite sides parallel

7. Not all quadrilaterals have
   A. 4 right angles
   B. 4 sides
   C. closed sides
   D. straight sides
   E. 4 angles

8. All plane closed figures with 4 sides may be called
   A. rhombuses
   B. trapezoids
   C. rectangles
   D. quadrilaterals
   E. squares

9. *All* quadrilaterals are
   A. plane closed 4-sided figures
   B. plane closed 3-sided figures
   C. plane open 4-sided figures
   D. plane closed 4-sided figures with opposite sides equal
   E. plane closed 4-sided figures with no sides equal

10. All quadrilaterals are also
    A. rhombuses
    B. kites
    C. triangles
    D. trapezoids
    E. polygons

11. Which is true?
    A. All hexagons are also quadrilaterals.
    B. All trapezoids are also quadrilaterals.
    C. All circles are also quadrilaterals.
    D. All triangles are also quadrilaterals.
    E. All pentagons are also quadrilaterals.

12. Which heavy line shows the perimeter of a quadrilateral?

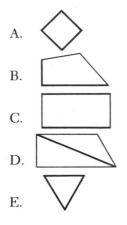

A.

B.

C.

D.

E.

ANALYZING AND MEASURING THE LEARNING OF COMMUNICATION ARTS CONCEPTS[9]

In this illustration, the concept *noun phrase* is analyzed, and then sample measurement items are presented—this time in a *verbal* mode to indicate the similarities with the alternative mode.

Concept Analysis

Concept label: *noun phrase*

Criterial attributes: noun phrase position, noun, noun marker.

Irrelevant attributes: meaning, gender, adverb, verb.

Concept examples: *seven men, he, all the gold, only the lonely, our aunt.*

Concept nonexamples: *have been slowly declining, going to go, happy.*

Concept definition: A word or group of words appearing in any one of five positions in a kernel sentence and which consists of a noun in the last slot and any noun markers preceding it [or in short-hand, NP = (NM) + N].

Supraordinate concept(s): *sentence, sentence constituent.*

Coordinate concept(s): *verb phrase, subject group.*

Subordinate concept(s): *noun phrase completer, noun, noun marker subject group.*

[9] *Ibid.*, pp. 17–21.

Principles: The subject group of a kernel sentence is a noun phrase. The noun phrase following such prepositions as *to, in, over,* etc., is the object of the preposition.

Sample Items

1. Write a word that is usually a noun marker.
2. What term describes the underlined words? In <u>the</u> garden, <u>several</u> men picked <u>some</u> flowers.
3. Write a noun phrase.
4. Complete this sentence without using a noun phrase. "The sheriff is _____ ."
5. What is the underlined portion of <u>this sentence</u> called?
6. A noun phrase consists of _____ and_____ .
7. Which types of words are *not* present in a noun phrase?
8. A group of words consisting of a noun marker followed by a noun would be called _____ .
9. What is the meaning of *noun phrase?*
10. A noun phrase and a verb phrase are the two necessary parts of a _____ .
11. Name one sentence position that a noun phrase can fill.
12. What is the relationship between a noun phrase and a subject group?

ANALYZING AND MEASURING THE LEARNING OF SCIENCE CONCEPTS[10]

The concept *mammal,* discussed earlier in Chapter 6, is presented. Its sample items will be presented in the nonverbal mode.

Concept Analysis

Concept label: *mammal*
Criterial attributes: Mammals
1. Feed their young on mother's milk.
2. Have hair.
3. Are warm-blooded.

[10]A. M. Voelker and J.S. Sorenson, *Items for Measuring the Level of Attainment of Selected Classificatory Science Concepts by Intermediate Grade Children,* Working Paper No. 58 (Madison, Wis.: Wisconsin Research and Development Center for Cognitive Learning, 1970).

Irrelevant attributes: include
1. Color: black, brown, yellow, etc.
2. Pattern of coat: plain, striped, spotted.
3. Habitat: lives on land, water.
4. Eating habits: eats other animals, eats plants.
Concept examples: *cow, dog, cat, pig, goat.*
Concept nonexamples: *chicken, duck, toad, bird, fish.*
Concept definition: A warm-blooded animal that has hair and feeds
its young on the mother's milk.
Supraordinate concept(s): *vertebrate, animal.*
Coordinate concept(s): *fish, reptiles, birds, amphibians.*
Subordinate concept(s): *dog, cat, squirrel, lion, rabbit.*
Principle: Mammals use lungs for breathing.

Sample Items

1. Which picture shows the young feeding on the mother's milk?

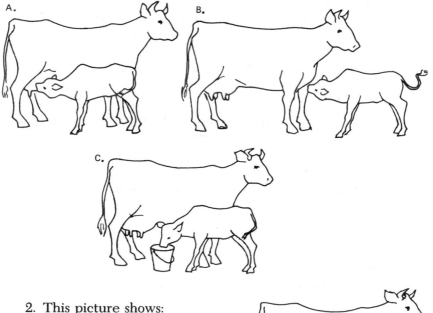

2. This picture shows:
   A. The young feeding on the
      mother's milk.
   B. The young feeding on
      grass.
   C. The young cleaning the
      mother's hair.

3. Which of these is a mammal?

A.

B.

C.

D.

4. Which of these is *not* a mammal?

A.

B.

C.

D.

5. The picture shows:
   A. A reptile
   B. A mammal
   C. A fish
   D. An amphibian

6. What is true for *all* mammals?
   A. They live in warm places.

   B. They have a spotted coat.
   C. They feed their young on the mother's milk.
 7. Which is *not* true for all mammals?
   A. They feed the young on the mother's milk.
   B. They are warm-blooded.
   C. They have hair.
   D. They are brown in color.
 8. An animal which feeds its young on the mother's milk and is
    warm-blooded is called a
   A. Mammal
   B. Bird
   C. Reptile
   D. Fish
 9. A mammal is an animal that
   A. Is cold-blooded and lays eggs.
   B. Is warm-blooded and feeds its young on the mother's
      milk.
   C. Is warm-blooded and has feathers.
   D. Has a body the same temperature as the air around it.
10. *All* mammals are kinds of
   A. Reptiles
   B. Plants
   C. Vertebrates
   D. Fish
11. Which of these is a kind of mammal?
   A. Chicken
   B. Frog
   C. Fish
   D. Dog
12. Which is true about mammals and lungs?
   A. Mammals use lungs for picking up sounds.
   B. Lungs are usually found on the mammals' legs.
   C. Mammals use lungs for breathing.
   D. Lungs are the digestive organs of mammals.

ANALYZING AND MEASURING THE LEARNING OF
SOCIAL-SCIENCE CONCEPTS

The social-science concept *organization* is used in this example. A
nonverbal mode is required for the sample items.

Concept Analysis[11]

Concept label: *organization*
Criterial attributes: An organization
1. Is made of a group of two or more people.
2. Has accepted rules—often a leader or officer(s).
3. Has members who cooperate with one another on a common problem or purpose.

Irrelevant attributes: include
1. particular problem or interest of the group.
2. age, sex, race, etc., of the members or leaders.

Concept examples: *Girl scout troop, the United Nations, the school safety patrol, the baseball team in your neighborhood, the Fishing and Hunting Club.*

Concept nonexamples: *all the people driving down Pine Street, the President of the United States, the children playing at the beach, the children at the zoo.*

Concept definition: a group of people with accepted rules who do things together because they have the same interests or problems.

Supraordinate concept(s): *group*
Coordinate concept(s): *institution*
Subordinate concept(s): *club, team, troop, pack*
Principle: Families are organizations to take care of basic needs.

Sample Items[12]

1. Which of these is a group?
   A. The tallest child in your class
   B. Your best friend
   C. The children on the swing set at the park
   D. The principal of your school
2. The children on the swing set at the park make up
   A. A person
   B. A group
   C. An organization

[11]B. Robert Tabachnick, Evelyn B. Weible, and Dorothy A. Frayer, *Selection and Analysis of Social Studies Concepts for Inclusion in Tests of Concept Attainment*, Working Paper No. 53 (Madison, Wis.: Wisconsin Research and Development Center for Cognitive Learning, November, 1970), pp. 92–93.

[12]B. Robert Tabachnick, Evelyn B. Weible, and Diane Livermore, *Items to Test Level of Attainment of Social Studies Concepts by Intermediate Grade Children*, Working Paper No. 54 (Madison, Wis.: Wisconsin Research and Development Center for Cognitive Learning, November, 1970), pp. 57–58.

3. Which of these is an organization?
   A. All the people driving down Pine Street
   B. A Girl Scout troop
   C. The President of the United States
   D. The children playing at the beach
4. Which of these is *not* an organization?
   A. The baseball team in your neighborhood
   B. The United Nations
   C. The children at the zoo
   D. The school safety patrol
5. The Fishing and Hunting Club is
   A. A country area
   B. A company
   C. A government
   D. An organization
6. Which is true about *all* organizations?
   A. They have rules and they often have a leader.
   B. They must have at least ten members.
   C. The leader is always the oldest member.
7. Which is *not* always true about an organization?
   A. The members of an organization are all the same age.
   B. The members of an organization have the same problems or interests.
   C. There is more than one member of an organization.
8. A group of people who do things together because they have the same interests or problems is
   A. A city
   B. The people walking past a movie theater
   C. An organization
   D. A baseball player
9. An organization is
   A. A group of children who have no cavities
   B. A group of people who drive down the same street because their houses are on that street
   C. A group of people who work together because they have the same interests or problems
   D. A group of people who vote for the same man for president
10. An organization is a kind of
    A. Country
    B. Person
    C. Group
    D. Building

11. Which of the following may be one kind of organization?
   A. A team
   B. A grove
   C. A park
   D. A president
12. What is true about organizations and families?
   A. One person in a family makes an organization within the family.
   B. A group of people in an organization make a family.
   C. Families are organizations to take care of basic needs.
   D. Families are not an organization if they live in the wilderness.

CONCLUSION

A schema for developing measurement items for concepts in any subject matter area allows one to analyze different dimensions of learning. Apart from determining whether a learner can simply discriminate examples of a given concept from nonexamples, the schema provides measures of attribute knowledge, rule identification, and relationships to other concepts.

The prototype and the sample items provided may be expanded or applied selectively, as the schema authors have noted.[13]

> For example, items of Type 1 and 2 may be written for all attributes of a concept. Several items of Types 3 and 4 may be written, contrasting examples of the concept with nonexamples differing in the number of relevant attributes which they lack. . . .
> This schema can be used to test in detail the student's ability to discriminate between examples and nonexamples of the concept. By presenting the student with an array of instances (both examples and nonexamples) and having him check those which are examples, one could detect incomplete concepts (some examples not checked) and overgeneralization (nonexamples checked). This approach would be equivalent in combining Item Types 3 and 4.
> Item types may be omitted when they are not of interest to the test constructor, or when the appropriate information does not exist, or is unavailable. . . .
> Some concepts are not defined in terms of relevant attributes, but rather semantically, operationally, or axiomatically. In these cases, Item Types 6 and 7 are not appropriate, and modifications are necessary. For example, when a concept is defined semantically, the student

[13]Frayer, Fredrick, and Klausmeier, op. cit., pp. 29–30.

may be required to select or produce a synonym and antonym, given the concept name (e.g., *beautiful:* synonym, *pretty:* antonym, *ugly*). When a concept is defined axiomatically, the student may be requested to name the components which are related to form the concept (e.g., *mass:* components, *force* and *acceleration*). In the case of operationally defined concepts, no obvious parallel exists, and Item Types 6 and 7 may be omitted.

Measures, such as those provided in the chapter, may be used either as pretests or posttests; that is, the teacher may wish to diagnose existing conceptual states of a class *prior* to an instructional sequence to determine what type of instruction is required, or to evaluate whether desired mastery has been acquired *as the result of* instruction. In either case, the schema should prove to be useful for classroom instruction.

SUGGESTED READINGS

Block, James H. (ed.), *Mastery Learning: Theory and Practice* (New York: Holt, Rinehart & Winston, Inc., 1971).

A collection of six papers dealing with different dimensions of mastery learning. Also included is a series of abstracts of studies dealing with the same topic.

Frayer, Dorothy A., Wayne C. Fredrick, and Herbert J. Klausmeier, *A Schema for Testing the Level of Concept Mastery*, Working Paper No. 16 (Madison, Wis.: Wisconsin Research and Development Center for Cognitive Learning, April, 1969).

Presents a logical system for analyzing and measuring all types of concepts from all subject-matter areas.

Wittrock, M.C., and David E. Wiley (eds.), *The Evaluation of Instruction: Issues and Problems* (New York: Holt, Rinehart & Winston, Inc., 1970).

Includes the proceedings of a symposium concerned with issues related to the evaluation of instruction. Discussions center primarily on theoretical aspects of evaluation.

Peter H. Martorella and Rosalie S. Jensen

CHAPTER 9

Concept-Learning Exercises for Teachers and Students

At this point the reader may find it useful to engage in some exercises relating to various dimensions of concept learning. Through actual involvement in some of the processes associated with concept learning, it may be possible to use more readily the meaning and significance of the conclusions reported in earlier chapters and to apply them better to the design of instructional strategies.

The exercises are designed to acquaint the reader with some of the dimensions involved in preparing students for a concept-learning task, and further, to sensitize him to some of the potential difficulties that students may encounter in learning concepts. In the exercises, opportunities are provided for the analysis of one's own behavior specimens, and for the determination of progress.

Six general concerns related to concept learning will be treated in the first sequence of exercises: (a) what it is like to learn a new concept, (b) how to informally diagnose pupils concept states, (c) making inferences, as contrasted with (d) drawing conclusions, (e) illustrating a concept "at work," and (f) systematically examining the effects of instruction. Following these general exercises, six exercises, all relating to mathematics instruction, are provided. These latter exercises might most profitably be considered in conjunction with Chapter 4.

It is suggested that the reader follow these steps in completing each exercise: (1) perform the exercise, (2) analyze the cognitive and affective processes that were taking place during the exercise, (3) analyze the objectives of the exercise, (4) draw conclusions concerning the general value of the exercise and its applicability to concept learning instruction, and (5) where applicable, consult the Appendix for answers and related comments.

THE LEARNER'S PERSPECTIVE

This exercise is designed to put the reader "in the skin" of a student who is learning a concept anew. Since it may be fairly safely assumed (as the reader will see) that the prerequisite learnings have already been acquired, the reader is "prepared" for instruction. And since the concept is "new" *(having just been created)*, the reader could not have learned it prior to this instructional experience. What follows then should not only be an experience in empathizing with a student in a concept-learning situation, but also a *test* of the effectiveness of the instructional model used. Consider both of these dimensions as you proceed through the exercise and then analyze your observations.

Learning a Concept of Blarp

You are about to encounter a concept that you have never learned before; its name is "blarp." Please pay close attention, because at the end of my instruction, you will be given a test.

Look closely at Fig. 9-1; it is a blarp.

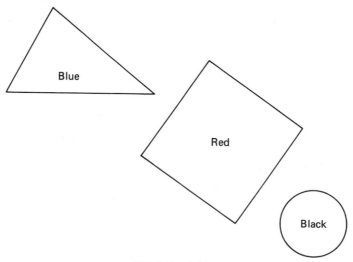

Fig. 9–1. A blarp.

Figure 9-2 is also a blarp.

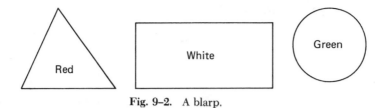

Fig. 9–2. A blarp.

But Fig. 9-3 is *not* a blarp. And Fig. 9-4 is *not* a blarp.

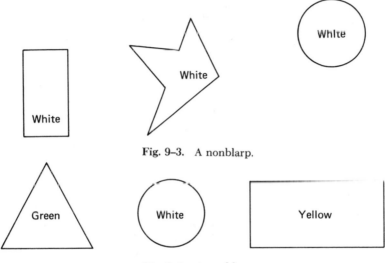

Fig. 9–3. A nonblarp.

Fig. 9–4. A nonblarp.

Figure 9-5, however, *is* a blarp. Compare Fig. 9-5 with Fig. 9-4, which is *not* a blarp.

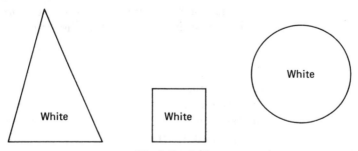

Fig. 9–5. A blarp.

Are you ready for a test? If not, reexamine the exemplars in Figs. 9-1–9-5. For your first test, you are asked to examine the four illustrations in Fig. 9-6, and to identify any instances of blarp.

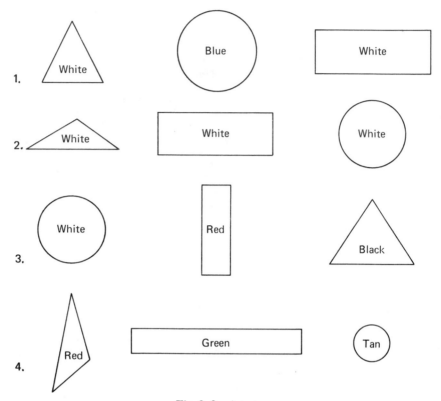

Fig. 9–6. A test.

Check the Appendix to see if you were correct. If not, repeat your examination of Figs. 9-1–9-5, and the corresponding instructions. As a second test, state the *definition* or *rule* of blarp in your own words, and then compare your conclusion with the answer in the Appendix.

Discussion

As the reader may have realized by now, learning the concept of blarp requires one to classify old knowledge (prerequisite learning) in a new way. Also, if he has examined the instructional sequence carefully (or did not learn the concept!), he will notice that it has some shortcomings. Or, put more specifically, addition of more illustrations and/or instructions could have kept the learner from attending to irrelevant attributes such as *color* or *shape*. Without such additional instructions, some students invariably will acquire an erroneous concept of blarp or a *misconception*.

DIAGNOSING PUPIL CONCEPT STATES

In the earlier discussion of the Taba cognitive tasks, it was suggested that the first task, concept formation, was essentially a *diagnostic* strategy to determine what students already knew about a given concept. The game that is described below performs a similar function for classes of any age. It is called "Would You Like to Be . . . ," and there is no limit to the number that can play, nor to the type of concepts that may be used. There are no "winners" or "losers" as such, but one may be considered successful if he is able to respond and unsuccessful if he fails to answer. If played with a group, one member acts as a leader and asks each person in turn the questions. When the game is played by only one person, he answers all the questions. In either event, the game proceeds until the questions are exhausted. Analysis then follows.

Game Rules

1. You may not respond to questions with just a "Yes" or "No."
2. In responding, your answer must be in the form "(Yes) (No), I (would) (would not) like to be _____."
3. You may *not* complete your response by using the same word(s) as the one(s) used in the questions.
4. Questions must be in the form "Would you like to be (a) (an) _____?"

Example: "Would you like to be a carrot?"
Answer: "No, I would not like to be a vegetable."

Discussion

This game was devised by a three-year-old, and has been used with groups ranging from preschool children to graduate students. A list of sample items that the reader may wish to use with his *peers* to try out the same is provided below. This list has been found to be effective in discussions with adults, although any comparable list may be used. Lists, however, should include *concrete* and *abstract* items.
Sample Questions. "Would you like to be (a) (an) _____?"

(banana, dog, car, chair, suit, hammer, door, triangle, river, television set, house, forest, sentence, soldier, enemy, army, atom, economy, colony, government, nation, century, theory).

Transcript of a Game Session. To illustrate how this game may reveal some of the students' problems in categorizing basic concepts, a short extract from an unedited preschool classroom transcript is included. Several of the youngsters in the class are unable to classify phenomena that are common to them. In this session the teacher does not know the students' names, and the group is playing the game for the first time. The transcript picks up after the children have been briefed on "taking turns" and are listening, while waiting for their turn. As the dialogue begins, the teacher is explaining the rules, after which each of the class in turn is given an item for a response.

Teacher   Here's how the game goes. It's called "Would you like to be . . ." and it's a pretend game, where I ask you if you would like to be something, and then you have to tell me, "Yes, I would like to be . . . ," or "No, I would not like to be . . ." That's easy, isn't it? "Yes, I would like to be . . ." or "No, I would not like to be. . . ." Now there is one other rule, because all games have rules. There are certain things that you can do and certain things that you can't do in games. You have to answer with a different word than the one that I give you. Let me give you an example. Let me show you how the game is played. OK? Suppose I said, "Would you like to be a carrot?"

Class   *(laughter)* I would like to be a carrot.

T   OK, then you would answer, "Yes, I would like to be a _____ " but you can't say the same word, you can't say "carrot." So, you would have to say something like this, "Yes, I would like to be a vegetable."

Class   *(laughter and talking)*

T   Let me try one more example; let me show you one more, and I'll start to ask each one of you, "Would you like to be . . ." Everybody is going to get asked. Would you like to be a pencil?

Class   Ummm.

T   Umm. Yes, and what could you say?

Student   Yes, I want to be a . . .

T   You can't say "pencil," can you?

S   . . . a piece of paper.

T   Oh, but a pencil isn't a piece of paper, is it? It has to be the same thing, only a different word. What would you say?

S   I would like to be a piece of wood.

T   OK, yes, "I would like to be a piece of wood." Well, a pencil is a piece of wood, isn't it—with lead down the middle? Or you could say, "Yes, I would like to be something that you write with." That's right, too, isn't it?

Class   *(nods and verbal agreements)*

T   Very good, now you all know how to play the game. That's fine; you are doing very well, because lots of times it's very hard to learn the rules to a game. Let's hurry now and get on with the game. Remember, too, not to tell anyone the answer. Let them try and figure it out themselves. OK, we'll start with the first one. Would you like to be a banana?

S   No, I would not like to be a fruit.

T   Very good. Would you like to be a flower?

S   Uh, uh, no, I would not like to be a plant.

T   Very good. Would you like to be a chair?

S   No, I would not like to be a sitting thing.

T   "No, I would not like to be something that you sit in or a sitting thing." Very good. Would you like to be a sock?

S   No, I would not like to be something that you wear.

T   "Something that you wear." Would you like to be a hamburger?

Class   (laughter)

S   No, I would not like to be something that you eat.

T   "Something that you eat." Would you like to be a rug?

S   No, I would not.

T   . . . like to be . . .

S   . . . walked on.

T   "Something that you walk on." Very good. Would you like to be a television set?

S   No, I would not like to be a television.

T   Oh, you can't say the same word, remember?

S   Oh, I forgot.

T   No, you would not like to be . . .

S   *(no response)*

T   Let me ask you the question again, while you are thinking. Would you like to be a television set? That's a hard one.

S   I don't know.

T   OK, how about if we go on to someone else, and then we will come back and ask you another one?

S   OK.

T   Would you like to be a dog?

S   *(long pause)*

T   Think it would be fun to be a dog? *(pause)* What kind of things are dogs? *(pause)* What is another name for a dog?

Class   (Students are whispering to one another, and saying aloud, "I know.")

T   Where do you sometimes buy dogs?

S   Store.

T   What kind of store? A special kind of store, isn't it?

S   *(long pause)*

T   Well, it could be a pet store. So, you might like to be a pet.

S   Yah, I would like to be a pet.

T   That's another name for a dog, isn't it—a pet. OK, let's see if the rest of these boys and girls have been thinking about being a television set. Who shall I ask first? Would you like to be a television set?

S   *(no answer)*

T   Let's ask somebody else, and then we'll come back and give you another one.

T   Would you like to be a television set?

S   Yes, I would like to be something that you watch.

T   Very good. Let's come back to these two people and give them another turn before we move on. Would you like to be an orange?

S   No, I would not like to be a vegetable.

T   Well, an orange is not a vegetable, it's a fruit. But that's pretty close. Would you like to be a celery stick?

S   I would like to be a flower.

T   But a celery stick is not a flower. It has to be the same thing as celery.

S   *(no answer)*

T   Let's try another one. Would you like to be a ball?

S   No . . .

T   What is a ball? *(pause)* What do you do with balls?

S   You play with them.

T   OK, you would not like to be something that you play with. Now we have a new one. This is going to be a hard one. Remember to listen, class, and try to answer to yourself quietly—to yourself. Would you like to be a cup?

S   Yes, I would like to be something that you drink out of.

T   You would like to be something that you drink out of. OK. Would you like to be a refrigerator?

S   *(no answer)*

T   We'll give you another one. Would you like to be a table?

Class   *(laughter)*

T   Remember to say, "Yes, I would . . ." or "No, I would not. . . ."

S   *(no answer)*

T   OK, you think about table, and we will come back and ask you about table again. Would you like to be a refrigerator?

S   No, I would not like to be something that you freeze in.

T   She would not like to be something that you freeze in. Very good. Would you like to be a book?

S   Yes, I would like to be something that you read.

T   Fine. Would you like to be teeth?

S   Yes . . .

T   Yes, you would like to be. . . . Remember you have to use a different word.

S   No . . . *(long pause)*

T   OK, we will try another one. Would you like to be an apple?

S   No, I would not like to be an apple.

S   No, you can't say the same word. What do you call apples and bananas?

S   *(no answer)*

T   We will come back later then, and give you another turn. Let's ask somebody over here. Would you like to be teeth?

S   Yes, I would like to be something that's in your mouth.

T   That's right, isn't it. Teeth are in your mouth. Would you like to be an ant?

S   No, I would not like to be something that bites you.

T Ants do sometimes bite, don't they? Would you like to be a rock?

S No, I would not like to be something that you throw.

T OK, you boys and girls play the game very well. Let's come back to you now. Do you think you have an answer for "table," or do you want to try another one?

S Another one.

T Would you like to be . . . ah, water?

S No, I would not like to be drinked.

T Something that you drink. That's very good. You do drink water. Would you like to be . . . oh, let's see, would you like to be a sweater?

S Yes, I would like to be something that you wear.

T Would you like to be a light?

S No, I would not like to be something that you use to see with.

T Girls, can we have your attention for just a little while longer? Fine. Would you like to be a grandfather?

S No, I would not like to be someone who smokes.

T "Someone who smokes." I'll bet you have a grandfather who smokes. Would you like to be a plant? (*to another student*)

S No, I would not like to be something what you grow.

AN INFERENCE EXERCISE

The ability to generate an inference involves going beyond data immediately present in a situation to draw a conclusion that appears likely. For example, I look at the sky and observe dark clouds, from which I conclude that it will rain. A classical illustration of inference is Sherlock Holmes, who consistently goes well beyond the data at his disposal to draw "elementary" conclusions, much to the amazement of his colleague, Dr. Watson.

In concept learning, inferences play a key role in allowing a person to establish a class identity for a set of observed attributes and then to draw additional, tentative conclusions about these properties. The sample exercise that follows is taken from a classroom session. After having engaged in a case study of a primitive society, students were asked to develop a profile of an imaginary society of their own choosing. They were to (a) give the society a name and (b) state some salient facts (about fifteen or twenty) about the society, which might include such things as general customs or artifacts. The students were also told that when they completed their assignment, several papers would be selected, dittoed and distributed to the class without identification of the author. In using the class members' lists, each bit of evidence was examined analytically with the question in mind, "What else does the information tell you about the society?" A sample of portions of one student's list is provided below.

Examine each item separately, and respond to the same question that the students were given. Use only *one* item at a time.

The Oboas

1. They eat mainly shrimp and fried potatoes.
2. Their education is mainly at home except their music and art.
3. Most of them go barefooted.
4. The husband and wife share household duties.
5. They have a language of 1,000 words.

Discussion

It is important to note that this is an *inference* exercise, since *none* of the hypotheses generated could actually be verified or tested. The plausibility of inferences, of course, may be analyzed, by relating the imaginary material to analogous reality. In essence, exercises of this type provide students with practice in going beyond literal observations.

LOGICAL RELATIONSHIPS

Whereas *inferences* suggest a likely conclusion, *implications* order a necessary conclusion. Black clouds *suggest* rain, but rain, in turn, *assures* wetness. A basic element in accurate and sophisticated categorization, as well as logical analysis, is the ability to appreciate and identify this nuance.

A quiz, containing nine simple arguments, allows the reader to focus on a statement in a relatively straightforward, syllogistic form. In "real life" oral and written arguments, of course, seldom appear in this simplistic form. By presenting the arguments in the manner of a basic quiz, however, the intent is to allow the reader to focus more clearly upon the structural relationship of the statement units.

Directions

Read over each of the following purported arguments and decide whether one who accepts its premises must *accept* its conclusion. That is, whether the conclusion is an *implication* of the premise. If your answer to this question is "yes," write "valid" on a separate answer sheet next to the number corresponding to the question. If your answer is "no," write "invalid."

Once you have completed the quiz, return to each question and analyze the categorical relationship among the items within each unit.

Quiz

1. Only a clever lawyer could have won an acquittal in this case. Mr. A won an acquittal in this case. Mr. A is therefore a clever lawyer.
2. This must be my cigarette; for all my cigarettes are on this table, and this cigarette is on this table.
3. All citizens are interested in political matters affecting the nation. All workers are citizens and therefore are interested in political matters affecting the nation.
4. All true humanitarians believe in the brotherhood of all men. All true Christians believe in the brotherhood of all men. Therefore, all true Christians are true humanitarians.
5. All machines are man-made. This automobile is man-made. It is therefore a machine.
6. Some communists are idealists. No idealists believe in the materialism of Karl Marx. Therefore, some communists do not believe in the materialism of Karl Marx.
7. All poisonous things are bitter. Potassium cyanide is not bitter. Therefore, potassium cyanide is not a poison.
8. All artists appeal to our emotions. All propagandists appeal to our emotions. All propananandists, therefore are artists.
9. Most Americans speak of the United States as Anglo-Saxon and Protestant country. Most Americans are neither Anglo-Saxon nor Protestant. Therefore, some persons who are neither Anglo-Saxon nor Protestant speak of the United States as an Anglo-Saxon and Protestant country.

Discussion

Answers to the quiz may be compared to those provided in the Appendix. Additionally, the categorical relationships among the statements are indicated through a series of circle diagrams.

It is recommended that those who feel they require more work in this area of logic consult a fundamental reference source.[1]

A CONCEPTUAL NETWORK

In Chapter 1 a concept was defined as a continuum of inferences by which a set of observed characteristics of an object or event suggests

[1]For example, Robert H. Ennis, *Logic in Teaching* (Englewood Cliffs, N.J.: Prentice-Hall, Inc., 1969).

a class identity, and then additional inferences about other unobserved characteristics of the object or event. The notion of concept as sequential inferential chains was further illustrated by Gaston Viaud's schematic relating to the observed properties "solid-head-at-right-angles-to-handle," as shown in Fig. 9–7.

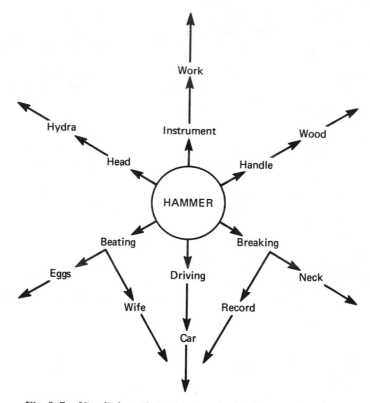

Fig. 9–7. Viaud's hypothetical network of inferences. An object or event is categorized as "hammer." This process generates an inference network with "hammer" having the rule "an instrument for beating, breaking, driving nails, etc., with a solid head at right angles to its handle." (Source: Gatson Viaud, *Intelligence: Its Evolution and Form*, E. J. Pomerans, trans., New York: Harper, 1960, p. 76.)

The reader now is asked to reflect upon his own conceptual network set in motion by an act of categorization. Consider the object in

Fig. 9–8, and then create a schematic similar to Viaud's model of *your* immediate chain of inferences. Take no more than three minutes and then compare your results with those of others.

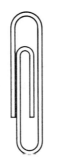

Fig. 9–8.   An object.

Discussion

In what ways was your schematic *similar* to those of others? In what ways was it *different*? What accounts for the similarities and differences in the various inferential chains? Questions such as these might be considered in the analysis, as well as some discussion of how the schematic generated by the *concrete* object in Fig. 9–8 might differ from that produced by an *abstract* event. Any object or event may be substituted for the item given.

SYSTEMATICALLY EXAMINING THE EFFECTS OF INSTRUCTION

This exercise takes the form of an experimental research study to measure the extent to which a given population of students have mastered a given concept. Experimental research is that which applies a true experimental research design to a setting in which carefully prescribed and manipulated conditions are operative.[2] Its value is that it affords a teacher some reasonably well-regulated measures of the effect of an instructional sequence. With this approach a teacher need not interrupt her usual teaching procedures to any great extent, and she is better able to make supportable generalizations concerning the impact of her teaching procedures under usual operating conditions.

Although experimental research is not a common occurrence among classroom teachers, the project recommended herein should be

[2]See the discussion in Donald T. Campbell and Julian C. Stanley, "Experimental and Quasi-Experimental Designs for Research on Teaching," in N.L. Gage (ed.), *Handbook of Research on Teaching* (Chicago: Rand McNally & Company, Inc., 1963), pp. 171–246.

within the capabilities of neophyte researchers.[3] Its design is basic but rigorous and only fundamental statistical procedures are required to generate the conclusions.

Design and Procedures

This design is referred to as "The Post-test Only Control Group Design."[4] It involves assigning one's total population of students (N) to two groups by randomized selection procedures. This process provides the greatest assurance that the two groups initially are basically equal in their potential ability to learn a given concept. The group designated as the experimental group may then be assigned the treatment (concept-learning instruction), while the remainder of the population (control group) receives alternate or no instruction. Both groups are then measured as to their level of concept mastery by some criterion measures immediately upon completion of the experiment.

The degree of difference between the measures may be evaluated by a simple t test[5] to determine if the experimental group has performed significantly better than the control group. One's hypothesis is that indeed there *will* be a significant difference in favor of the population receiving the favored instruction, and by recasting this assumption in the form of the null hypothesis: "There will be no significant difference between the two groups with respect to scores on a concept-mastery test," one is able to reject or accept the notion through basic statistical means.

Discussion

While this project is limited in its scope, it provides at least a basic index of the degree of success a teacher is having in concept teaching. It also suggests a means by which a teacher may compare various strategies for teaching concepts, since the instructional treatment may take any form or format that the teacher wishes. Similarly, a criterion measure of mastery might take a variety of forms, either those suggested in Chapter 8 or ones of the teacher's making.

One may regard an individual class or a series of classes as his total population. An elementary teacher might wish to make her self-contained class the N, whereas a secondary teacher might use his entire five classes in the total population.

---

[3]For additional assistance, consult a basic educational research text such as Gilbert Sax, *Empirical Foundations of Educational Research* (Englewood Cliffs, N.J.: Prentice-Hall, Inc., 1968).
[4]Campbell and Stanley, *op. cit.*, p. 195.
[5]*Ibid.*, p. 196.

One of the more critical considerations in this exercise is that of time. The sooner that the instructional process can be completed after its initiation and the sooner that the criterion measure can be administered after the completion of instruction, the less likely is the experiment to be invalidated by extraneous variables.

EXERCISES RELATED TO MATHEMATICS INSTRUCTION

Answers for the following sections, where required, will be found in the Appendix.

Developing the Concepts of Prime Number, Composite Number, and Unit Intuitively

The following set of exercises is adapted from Jerome Bruner's example about a boy playing with shells. A different criterion than Bruner's, however, will be developed for determining whether a number is prime.

Materials. Twenty-five small objects of uniform size. (*Suggestions:* small squares of paper, wooden or ceramic tiles, dried beans, or bottle caps.)

Objective. To develop the concepts of prime number, composite number, and unit on an intuitive level.

Procedures

1. Consider the following example. We wish to arrange small objects in rectangular patterns. We obtain the following patterns:

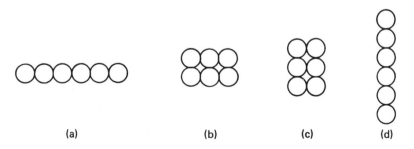

(a)   (b)   (c)   (d)

Each rectangular pattern has a certain number of rows and a certain number of columns. In (a) there is 1 row and 6 columns, in (b) there are 2 rows and 3 columns, in (c) there are 3 rows and 2 columns, and in (d) there are 6 rows and 1 column. Each of the rectangular patterns embodies a "multiplication fact" involving a product of 6. The representations are: (a) $1 \times 6 = 6$; (b) $2 \times 3 = 6$; (c) $3 \times 2 = 6$; (d) $6 \times 1 = 6$.

2. Now that you have seen an example, try this exercise:
   (a) Determine all rectangular patterns for 8 objects.
   (b) The "multiplication facts" involving a product of 8 are: ____
       × ____ = 8; ____ × ____ = 8; ____ × ____ = 8; ____ × ____
       = 8; ____ × ____ = 8.
3. (a) Determine all rectangular patterns for 5 elements.
   (b) The "multiplication facts" involving a product of 5 are ____;
       ____.

In exercise 3 we found that with 5 objects we can make exactly two arrays. On the other hand, we found in the previous examples that with 6 objects or with 8 objects we can make more than two patterns. We call a whole number that yields exactly two rectangular patterns a *prime number;* a number that yields more than two rectangular patterns a *composite number.* One object will yield only one pattern. We call the number 1 a *unit.*

4. Use rectangular arrays to determine the multiplication facts involving each number in the Table 9–1 as a product. List the multiplication facts in the second column and write "unit," "prime," or "composite" in the third column.

TABLE 9-1

Number	Multiplication Facts	Classification
(a) 1		
(b) 2		
(c) 3		
(d) 4		
(e) 7		
(f) 9		
(g) 12		
(h) 18		
(i) 20		
(j) 23		
(k) 24		

It should be noted that Bruner's idea of prime differs from the concept of prime developed here in that Bruner assumed that a "rectangular array" contained more than one column *and* more than one row. If the child could not construct any array with more than one column *and* more than one row he must construct an array with one shell "left over." For example, given 7 shells the boy might construct the following arrays:

5. Using either Bruner's criterion for a prime number or the criterion we developed, use your objects to find all prime numbers less than 25.

Logic-Blocks Exercise

This set of exercises is a follow-up for the examples in Chapter 4 which are built around the Logical Blocks.

Materials. A set of Dienes blocks or the ability to visualize the blocks given a verbal description.

Objectives

1. To indicate relations by the notation suggested by Dienes.
2. To determine whether a given relation is a function.

Procedures

1. Choose as your universe the following set of blocks:
   small thin red circle
   small thin blue circle
   large thin blue circle
   (a) indicate with arrows the correspondent(s) of each element of the universe with respect to the relation "has a different color from."
   (b) Is this relation a function? If not, give a counterexample (a specific example that shows an element with more than one correspondent).
2. Choose as your universe the following set of elements.
   small thin red circle
   small thin blue circle
   large thin blue circle
   large thick blue circle
   (a) Indicate with arrows the correspondents of each member of the universe with respect to the relation "differs in exactly one attribute form."
   (b) Is this relation a function? If not, supply a counterexample.
3. Choose as your universe the following set of elements:
   large thick yellow triangle
   large thin yellow circle
   large thick red square
   small thin yellow square
   (a) Indicate with arrows the correspondents of each member of the universe with respect to the relation "has the same color *and* shape as." (*Note:* Each element is related to itself.)
   (b) Is the relation a function? If not, supply a counterexample.

Function Machines

The following set of exercises present examples of different types of "function machines."

Objective. To provide the output, given a particular function machine and a specific input.

Procedures. For each input and each machine, provide the unique output.

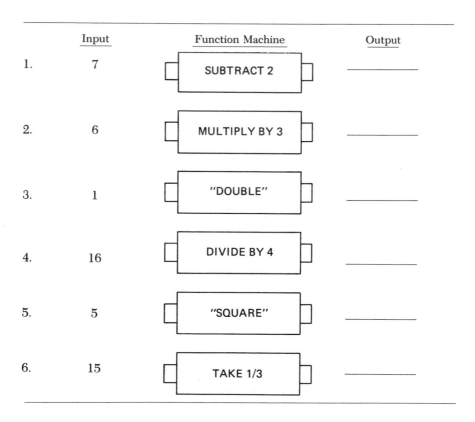

	Input	Function Machine	Output
1.	7	SUBTRACT 2	_____
2.	6	MULTIPLY BY 3	_____
3.	1	"DOUBLE"	_____
4.	16	DIVIDE BY 4	_____
5.	5	"SQUARE"	_____
6.	15	TAKE 1/3	_____

Each of the machines in the table takes a single number as an input. Some function machines take pairs of numbers, such that each pair is in a given order. For example, an "addition machine" takes a pair of numbers and yields the sum of the pair. Such a pair is sometimes written in the form *(a,b)* and called an *ordered pair.* For instance, the pair consisting of the numbers 1 and 5, in the order specified, is written (1,5). The illustration below indicates (1,5) as an input for the "addition machine." The output is the sum of 1 and 5.

Input	Machine	Output
(1,5)	ADDITION	6

For each exercise below, find the output of the machine for the given input. The examples are chosen in such a way that the output will always be a whole number.

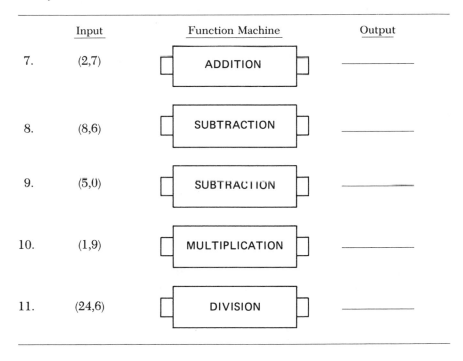

	Input	Function Machine	Output
7.	(2,7)	ADDITION	————
8.	(8,6)	SUBTRACTION	————
9.	(5,0)	SUBTRACTION	————
10.	(1,9)	MULTIPLICATION	————
11.	(24,6)	DIVISION	————

A Rule-Finding Game

In this set of exercises, we present two strategies for finding the rule in the game described by Robert Davis in Chapter 4. The instruction uses an expository approach with examples.

Objectives. Given a set of ordered pairs which satisfy a "rule" of the form $(a \times \square) + b = \triangle$, to find the numbers a and b.

Procedures. Recall that in the game described by David, a group of children make up a rule such as "If you give me a number, I will double it and add 4." In symbols, the particular rule "double it and add 4" can be symbolized as follows: $(2 \times \square) + 4 = \triangle$.

Each time that a member of the class supplies a number to substitute for ☐, the team gives the number which results. This other number is the corresponding replacement for ☐. In this particular case, if a class member provides the number 3, the team computes

$$(2 \times 3) + 4 = 10,$$

and gives the number 10 as the correspondent of 3 with respect to the rule. Thus one pair of numbers in the table that the class makes consists of 3 and 10. With pairs of numbers obtained in this manner, the class makes a table such as the one below.

☐	△
1	6
3	10
4	12
0	4

From the table (or an extension of it), the class is supposed to find the rule $(2 \times \square) + 4 = \triangle$. It is hoped that in the process they will discover a general strategy for finding rules of the form

$$(a \times \square) + b = \triangle.$$

We now present two strategies that the children might use in "guessing" the rule.

Strategy I

Step 1. Notice that the correspondent of the number 0 in the first column is the number 4. We know that the rule we are seeking is of the form $(a \times \square) + b = \triangle$. Therefore, we substitute 0 for ☐ and 4 for △ and reason

$$\begin{aligned}
(a \times 0) + b &= 4, \\
0 \quad + b &= 4, \\
b &= 4.
\end{aligned}$$

Thus $b = 4$, and we now need only find a.

Step 2. At this point we substitute 4 for b, and obtain $(a \times \square) + 4 = \triangle$. Another pair in the table consists of 1 and 6. Substituting 1 for ☐ and 6 for △, we reason:

$$\begin{aligned}
(a \times 1) + 4 &= 6, \\
a \quad + 4 &= 6, \\
a &= 2.
\end{aligned}$$

Thus $a = 2$. The completed rule is $(2 \times \square) + 4 = \triangle$.

For each exercise a table provides pairs which satisfy a rule of the form $(a \times \square) + b = \triangle$. Find a and b, and write the rule.

1.

□	△
0	3
1	7
2	11
3	15

2.

□	△
1	6
0	0
3	18
5	30

3.

□	△
2	7
4	9
0	5
6	11

Strategy II

Consider the Table for Exercise 1 above. We wish to find the "rule," given the table

□	△
0	3
1	7
2	11
3	15

Step 1. Check the table to make certain that the numbers in the first column are in serial order, beginning with 0. If they are not in order, arrange them in order, being careful to keep each number in the first column with its correspondent in the second column.

Step 2. Find the number b for the rule $(a \times \square) + b = \triangle$, as in Strategy I. In this case, $b = 3$. Now notice that b is always the number which corresponds to 0. Check the exercises you performed above to verify this fact for those particular examples.

Step 3. Note that the difference between consecutive values for $\triangle$ is 4 in each case on the table (see below).

□	△	
0	3	
1	7	$7 - 3 = 4$
2	11	$11 - 7 = 4$
3	15	$15 - 11 = 4$

This "constant difference" is found only if we have the numbers in the first column arranged in proper order. The constant difference between consecutive values in the second column, in this case 4, is the number a in the rule $(a \times \square) + b = \triangle$. (In the Madison Project development, the teacher would attempt to lead the children into making a discovery that the constant difference yields the number a.)

Using step 2 and step 3, we find the rule to be $(4 \times \square) + 3 = \triangle$.

Use Strategy II to find the rule of the form $(a \times \square) + b = \triangle$ for each Table.

4.

$\square$	$\triangle$
0	7
1	11
2	15
3	19

5.

$\square$	$\triangle$
2	7
3	10
0	1
1	4

The following exercise provides the reader with an opportunity to make a modest discovery.

6. Using either Strategy I or Strategy II, we need only *two* pairs of numbers in order to find the rule. Suppose you are playing the game with me. I have a rule in mind of the form $(a \times \square) + b = \triangle$. Give me exactly two numbers to substitute for $\square$ so that you can be assured of finding the rule by *either* strategy. Explain why you chose the particular numbers.

7. Use Strategy II to "guess the rule."
   Player 1. I have a rule. Give me a number to substitute for $\square$.
   Player 2. 0.
   Player 1. The corresponding number is 5.
   Player 2. 1.
   Player 1. The corresponding number is 11.
   Player 2. The rule is _____.

Programmed Unit to Teach the Concept of Function

The following programmed unit was written in an effort to lead the reader into an understanding of an abstract concept of function. An analysis was performed to determine prerequisite concepts and notational devices which needed to be built into the program. It is assumed that the reader has performed exercise sets *A* through *D* before attempting this abstract approach to the concept of function.

Author's Objectives

1. To introduce a pair of braces { } as notation for denoting a set of elements.
2. To define what we mean by *equal* sets.
3. To define *ordered pair* and *equality* of ordered pairs.
4. To introduce the convention of using capital letters to name sets.
5. To define a *function* from one set to another in terms of ordered pairs.

Principal Student Objective. Having completed the program, given two sets *A* and *B* and a set of ordered pairs, the student should be able to determine whether the set of ordered pairs is a function from *A* to *B*.

1. In mathematical language, we have many symbols which act as devices for communicating information precisely and concisely. One of these devices is a pair of braces { } which we use to enclose elements of a set. If we wish to denote the set containing the numbers 0, 1, and 2, we write:

$$\{0, 1, 2\}$$

   If we wish to denote the set containing the elements *a, b, c,* and *d,* we write_____. (Notice that braces should enclose the elements.)

Ans. $\{a, b, c, d\}$

2. We say that two set representations are *equal,* or *identical,* if they represent precisely the same set of elements. For instance, $\{0, 1, 2\}$ represents the same set as $\{1, 0, 2\}$. Even though the elements are listed in a different order, the two representations embody precisely the same set of elements. We write

$$\{0, 1, 2\} = \{1, 0, 2\}$$

   to indicate that the set represented is the same in each case. Are $\{a, b, c, d\}$ and $\{d, c, a, b\}$ representations of the same set? _____

Ans. Yes, each representation displays precisely the same elements. We may write

$$\{a, b, c, d\} = \{d, c, a, b\}$$

3. The examples above indicate that the order in which elements of a set are listed is not important in determining whether we have two representations of the same set. For each example below, write "yes" if two representations are equal and "no" if they are not.

   _____ (a) $\{0, 3, 6\} = \{3, 0, 6\}$ _____ (c) $\{0, a\} = \{a, 0\}$
   _____ (b) $\{a, e, i\} = \{a, e\}$ _____ (d) $\{1, 2, 3, 4\} = \{1, 3, 2, 5\}$

Ans. (a) yes   (b) no   (c) yes   (d) no

4. There is a particular type of set in which the order of listing elements is crucial. We call this type of set an ordered pair. An *ordered pair* is a two-element set for which the elements must be listed in a particular order. We enclose the two elements of an ordered pair in parentheses, ( ), instead of braces to distin-

guish it from an ordinary two-element set. Using this convention, $\{0, 1\}$ indicates a set containing the two elements 0 and
1, while (0, 1) represents an ordered pair with first element 0
and second element 1.

This statement is true: $\{0, 1\} = \{1, 0\}$

This statement is not true:$(0,1) = (1,0)$

We sometimes write $(0, 1) = (1, 0)$.

Beside each statement, write either "true" or "false."

——— (a) $(2, 7) = (7, 2)$ ——— (c) $\{b, g\} = \{g, b\}$

——— (b) $\{1, 5\} = \{5, 1\}$ ——— (d) $(x, y) = (y, x)$

Ans. (a) false   (b) true   (c) true   (d) false

5. Two ordered pairs are *equal* if and only if their first elements
   are the same and their second elements are the same.

   Example: Fill in the blank to make a true statement: $(3, \text{—}) =$
   $(3, 5)$. We place 5 in the blank to obtain $(3, \underline{5}) = (3, 5)$.

   Fill in each blank to make a true statement:

   ——— (a) $(\text{—}, 8) = (1, 8)$

   ——— (b) $(4, \text{—}) = (\text{—}, 7)$.

Ans. (a) $(\underline{1}\ 8) = (1, 8)$ (b) $(4, \underline{7}) = (\underline{4}, 7)$

6. We often name a set by a capital letter in order to avoid the necessity of listing its elements each time we wish to refer to it. For
   example, let A be the name of the set $\{0, 1, 2, 3, 4, 5\}$ and let B be
   the set $\{1, 2, 3, 4, 5, 6\}$. We write:

   $$A = \{0, 1, 2, 3, 4, 5\}$$
   $$B = \{1, 2, 3, 4, 5, 6\}.$$

   The "Add 1" function represented in Figs 8-7 and 8-10 can also
   be represented in the following way:

$0 \longrightarrow 1$	$3 \longrightarrow 4$
$1 \longrightarrow 2$	$4 \longrightarrow 5$
$2 \longrightarrow 3$	$5 \longrightarrow 6$

   The function denoted is called a *function from A to B*, for it
   pairs with each element of A one and only one element of B.
   Does the following pairing represent a function from A to B?

$0 \longrightarrow 6$	$3 \longrightarrow 3$
$1 \longrightarrow 5$	$4 \longrightarrow 2$
$2 \longrightarrow 4$	$5 \longrightarrow 1$

Ans. Yes, each element of A is paired with one and only one element of B.

7. Does the following pairing represent a function from S to B?

$$0 \longrightarrow 2 \qquad 3 \longrightarrow 1$$
$$1 \longrightarrow 1 \qquad 4 \longrightarrow 2$$
$$2 \longrightarrow 2 \qquad 5 \longrightarrow 1$$

Ans. Yes, each element of A is paired with one and only one element of B. Notice that an element of B may be the correspondent of more than one element of A, and that it is possible that not every element of B is a correspondent of an element of A.

8. Consider again the "Add 1" function from A to B represented by

$$0 \longrightarrow 1 \qquad 3 \longrightarrow 4$$
$$1 \longrightarrow 2 \qquad 4 \longrightarrow 5$$
$$2 \longrightarrow 3 \qquad 5 \longrightarrow 6$$

This function can be represented as a set of ordered pairs as follows: $\{(0, 1), (1,2), (2, 3), (3, 4), (4, 5), (5, 6)\}$.
The first element of each ordered pair is an element of A and the second element of each ordered pair is an element of B. Represent the function below as a set of ordered pairs:

$$0 \longrightarrow 6 \qquad 3 \longrightarrow 3$$
$$1 \longrightarrow 5 \qquad 4 \longrightarrow 2$$
$$2 \longrightarrow 4 \qquad 5 \longrightarrow 1$$

Ans. $\{(0,6), (1,5), (2,4), (3,3), (4,2), (5,1)\}$.

9. We generalize the concept of a function from one set to another as follows:
   Definition. Let S and T be any sets (where S may be equal to T). A *function from S to T* is a set of ordered pairs (s, t) such that
   (1) s is an element of S and t is an element of T, and
   (2) each element of S is the first element of one and only one ordered pair.
   Notice that a function from S to T must satisfy both criteria in the definition.
      Let C be the set $\{0, 1, 2, 3\}$ and let D be the set $\{0, 2, 4, 6, 8\}$.
   For each example below, write "yes" if the set is a function from C to D and "no" if the set is not a function from C to D. If it

is not a function from C to D, give an example to show that one of the criteria is not satisfied.

_____ (a) $\{(0,0),(1,2),(2,4),(3,6)\}$
_____ (b) $\{(0,0),(0,2),(1,2),(2,4),(3,6)\}$
_____ (c) $\{(0,2),(1,2),(2,4),(3,6)\}$
_____ (d) $\{(0,0),(1,4),(2,6)\}$

Ans.

(a) yes
(b) no, the number 0 is the first element of two ordered pairs—
(0, 0) and (0, 2).
(c) yes
(d) no, the element 3 in C is not represented as the first element of any ordered pair.

10. Let G be the set $\{a, b, c\}$ and let H be the set $\{1, 2, 3, 4\}$.

For each example, write "yes" if the set is a function from G to H and "no" if the set is not a function from G to H.

_____ (a) $\{(a,1),(b,3),(c,2)\}$
_____ (b) $\{(a,2),(b,2),(c,2)\}$
_____ (c) $\{(1,a),(2,b),(3,c)\}$
_____ (d) $\{(a,1),(b,2),(c,3),(c,4)\}$

Ans.

(a) yes (b) yes
(c) no, this is a function *from H to G.*
(d) no, the element c is the first element of two ordered pairs
—(c, 3) and (c, 4)

Application of Functions

The following set of exercises extends the scope of functions by offering examples outside the field of mathematics.

Objectives

1. Given the domain and rule for a function,
   (a) to represent the function as a set of ordered pairs, and
   (b) to determine the range.
2. Given a function written as a set of ordered pairs, to find the rule.

Procedures

1. In each case below, you are given a domain and a rule. Write the function as a set of ordered pairs and determine the range.

	Domain	Rule
(a)	{0, 2, 4, 6, 8}	Divide by 2
(b)	{Beethoven, Michaelangelo, Thomas Edison, Galileo}	Pair with principal "vocation"
(c)	{United States, Canada, Italy, Spain}	Pair with its capital city
(d)	{dog, robin, cat, trout, bluejay}	Pair with its biological "class"
(e)	{*Hamlet, The Glass Menagerie, A Doll's House, Romeo and Juliet, Death of a Salesman*}	Pair with its author (playwrite)

2. Given the function, determine the rule which pairs each first element with its correspondent.

Function

(a) $\{(0,3),(1,4),(2,5),(3,6)\}$
(b) $\{(3,1),(4,2),(5,3),(6,4)\}$
(c) {(blue and red, violet), (yellow and blue, green), (red and yellow, orange)}
(d) {(New York, New York City), (Illinois, Chicago), (Louisiana, New Orleans), (California, Los Angeles)}

CONCLUSION

A variety of exercises relating to some dimensions of concept learning have been suggested. Several were expressly designed for the reader, as a way to assist in clarifying, internalizing, and expanding upon ideas discussed in earlier chapters. Others, while meant to serve a similar purpose, also may be applied directly to classroom situations for use with students.

SUGGESTED READINGS

Ennis, Robert H., *Logic in Teaching* (Englewood Cliffs, N.J.: Prentice-Hall, Inc., 1969).

An in-depth examination of fundamental principles of logic designed for teachers. This book is of particular value to those who have had little or no formal training in logic.

Sax, Gilbert, *Empirical Foundations of Educational Research* (Englewood Cliffs, N.J.: Prentice-Hall, Inc., 1968).

A lucid, cogent, well-written text outlining principles and practices of educational research in a form that is easily applied by teachers.

CHAPTER 10

Future Directions for Instructional Design

Instructional materials that were designed to take into account the concept-learning considerations discussed in earlier chapters might vary considerably in their details. Generically, however, materials that purport to aid in the learning of explicit concepts would share at least three fundamental common properties.

1. The concept(s) to be learned from the materials would be operationally delineated in the teacher's instructions.
2. They would contain explicit exemplars and nonexemplars of the concept(s) in question and would be identified as such in a variety of subject matter contexts.
3. Insofar as possbile, criterial attributes of the concept(s) would be featured or emphasized through verbal or pictorial cues or some other form of focusing.

The bulk of what currently may be broadly construed as "instructional materials" would be altered seriously if these implications were translated into practice. Gagné has criticized instructional texts, for example, for their insensitivity to proper conditions for learning.[1]

> Many textbooks, after all, are poorly written from the standpoint of establishing the proper conditions for learning. For example, does the printed text introducing a topic direct attention to the

[1]Robert M. Gagné, *The Conditions of Learning*, 2nd ed. (New York: Holt, Rinehart & Winston, Inc., 1970), p. 357.

proper stimuli? . . . Designing a printed text that will efficiently instruct a ten-year-old is not simply a matter of matching his vocabulary. Primarily, it is a matter of *organizing* the statements in such a way that they will perform the instructional functions that have been described. . . . Each sentence has a purpose, and sets of sentences are organized in such a way that learning will occur most readily.

Instructional materials, of course, frequently are advertised as being capable of teaching concepts for the reasons that Markle and Tieman have stated,[2] "Conceptual learning is a Good Thing. Seldom do educators want to teach 'mere' facts; rather they want students to really understand the concepts and principles of the subject being studied. Claims that a set of instructional materials teaches concepts provide a strong sales point."

The difficulties in designing appropriate materials for concept learning, however, are both considerable and subtle, as Markle and Tieman note further. They offer the example of a set of published materials for preschool children, designed to teach the concept "pair."[3]

> There were pairs of shoes and skates and mittens and skis. The potential hypothesis that *pair* applies only to things worn by people was dealt with by including a pair of deuces from a deck of cards and a pair of dice. The potential hypothesis that members of a pair were always in some way different (as with the opposite orientation of thumbs on mittens) was dealt with by including socks and earrings. Nonpairs consisting of two related but not paired items, such as cup and saucer were included to teach discrimination of nonexamples. The concept is a subtle one, as anyone attempting to analyze it will discover, and the materials were well designed.

The materials, however, were considered by Markle and Tieman to be *deficient* in one important characteristic. In all the examples given, an irrelevant attribute occurs; all the illustrations of pair contain *discrete* objects.[4] Given the set of examples, and given the single objects that were used as nonexamples of *pair*, it is not likely that learners can generalize correctly when they first confront a pair of pants or a pair of eyeglasses. These are, however, true examples of the concept."[5]

[2]Susan M. Markle and Philip W. Tiemann, "Conceptual Learning and Instructional Design," in M. David Merrill (ed.), *Instructional Design: Readings* (Englewood Cliffs, N.J.: Prentice-Hall, Inc., 1971), p. 284.
    [3]*Ibid.*, p. 290.
    [4]*Ibid.*
    [5]*Ibid.*

ORGANIZATION OF INSTRUCTIONAL MATERIALS

Some selected specific considerations for the design of instructional materials in a variety of formats are outlined below. While not exhaustive, they should suggest some directions that could be taken to construct more efficient learning materials.

Books and Texts. If organized to promote concept learning, textual materials might be organized around concept units containing sequenced exemplars and nonexemplars reflecting a variety of different contexts. Focusing instructions, questions, reviews of prerequisite learning, and practice opportunities would be provided within the unit. Exemplars and nonexemplars might consist of case studies or sketches, pictures, graphs, tables and charts, or drawings arranged in a variety of patterns.

Films and Videotapes. Films and videotapes represent a potentially excellent vehicle for regulating, through visual cues and oral prompts, one's focus upon exemplars and nonexemplars. Designs to maximize concept learning, however, would give priority to emphasis on relevant concept attributes, rather than to narrative or continuity considerations. And as Gagné has already noted, with a few exceptions, this area of media has not yet developed its full instructional potential.[6]

The author *has* located two films which, while *not* designed for this purpose nor advertised as such, fit many of the general specifications cited for concept-learning materials: *Neighbors*, a 9-minute film by Norman McLaren, using human animation, dealing with "conflict;"[7] and *"Model Man,"* a 17-minute film produced by the Econ 12 social-studies project dealing with "models."[8]

A parenthetical note here is appropriate concerning the much heralded 8-mm "single-concept" loop films. While so proclaimed, many of the 8-mm loops currently available in general are *not* designed to meet the three general criteria, cited for the organization of materials. What they *do* provide, and many reasonably well, is a short (three- to five-minute) film-clip of a particular event, normally without sound or focusing instructions and exclusive of descriptive comments.

Slides, Drawings, and Pictures. At the expense perhaps of some visual impact, slides, drawings, and pictures afford an added opportunity to edit and shape more carefully than films, exemplars, and nonexemplars. When synchronized with a dialog focus and instructions, they allow for considerable control over the characteristics of the material *actually* presented to the learner. De Cecco has drawn the

[6]Gagné, *op. cit.*, p. 362.

[7]Available from International Film Bureau, Chicago, Ill.

[8]Available from Joint Council on Economic Education, New York, N.Y.

interesting conclusion, too, that "direct experience of realistic examples are usually not preferable to simplified presentations of the concepts, such as line drawings, cartoon, diagrams, and charts."[9]

Audiotapes. Audiotapes may be seen as functioning in essentially the same way as strictly textual material, only providing an auditory substitute for the written page. While the advent of cassettes provides a technologically efficient way to harness audio material, the chief values of tape would seem to be for *non*readers and for use in conjunction with other media forms.

Field Trips. Field trips, perceived in a special perspective, can provide powerful concrete exemplars and nonexemplars. A high school social-studies class studying about "central business districts," for example, has an easy opportunity to use field trips for purposes of examining concrete exemplars and nonexemplars, if appropriate focusing instructions and questions are provided. Field trips, then, seen as opportunities for single-focus examination of examples and nonexamples of concepts rather than global cognitive assaults on "interesting places," provide yet another source of concrete materials available to teachers.

Combined Media. The reference to "combined" is simply to situations in which media are used in a *complementary* way. Usually, this will be done for purposes of variety (e.g., texts, then pictures, then charts, etc.), to supplement the limitations of one form of media (e.g., adding needed pictoral features to text, providing aural instructions with slides or still pictures, etc.), or to compensate for student limitations (e.g., inability to read, physical handicap such as deafness).

Certainly it would be inappropriate and pointless for *all* curricular materials to be designed along the lines indicated in the foregoing discussion, and no such suggestion is intended. Rather the intent is to suggest that if one's objective is to teach *concepts* instead of specifically relating descriptive information, developing fact connections, examining values, teaching motor skills, or even teaching generalizations, the curricular materials he uses should be so structured as to maximize a student's likelihood of learning the concept. That not all these competing goals are mutually exclusive and incompatible with the simultaneous goal of concept learning is perhaps true. But curricular development has not begun to even approach the stage where materials are constructed in this complex fashion to achieve multiple goals, and moreover, it is difficult to analyze logically what the theoretical structure of such materials might be.

[9]John P. De Cecco, *The Psychology of Learning and Instruction* (Englewood Cliffs, N.J.: Prentice-Hall, Inc., 1968), p. 412.

ORGANIZATION OF INSTRUCTIONAL SEQUENCES

All of the traditional unresolved questions and issues relating to the articulation of generically similar and dissimilar instructional objectives apply to the teaching of concepts. Namely, what is the sequential relationship of concept teaching to other instructional processes, such as aesthetic development and humanistic considerations, teaching valuing, and developing skill in questioning, research, inference generation, logical analysis, and sensitivity for the concerns of others—to list just a few processes. The sequential and emphasis priority of these instructional processes needs to be established, at least as working hypotheses, for inter- and intragrade levels generally.

Moreover, there are important considerations concerning the relationship of coordinate, subordinate, and supraordinate concepts that are nested within the preceding issues. Hence there is a need to examine not only the sequential relationship between all types of instructional sequences, but also the interrelationship of instructional sequences designed explicitly for teaching concepts. Considerable assistance toward this goal has already been provided in the concept analyses developed at the Wisconsin Research and Development Center for Cognitive Learning, and reported in part in Chapter 8.

A related area of needed study is the investigation of what concepts in specific subject-matter areas students may normally be expected to learn at a given grade level. A recent study of the Center offers one approach to this issue. In the study, fourth-grade social studies programs and textbooks in a city system were analyzed to determine familiar concepts.[10] A survey of materials suggested 200 possible concepts.[11]

> To summarize, the basic concepts taught in fourth-grade social studies were identified by using curriculum guides and social studies textbooks as source materials, by tabulating words and ideas in these sources, and by conferring with school district personnel (both central office and teachers). Our knowledge as subject specialists was used to classify the concepts into three areas. Ten concepts were randomly selected from each of the three areas for inclusion in the study. Table [10-1] lists all of the concepts identified within each area; concepts selected for testing are noted with asterisks.

All of the fourth-grade teachers within the system were questioned concerning whether the concepts were taught, and whether their stu-

---

[10]B. Robert Tabachnick, Evelyn B. Weible, and Dorothy A. Frayer, *Selection and Analysis of Social Studies Concepts for Inclusion in Tests of Concept Attainment*, Working Paper No. 53 (Madison, Wis.: Wisconsin Research and Development Center for Cognitive Learning, November, 1970).

[11]*Ibid.*, pp. 77–78.

TABLE 10-1

MAJOR SOCIAL STUDIES CONCEPTS CATEGORIZED BY AREA

Geographic Region	Man and Society	Map and Globe Study
Bay	Agriculture	Area (square miles)
Canal	* Airway	Axis
Climate	Basic needs	Boundary
* Coastline	* City	Continent
* Delta	Commerce (trade)	* Country
* Desert	Country	Day
Elevation	* Democracy	* Distance
Geography	Economy	Earth
* Gulf	Educational institution	* East-West (lines of
Harbor	* Exchange	latitude)
Highland	Family	Equator
Hills	Farming	* Globe
Island	Fishing	Gravity
Isthmus	Forestry	Hemispheres
Lake	* Government	Legend
Location	Industry	Map
Mountain	Institutions	* Map directions
* Mountain region	International	* Map measurement
Mountain pass	* Land routes	Meridians
Mountain peak	Man	Model
Ocean currents	Man as an individual	Night
Ocean tides	Man as a member of a	* North-south (lines
Peninsula	group	of longitude)
Plain	Manufacturing	Ocean
Precipitation	Market	Orientation
Prairie	Nation	Parallels
Ridge	Nature	* Physical feature map
Region	* News	Planet
* River	* Organization	Political map (of nations,
* River mouth	President	countries)
River source	Republic	Revolution
* Strait	* Countryside	Rotation
Subtropical region	Service organization	* Map scale
Swamp	Society	Sea level–below sea
Temperature	State	level
Topography	Suburban	Seasons
Transitional region	Transportation	Solar system
* Tributary	Urban	* Symbol map
* Tropical region	Village	Topographical map
Waterway	* Waterway	(map of land forms)
Weather		
Valley		

*Concepts randomly selected to be tested.

dents would be likely to know the concepts names and their meanings. Responses generally were affirmative.[12] A further measure of appropriateness of concept selection was a study of selected students in the first semester of the *fifth* grade.[13] The study's objective was "to determine for each of the 30 concepts whether the children could read the concept name and whether they were familiar in a rudimentary way with its meaning."[14] This study of readability indicated that the names and general meanings were known by most of the students.[15]

A final instructional concern that should be cited relates to distinctions between concept *types,* and the corresponding requirements for alternative instructional strategies. As noted in an earlier chapter, Gagné, for example, has suggested that *disjunctive* and *relational* concepts should be taught using the model he has established for *defined* concept learning.[16] Similarly, Markle and Tieman have argued for differential instructional strategies for disjunctive concepts or what they refer to as "multiple situations."[17] "Danger," for example, they illustrate, must be taught to a youngster much differently than if it were a concrete concept.[18]

An implication of the foregoing analyses, is that efficient instructional procedures require the discrimination of concept *types* in order to effect appropriate strategies. Before initiating instruction, a teacher should determine whether the concept in question is of the disjunctive, relational, or conjunctive variety. As a measure of assistance to teachers, curriculum developers also might themselves begin to specify such distinctions.

INDIVIDUALIZING CONCEPT LEARNING: INSTRUCTIONAL CONSIDERATIONS FOR STUDENTS AND TEACHERS

Operating within the context of a concept-oriented approach to instruction, flexibility is provided for the selection of alternative subject-matter areas and varying degrees of analysis and study. From the perspective of a student, freedom is provided for selecting subject-matter exemplars that match with some interest areas, and for pursuing a topic to any depth he wishes beyond the basic criterion measures for the concept-learning task. A student who expressed some interests in contemporary "pop" music might have his exemplars of the concept

[12]*Ibid.,* p. 9.
[13]*Ibid.*
[14]*Ibid.*
[15]*Ibid.,* p. 13.
[16]Gagné, *op. cit.,* p. 310.
[17]Markle and Tieman, *op. cit.,* p. 292.
[18]*Ibid.*

"counterpoint" selected from this domain, rather than from that of classical music.

Similarly, a teacher has some measure of freedom to select exemplars from areas in which his competencies and interests are greatest. A teacher, for example, with a high degree of competency in facets of primate behavior could draw upon these contexts, rather than insect life about which he is relatively ignorant, in framing his exemplars for the concept "adaptation." To the extent that such student-profile-subject-matter-teacher-profile matches are possible, concept-oriented curricula provides a dual measure of individualization not possible in programs where specific textual material itself is an end. In the latter approach, teacher and student learning goals are shaped almost exclusively and narrowly by their curricula. Individualization therein, to the extent that it exists at all, is a function largely of learning rate and media format options.

A THEORY OF INSTRUCTION

Instructional sequences designed to produce the learning of given concepts may take on a variety of forms or include different considerations, as much of this book has tried to indicate. All of the related perspectives in turn, however, reflect some notions of how the totality of instruction may be perceived or a *theory of instruction.*

It may be recalled that in a preceding chapter a theory was regarded as a category under which related concept- and interrelated fact-clusters are subsumed in a special logical structure. A theory of instruction, then, may be viewed as a network of logically realted notions of how, why, and under what circumstances instruction should occur, the diverse properties of instruction, and ways in which its impact may be detected. In relationship to teachers and students, a theory of instruction would include specifically, for example, considerations such as: (a) knowledge of methodological alternatives; (b) knowledge of categories of objectives and related teaching strategies; (c) a repertoire of instructional techniques; (d) generalizations concerning a teacher's and students' assumed roles; (e) resources required to implement instruction; (f) procedures for evaluating instruction.

A possible model for a theory of instruction encompassing the foregoing points in relationship to effecting concept learning is suggested by the author in Fig. 10-1.

"Method," similar to the definition applied by Hunt and Metcalf, [19]

[19]Maurice P. Hunt and Lawrence E. Metcalf, *Teaching High School Social Studies,* 2nd. ed. (New York: Harper & Row, Publishers, 1968), p. 171.

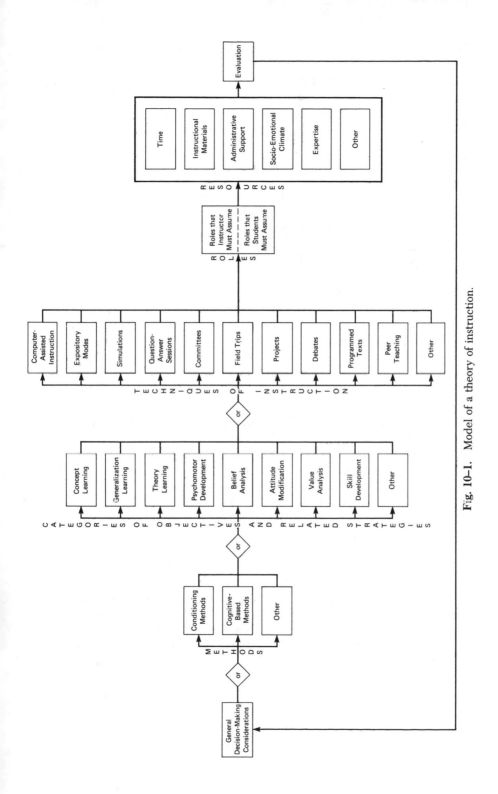

Fig. 10-1. Model of a theory of instruction.

is assumed to be one's perspective concerning under what psychological conditions most significant learning takes place and concerning what the goals and functions of education should be. "Strategy" is defined as the specific way in which a method is applied to a particular instructional task or set of tasks. The structural relationship of facts then defines the individual identity of a strategy, and consistent with a given methodology, one may opt for a variety of compatible strategies related to a particular objective for instruction. "Technique," again using Hunt and Metcalf's definition, refers to the format or setting used to convey a strategy; expository modes such as lectures and films, as well as simulations, and the like may *all* be viewed as techniques.[20]

Also illustrated in Fig. 10-1 is the *order* of operations, from left to right, that a teacher would follow in applying some components of a theory of instruction, once entry behaviors have been ascertained. Thus method options, is one of the initial considerations while evaluation, a feedback mechanism for the theory, is a concluding step.

In adapting or modifying the model, it is possible to refine categories or increase their number. One might wish to discriminate further between methods, add strategies to the sample ones listed, or list new techniques, as they are derived by the teacher. Additionally, from some readers frames of reference, it may be more useful to combine the first two or the second and third steps. It is the sequence of considerations and the necessity for distinctions between instructional considerations that are basic to the model, rather than the illustrative segments provided. Similarly, the illustrative segments are *suggested* possible categories rather than *established* ones inferred from all possible instructional contexts.

Objectives and a Theory of Instruction

Any instructional sequence reflects an overall objective or general decision-making considerations, either defensible or indefensible. Not infrequently beginning teachers, on particularly traumatic days, have as their general objective (often explicitly stated and almost always defensible): "to get through this day (week)!" Stating one's overall objective for teaching not only opens one's approach to rational scrutiny, but also allows for self-determination of what shall be given *priority* in classes where an excess of "worthwhile" subject matter always exists.

In concert with clear specification of objectives, there is reflected a knowledge base about instruction in general, and a systematic plan or conscious design. Included in this knowledge base are instructional

[20]*Ibid.*, pp. 171, 175–184.

models, related research on instruction, key variables that affect instruction, analysis of instructional failures, and most importanly of all, perhaps, direct experience with cause-effect relationships in real or simulated instructional settings in which one can analyze learning outcomes as a function of instructional sequences.

The notion of "conscious design" also includes a logical analysis of the learning tasks that have been planned, including contingencies predicated and hypothetical feedback anticipated. This step does not preclude instructional sequences that are "open-ended," or that have unpredictable outcomes; rather, it prepares the teacher for a variety of possibilities as an instructional sequence unfolds.

A word here concerning so-called "behavioral objectives" and the current emphasis being placed upon their specification seems pertinent. Seen as a *means* rather than an end, concern with the specification of objectives in terms of observable student behavior may help to focus needed attention upon the analysis of an appropriate instructional procedure, discriminating relevant from irrelevant details. Clearly, however, behavioral objectives of themselves do *not* imply corresponding instructional procedures, and consequently do *not* provide adequate guidance for the structuring of subject matter. To state an objective behaviorally concerning a concept-learning task, then, is *not* to state the design of a learning process. Presumably, however, one who follows some model of concept learning—either those discussed in preceding chapters or others—could supply on demand behaviorally oriented statements of his objectives.

What is at issue in this analysis is the matter of perspective concerning the role of behavioral objectives in developing instruction for facilitating concept learning. While they may serve as analytical tools, the reader is cautioned to observe the maxim, "Never let a behavioral objective interfere with your objective," and David Ausubel's conclsion, "it is probably more realistic and generally satisfactory to define educational objectives in grosser or more descriptive terms that are closer to the language of the curriculum worker than to that of the psychologist."[21]

CONCLUSION

As concern over issues such as "accountability," "individualized learning," and the "structure of knowledge" continue into the decade

---

[21]David P. Ausubel, *Educational Psychology: A Cognitive View* (New York: Holt, Rinehart & Winston, Inc., 1968), p. 35.

of the 1970's, *concept* learning is likely to remain an important instructional focus. Since man's society is spun of a vast interrelated and complex conceptual web, learning to operate within it effectively requires insight into its structural mysteries. To provide systematic conceptual links within the web will require constant attention to the affective, as well as cognitive states of learners. Similarly, the progress and conerns of the learner must be chartered carefully in order to determine the most efficient route.

Such is the basic task of instructional design for concept learning.

Appendix

In Chapter 9 a number of exercises relating to different dimensions of concept learning were provided. The premise of the chapter was that actual involvement in some of the processes associated with concept learning might make it possible for the reader to see more readily the meaning and significance of the conclusions reported in earlier chapters and to better apply them to the design of instructional materials. A general aim of the exercises was to acquaint the reader with some of the dimensions involved in preparing students for a concept-learning task, and further, to sensitize him to some of the potential difficulties that students may encounter in learning concepts.

Where applicable, answers and/or comparative comments for the exercises are provided below.

THE LEARNER'S PERSPECTIVE

A Concept of Blarp

As a test for the learning of this "new" concept, two measures of competency were provided: concept discrimination and rule or definition verbalization.

Concept Discrimination. Both *item 2* and *item 4* in Fig. 9–6 on page 236 are exemplars of blarp.

Rule Verbalization. A blarp may be defined nonrigorously as *a triangle, rectangle and circle placed in that order.* Another general statement of the rule might be *three figures, one of which is a triangle, another is a rectangle, and one is a circle, always arranged with the rectangle in the center, the triangle to the left of it, and the circle to the right of it.* Other similar versions are possible.

The rule reflects the fact that the *number, shapes* and *locations* of figures are *criterial* attributes; while *color* and *size,* for example, though present and varied in the concept exemplars, are *noncriterial* attributes. Incorrect responses reflect under-or overgeneralization of the concept, and suggest what additional instructional sequences are necessary to eliminate errors.

LOGICAL RELATIONSHIPS

The validity or invalidity for each of the nine arguments in Chapter 9 is indicated below. Then diagrams of the arguments are supplied to illustrate how the answers may be derived visually.

1. Valid	4. Invalid	7. Valid
2. Invalid	5. Invalid	8. Invalid
3. Valid	6. Valid	9. Valid

Diagrams

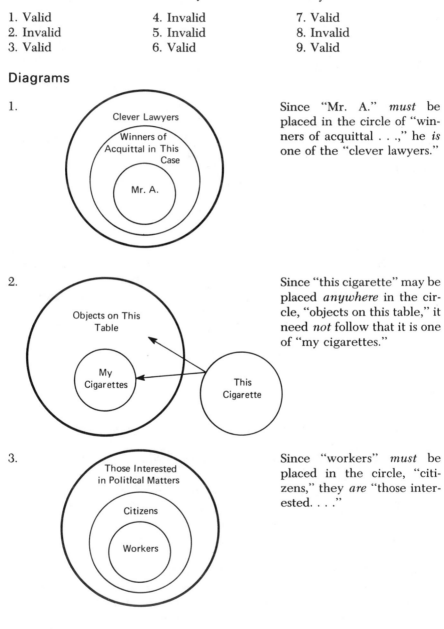

1.

Since "Mr. A." *must* be placed in the circle of "winners of acquittal . . .," he *is* one of the "clever lawyers."

2.

Since "this cigarette" may be placed *anywhere* in the circle, "objects on this table," it need *not* follow that it is one of "my cigarettes."

3.

Since "workers" *must* be placed in the circle, "citizens," they *are* "those interested. . . ."

4.

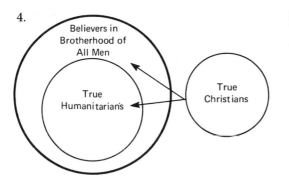

Since "true Christians" may be placed *anywhere* in the circle, "believers . . .," it need *not* follow that they are "true humanitarians."

5.

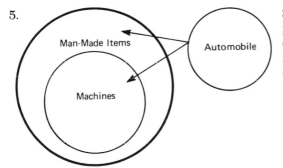

Since "automobile" may be placed *anywhere* in the circle, "man-made items," it need *not* follow that it is one of the "machines."

6.

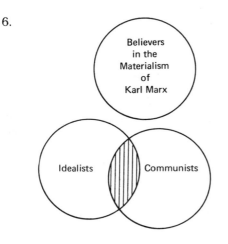

Some "communists" *must* be placed in the circle, "idealists," and since *no* "believers . . ." can be placed in the circle, "idealist," *some* "communists" *are* "*non*believers. . . ."

7.
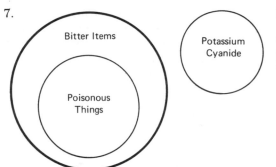

Since "potassium cyanide" *must* be outside the circle of "bitter items," it *is* impossible for it to be one of the "poisonous things."

8.
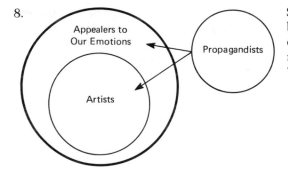

Since "propagandists" may be placed *anywhere* in the circle, "appealers . . .," it need *not* follow that they are "artists."

9.
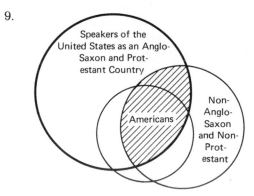

Since most "Americans" *must* be placed in both the circles "non-Anglo-Saxon and non-Protestant" and "Speakers . . .," at least *some* persons who are "non-Anglo-Saxon . . ." *are* in the circle, "Speakers. . . ."

EXERCISES RELATED TO MATHEMATICS INSTRUCTION

Developing the Concepts of Prime Number, Composite Number, and Unit Intuitively

Answers

2. (a) OOOOOOOO   8888

(b) $1 \times 8 = 8$, $2 \times 4 = 8$, $4 \times 2 = 8$, $8 \times 1 = 8$

3. (a) OOOOO

(b) $1 \times 5 = 5$, $5 \times 1 = 5$

4. (a) 1; $1 \times 1 = 1$; unit (b) 2; $1 \times 2 = 2$, $2 \times 1 = 2$; prime (c) 3; $1 \times 3 = 3$, $3 \times 1 = 3$; prime (d) 4; $1 \times 4 = 4$, $2 \times 2 = 4$, $4 \times 1 = 4$; composite (e) 7; $1 \times 7 = 7$, $7 \times 1 = 7$; prime (f) 9; $1 \times 9 = 9$, $3 \times 3 = 9$, $9 \times 1 = 9$, composite (g) 12; $1 \times 12 = 12$, $2 \times 6 = 12$, $3 \times 4 = 12$, $4 \times 3 = 12$, $6 \times 2 - 12$, $12 \times 1 = 12$; composite (h) 18; $1 \times 18 = 18$, $2 \times 9 = 18$, $3 \times 6 = 18$, $6 \times 3 = 18$, $9 \times 2 = 18$, $18 \times 1 = 18$; composite (i) 20; $1 \times 20 = 20$, $2 \times 10 = 20$, $4 \times 5 = 20$, $5 \times 4 - 20$, $10 \times 2 = 20$, $20 \times 1 = 20$; composite (j) 23; $1 \times 23 = 23$, $23 \times 1 = 23$; prime (k) 24; $1 \times 24 = 24$, $2 \times 12 = 24$, $3 \times 8 = 24$, $4 \times 6 = 24$, $6 \times 4 = 24$, $8 \times 3 = 24$, $12 \times 2 = 24$, $24 \times 1 = 24$; composite.

5. 2, 3, 5, 7, 11, 13, 17, 19, 23.

Logic-Blocks Exercise

Answers

1. (a)   small thin red circle $\nearrow$ small thin blue circle
   $\searrow$ large thin blue circle
   small thin blue circle→small thin red circle
   large thin blue circle→small thin red circle

 (b)   not a function; the small thin red circle has two correspondents

2. (a)   small thin red circle→small thin blue circle
   small thin blue circle $\nearrow$ small thin red circle
   $\searrow$ large thin blue circle
   large thin blue circle $\nearrow$ small thin blue circle
   $\searrow$ large thick blue circle
   large thick blue circle→large thin blue circle

 (b)   not a function; small thin blue circle has more than one correspondent

3. (a)   large thick yellow triangle→large thick yellow triangle
          large thin yellow circle→large thin yellow circle
          large thick red square→large thick red square
          small thin yellow square→small thin yellow square
   (b)   is a function

Function Machines

Answers

1. 5   2. 18   3. 2   4. 4   5. 25   6. 3   7. 9
   8. 2   9. 5   10. 9   11. 4

A Rule-Finding Game

Answers

1. $(a \times 0) + b = 3,$ $(a \times 1) + 3 = 7,$ Rule:
   $0 + b = 3,$ $a + 3 = 7,$ $(4 \times \square) + 3 = \triangle.$
   $b = 3.$ $a = 7.$

2. $(a \times 0) + b = 0,$ $(a \times 1) + 0 = 6,$ Rule:
   $0 + b = 0,$ $a + 0 = 6,$ $(6 \times \square) + 0 = \triangle,$
   $b = 0.$ $a = 6.$ or $6 \times \square = \triangle.$

3. $(a \times 0) + b = 5,$ $(a \times 2) + 5 = 7,$ Rule:
   $0 + b = 5.$ $a \times 2 = 2,$ $(1 \times \square) + 5 = \triangle,$
   $b = 5.$ $a = 1$ or $\square + 5 = \triangle.$

   (Since this Table did not contain 1 in its first column, we chose the
   pair consisting of 2 and 7 in order to find the value of *a*.)

4. $b = 7; a = 4; (4 \times \square) + 7 = \triangle.$
5. $b = 1; a = 3; (3 \times \square) + 1 = \triangle.$
6. Choose the numbers 0 and 1. Having chosen 0, you will receive the
   correspondent of 0, which is equal to *b*. Having chosen 1, you will
   receive the correspondent of 1. Using Strategy I, you can find *a* by
   substitution; using Strategy II, you can find the difference between the
   correspondent of 0 and the correspondent of 1. This difference is the
   number *a*. *Example:*
   Given:

$\square$	$\triangle$
0	3
1	8

   Solution: $b = 3; a = 5; (5 \times \square) + 3 = \triangle.$
7. $b = 5;$ the "constant difference" is 6 $(a = 6); (6 \times \square) + 5 = \triangle.$

Application of Functions

Answers

1. (a) $\{(0, 0), (2, 1), (4, 2), (6, 3), (8, 4)\}$; $\{0, 1, 2, 3, 4\}$

    (b) {(Beethoven, composer), (Michaelangelo, artist), (Thomas Edison, inventor), (Galileo, astronomer)}; {composer, artist, inventor, astronomer}; Note. This example does not furnish an example of a function unless we agree on a single vocation for each person. The vocation chosen by the reader for each man might be slightly different from the one chosen by the author. For example, the reader may wish to term Beethoven a "musician" rather than a "composer." The important point is that each person must be paired with only one vocation. The range will, of course, depend on the words chosen by the reader.

    (c) {(United States, Washington, D.C.), (Canada, Ottawa), (Italy, Rome), (Spain, Madrid)}; {Washington, D.C., Ottawa, Rome, Madrid}

    (d) {(dog, mammal), (robin, bird), (cat, mammal), (trout, fish), (bluejay, bird)}; {mammal, bird, fish}

    (e) {(*Hamlet*, William Shakespeare), (*The Glass Menagerie*, Tennessee Williams), (*A Doll's House*, Henrik Ibsen), (*Romeo and Juliet*, William Shakespeare), (*Death of a Salesman*, Arthur Miller)}; {William Shakespeare, Tennessee Williams, Henrik Ibsen, Arthur Miller}

2. (a) "Add 3"

    (b) "Subtract 2"

    (c) mix the two colors that form the first element and obtain the color that is the second element.

    (d) Pair each state with its most populous city.

Index